# The English Language Arts Handbook

**SECOND EDITION**

D1279742

# The English Language Arts Handbook

*Classroom Strategies for Teachers*

SECOND EDITION

**Susan J. Tchudi**
and
**Stephen N. Tchudi**

Boynton/Cook Publishers
Heinemann
Portsmouth, NH

**Boynton/Cook Publishers, Inc.**
A subsidiary of Reed Elsevier Inc.
361 Hanover Street
Portsmouth, NH 03801–3912
http://www.boyntoncook.com

*Offices and agents throughout the world*

**Library of Congress Cataloging-in-Publication Data**
Tchudi, Susan J. (Susan Jane), 1944–
    The English language arts handbook : classroom strategies for teachers /
Susan J. Tchudi and Stephen N. Tchudi. — 2nd ed.
        p.    cm.
    Stephen Tchudi's name appears first on the earlier edition.
    Includes bibliographical references and index.
    ISBN 0-86709-463-X
    1. Language arts.    2. English language—Study and teaching.    I. Tchudi,
Stephen, 1942-  .  II. Title.
    LB1576.T358 1999
    429.'0071'2—dc21
                                                                99-23090
                                                                CIP

*Editor: Lisa Luedeke*
*Production: Elizabeth Valway*
*Cover Design: Joni Doherty Design*
*Manufacturing: Louise Richardson*

Printed in the United States of America on acid-free paper
03   02   01   00   99   DA   1   2   3   4   5

*To all English language arts teachers everywhere who continue to dedicate their careers to students' meaningful engagement with language and literature.*

# Contents

# four ○ Ideas for Teaching Language    197

# five ○ The Profession of Teaching    249

# Preface

We are pleased to offer this new edition of *The English Language Arts Handbook*, continuing a publishing history that began in the mid-1970s. Almost a quarter of a century has passed since we launched *The Inkwell*, a monthly newsletter for English language arts teachers. Your entrepreneurial authors believed that a practical, classroom-oriented newsletter would provide a service for teachers in the field and possibly bring us modest fortune and early retirement. We had sensed in our university classes and at professional meetings a strong interest in how-to-do-it materials, and we found in *The Inkwell* a way of getting teaching ideas into the hands of a number of elementary and secondary teachers in the United States, the United Kingdom, Canada, New Zealand, and Australia.

Our entrepreneurial and writing efforts were less successful than we had hoped, however, and after two years we discovered that we couldn't keep writing, typing, and licking the stamps for *The Inkwell*. We condensed and reorganized the material into the first version of this book, which was called *The English Teacher's Handbook*. The second version of the book, published in 1991, was called *The English/Language Arts Handbook*; this is the second edition of that title.

If you're familiar with the earlier versions, you'll see we've retained the format that has proven popular and useful for both experienced and prospective English language arts teachers. Each chapter begins with a concise overview of current theory regarding a particular aspect of literacy education, which is then followed by numerous practical teaching ideas that grow from that philosophy.

We want to emphasize that this book isn't simply a grab bag of ideas or an eclectic smorgasbord. We're committed to a philosophy of English language arts education that's variously labeled *student centered*, *holistic*, *naturalistic*, *whole language*, *experience centered*, *interdisciplinary*, and *multicultural*. We believe you'll find our various activities consistent with those approaches to the teaching and learning of language. While continuing to elaborate on the core philosophy, we have added new materials for this edition: In particular, we have strengthened the materials on electronic communications and publication and infused the entire book with a greater sense of the possibilities for developing interdisciplinary and multicultural teaching materials.

As with the earlier versions, each major portion of the book concludes with a "Summary and Troubleshooting" section, where we recap the main ideas of the section and, more important, discuss some of the problems that may emerge when you move from the printed pages of this book to your own classroom. Our contact with readers over the years has convinced us that people do not see this book as "ivory tower," but we also want to emphasize that we do not offer this work as any sort of classroom magic or cure-all. In many cases, our readers survey the text, study the possibilities, then go on to make adaptations to their own classrooms that are far more interesting and imaginative than anything we've done here.

We welcome correspondence with readers (and college classes), and can be reached at the following e-mail addresses:

Susan Tchudi <tchudi@scs.unr.edu>
Stephen Tchudi <stuchu@powernet.net>

or c/o Department of English 098, University of Nevada, Reno, NV 89557
Let us hear from you!

# Introduction

We teach in dramatic, controversial times.

And the teaching of English language arts is, perhaps, the most complex discipline in the spectrum of education. Literacy is clearly the skill most directly linked to school success, and it provides the avenue to participation in civic affairs as well as to aesthetic enjoyment and appreciation. Although people may draw on their skills with mathematics or science or history several times during every day, they access those skills through language, and use their language, quite literally, second-by-second throughout the day.

In times of controversy, few combatants would argue against the value of high-quality instruction in English language arts.

However, in times of controversy, good teachers must be able to link their day-to-day practices consistently and defensibly to a coherent theory of instruction.

The teaching of English language arts has undergone extraordinary changes in the past quarter century. An older tradition of spelling drills, grammar practice, literary surveys of the classics, and expository writing in the plain style has given way (not without controversy) to an integrated view of literacy instruction that extends the opportunities for reading, writing, listening, and speaking to every corner of the world, using any mode or medium of communication that helps make connections between people. The new way of teaching English language arts is centered in a growing understanding of how language is acquired, how it is employed for business and pleasure, and how people learn to use it successfully. There has been a shift in teaching emphasis away from mastery of knowledge about language toward actual use of language. In schools where the newer philosophy is practiced, students spend more time reading and writing, less time learning rules of writing and syntax. The set list of "classics" has been broadened to include a much wider range of literature for children, young adults, and adults. An earlier obsession with surface correctness in writing has been replaced by an interest in teaching students the processes of composing so they can solve writing problems on their own. Narrow absorption with the printed word has been replaced by recognition that our subject is *language*, not just print literacy, and that in today's world students must be able to talk and discuss intelligently, to communicate with and through computers, and to interpret and critique visual images.

Most important, we think, is that in recent years the teaching of English language arts has progressed from being atheoretical—a collection of content and pedagogy loosely linked under the heading "English"—to having a coherent, if tentative, and research-based set of philosophies and practices.

All these changes have created new roles for teachers. Teaching language was once a matter of simply following the course outline or grammar or spelling book in sequences that were obvious, if dull: Sounding out syllables preceded reading whole words and whole texts; "the sentence" always followed "parts of speech"; "organizing a composition" followed "paragraphs." Methodology consisted largely of lecture or discussion, the latter with the teacher doing most of the talking. Literature was mostly explication for the students; language study meant grammar; composition meant having your errors in spelling, mechanics, and usage pointed out with a brightly colored (usually red) pencil.

Now standard practice includes "workshop" classes, where even the youngest children read whole texts of their own choice and write original compositions that are published and illustrated by the authors. The teaching profession has developed an interest in "response to literature," in which students' reactions to their reading are valued as contributing to literary knowledge rather than as an aberration from accepted critical interpretation. "Grammar" is now seen as including all of the systematic study of language, from doublespeak to advertising language, from dialect studies to sex and gender portrayals in language.

The new way of teaching English language arts is neither universal nor without controversy. Many people outside the classroom have been critical of what they see as a decline of interest in correctness and standards, confusing teachers' handling of such matters in context with an abandonment of concern. There are expressions of unrest that some of the standard classics have had to make room for contemporary literature, children's and young adult literature, and literature reflecting cultures and traditions other than the Anglo-American. Test scores—at best indirect measures of literacy—rise and fall, fall and rise, each blip on the graphs bringing cries of "I told you so" from competing views of language pedagogy.

Yet there is enough agreement at national and international professional meetings, at in-service workshops and gatherings, and in the hallways and teachers' lounges of elementary and secondary schools that we can safely and accurately describe a "new English language arts," born in the late 1960s and early 1970s, tested in the 1980s and 1990s, supported by a growing body of research and providing a professional core of knowledge for the twenty-first century.

This new English language arts is unquestionably exciting. It allows us to take a new look at what we are doing, to take fresh approaches to teaching—using new books, drawing on current media, looking for alternate directions in composition, and, above all, examining the learning styles and patterns and personalities of our students.

But contemporary English teaching is also terribly demanding, for its very diversity (and the diversity of our students) creates a drain on material resources and on our energy, originality, and creativity. Whereas we could once plan on teaching the same courses, books, and units over and over (stories about teachers who had memorized the textbook are not exaggerated), today we are constantly reading new texts, surveying fresh titles, and planning new units and activities for students.

And schools themselves are not always conducive to this sort of teaching. At the secondary level, despite fifty years of lobbying by the National Council of Teachers of English, class size often remains at thirty students or more, and teachers often see over 150 students a day. ("Why don't you teach more writing?" asks a critical administrator who will, next September, add two or two dozen students to the load of every English language arts teacher because of fiscal constraints.) At the elementary level, teachers are snowed under with paperwork and expected to include more and more in the curriculum, sometimes leading them to question where "home" ends and "school" begins. At both levels, there are cumbersome structures and traditions that make teaching difficult: bell schedules, grades, permission slips and tedious forms to complete, and public-address interruptions. In our time, too, innovative or progressive teaching is often viewed with suspicion. Growing unrest over the quality of schooling leads parents and administrators to call for a return to patterns of teaching remembered from their youth, even when those patterns may be part of the problem of education.

In such a milieu, it's easy for teachers to burn out. After a brief fling with contemporary techniques, many retreat in the direction of grammar books and old-fashioned anthologies. Some quit and go into real estate or law; others stay in the profession and simply become pessimists: unhappy with their teaching, their students, themselves.

Yet a great many English language arts teachers not only survive, but thrive. We're amazed by the commitment and resilience of teachers we meet, of enthusiastic newcomers to the profession who know they could make more money in business but choose not to, and of gray-headed experienced teachers who bubble over with enthusiasm at professional meetings, happy with their students, themselves, and their profession. But even if you're this kind of positivist teacher, you'll need support, and you'll get it from spouses and friends, from colleagues, from administrators, and, just possibly, from a helpful handbook of teaching ideas.

It's in support of such teachers that *The English Language Arts Handbook* has been prepared. Whether you're an undergraduate in a methods course getting ready for your student teaching or an experienced professional who occasionally feels overwhelmed by the job, we figure you need all the help you can get. At the same time, we feel it's important to enter two cautionary notes:

1. The teaching ideas presented here are meant to be catalysts to your thinking, not sure-fire gimmicks. Adapt these teaching ideas to your needs, to your students, to your classes. Don't simply pull strategies from here and there and expect them to work without modification. In our college pedagogy classes, we frequently have students write their own edition of an *English Language Arts Handbook*, a ring binder full of their own thinking, comprising the ideas that will truly bring success in their classrooms.

2. Don't use this book as a cookbook. The ideas aren't recipes, and the book is intended to supplement your course planning, not replace it. Further, don't pick ideas just because they are unusual or because they have shock value. Students can be tricked, manipulated, and "gimmicked" only so many times before the novelty wears off. The book begins with an intensive section on classroom planning, and we urge you to plan the broad dimensions of your work before selecting individual activities.

From time to time we've heard people say, "Well, any idea or method can work at some time in the hands of the right teacher."

We don't buy that idea, and we think such a philosophy leads to eclecticism of a very dangerous sort. So we've been highly selective in presenting ideas. The practices we recommend show internal consistency with what we interpret contemporary language arts philosophy and research to mean. Thus, we don't present "101 New Approaches to the Book Report," but we do discuss a variety of ways of helping students extend their responses to literature. We don't show you ways to "Make Grammar Fun!" but we do explore some ideas about engaging students profitably and with occasional laughter in thinking about the English language and their use of it. We don't offer you "The Five-Paragraph Theme" or the "Power Paragraph," but we do suggest dozens of ways of helping students write well-organized compositions.

Underlying all our discussion is the belief that teachers are at the heart of solving classroom teaching problems. We don't believe formulas can be applied to teaching, whether mandated by a curriculum guide or suggested by a book like this. Growth in the ability to teach evolves from within, from teachers who are willing to explore and experiment with new ideas, techniques, possibilities.

We anticipate that a reader who has gotten this far in the Introduction shares many of those assumptions. We hope you'll find this book a useful aid in teaching, as we said, the single most important skill/process/activity in the entire school curriculum:

The Art of Literacy

# o · n · e

# Planning for English Language Arts

The first section of *The English Language Arts Handbook* provides what we see as the context for teaching, the larger framework into which the daily activities, the weekly schemes, and entire course plans fit. In this section we discuss—and ask you to think about—the broad view of what it means to be an English language arts teacher.

While it is possible to begin by thinking about parts of the curriculum—activities for reading, writing, speaking, and listening—we've come to see having a handle on the large picture as essential to teachers. Knowing what you see as "basic" in the teaching of language arts, what your central goals are, who your students are, why you are teaching what you are teaching, how you can go about reaching all students, and how you can assess your success in all these, allows you to make solid decisions in your teaching and to be flexible and adaptable in response to your students, your colleagues and administrators, and the fads and fancies that come down the educational pipeline. Placing your particular plans into this larger theoretical context will allow you to become a *reflective practitioner*.

# Chapter One

# Aims and Priorities

Why do we "teach" English language arts, anyway? Virtually all babies learn the hardest part of language—its basic syntax and vocabulary—on their own, without any instruction from teachers. They learn by being in the world with parents, older brothers and sisters, friends, and caretakers who provide them with language and respond to their efforts at communicating in the course of their everyday lives. Babies learn language as they learn about their environment—as they are hungry and hear about oatmeal and spoons; as they are dressed and learn about putting on shoes and socks, shirts and pants; as they are taken places and learn about getting in their car seats, hurrying for the bus, or putting up an umbrella so they won't get wet. They learn through listening and responding, imitation, and trial and error as they and those around them use language to accomplish something or to say something about the world. Would such language learning come to an end if children didn't have language arts teachers to provide them with assignments and lessons?

As a matter of fact, there's a good deal of evidence to suggest that naturalistic learning of language does take place outside school, and it may be that some of the most significant learning happens there as people use language to engage with their world, to shape it, and to control their corner of it. We know some children even learn the print code—reading and writing—outside school: from signs, television, magazines, picture books, and caregivers who give attention to printed language.

Yet schooling can and obviously does affect the learning of language, and we'll argue vigorously that English language arts deserves its place in the curriculum as the most widely taught school subject, from kindergarten through college composition. At its best, school instruction produces students who have confidence in their ability to tackle new language situations, who have pretty good control of mechanics and grammatical usage, and who have read widely and intend to keep on reading after school. At its worst, English language arts instruction results in students who hate to read, believe they can't write, and groan about their inability to master grammar. One look at the discussion of literacy in your local papers or in the national news will demonstrate people's frustration about the failure of the schools to teach language.

The public response to the perceived failure of the schools to teach literacy has been expressed in a number of national political movements—the "back-to-basics" movement, the "effective schools" movement, and the "standards" movement. The leaders of these movements are often politicians, parents, and administrators who know little about language and language learning. Twenty-five years ago, those leading the "back-to-basics" movement argued that teachers needed to return to direct teaching of basic skills—rules about grammar, writing, and reading. More recently, the "effective schools" movement has promoted the model of business and industry, where (at least in myth) everything is tightly organized, goal directed, and efficient, leading to the highest quality product created at the lowest cost. Similarly, the "standards" movement assumes that if schools set high standards for student achievement and then test students on those standards, students' performance will improve.

All of these models fail to recognize both the simplicity and the complexity of humans' learning of English language arts. They fail to see that language learning is not something that can be rushed, mechanized, or treated as an assembly line project. Language is one of the most highly individual learning enterprises, growing from unique experiences with words and the world.

# Some Basic Premises About English Language Arts

To us, the rigid, monolithic, assembly line model of education posited by some political leaders and uninformed school administrators reflects their lack of understanding of language and language learning. Rather than being fixed and lockstep, instruction in English language arts requires that you have a sense of how young people learn language and a clear sense of the ways in which you can create a classroom that supports and encourages language learning. This often requires that you avoid "teacher-proof" materials, political admonitions of what and how to teach, and the glitzy teaching methods that promise quick results, and instead consider ways to achieve long-range, slow growth and development.

It further requires that you be willing and able to state your philosophy of English language arts instruction clearly and concisely. At this point we offer ours—a credo of sorts, a list of our fundamental beliefs, developed through teaching, sharing and debating issues with other teachers, and reading the professional literature.

1. *Reading, writing, listening, and speaking are learned by doing, not principally by studying abstractions or completing exercises.* More and more it seems clear that English is a learn-by-doing skill, that our most important task as teachers is not telling students about language but encouraging them to use it. To this end, *The English Language Arts Handbook* is aimed at helping you develop a language-centered classroom, a place in which students use language constantly, in a rich variety of ways. We've said "not principally" by exercises and study, because we know there are times when direct teaching and intervention can be of use to students. However, decades of research into language learning demonstrate persuasively that engagement in language use must be central and exercises and direct teaching peripheral.

2. *Language growth is bound up with the broader dimensions of human growth and development.* In contrast to all other subjects that are studied in school, language is a basic human activity. It is tied to every aspect of humans' perceptions, thoughts, feelings, and beliefs. As such, language grows in response to the human need to communicate. As people grow, their language expands. The implication is that English language arts classes need to focus on children's lives—what they do and have done, what they are thinking about or have thought about.

3. *Language teaching begins "where the student is" and moves him or her as far as possible.* Because students come to school with language, because they have used language since babyhood, and because their language has been shaped by their experiences, their homes, and their communities, teachers need to build on and develop the language skills students already possess. Students' varied experiences—both in and out of school—require that teachers provide highly individualized instruction for students who have widely different experiences and abilities. We believe that this diversity should not only be accepted but also celebrated.

4. *English language arts should broaden the range of discourse that students can employ, both as "consumers" (listeners and readers) and as "producers" (speakers and writers).* While we celebrate the language experience that our students bring with them to our classrooms, we also hope to help students extend their dimensions of literacy. Although we see the need for language arts classrooms to help students develop practical skills (those that emphasize language for the workplace), we believe that students also need opportunities to read and write in ways that develop imagination, creativity, and human awareness. In achieving this goal, we believe that students should have opportunities to create in and respond to a wide variety of media—both print and nonprint.

5. *Language study is naturally interdisciplinary.* For a long time, English limited itself to literature, but developments in the "language across the curriculum" movement in the past two decades have forged links with math, science, the arts, social studies, and history. English language arts programs increasingly draw on materials that go beyond the limits of traditional literature to include nonfiction and fiction on a variety of topics in many fields.

6. *A balanced English language arts curriculum looks at both the needs of individual students and the aims of an English language arts curriculum.* We strongly believe that these two goals are not incompatible, but need to be considered equally. The goals of the English language arts curriculum are to help students become readers, writers, speakers, and thinkers who use language effectively for a wide range of purposes. Views in public discourse often reflect worry that if we "just take students from where they are" and let them "grow from experience" they will never achieve. However, Jack Thomson (1987) has said in his discussion of students' response to literature, students can only start from where they are. As we have seen, efforts to force them beyond their experience will only backfire, creating resistance and hostility toward reading and writing. To achieve the goals of the curriculum, we must consider students.

7. *The teaching and learning of language is a natural, pleasurable, invigorating experience.* We're distressed by the way language arts classes have become feared, dreaded, or seen as sites of boredom by so many students, mostly because these classes overemphasize correctness and the standard literature. Using language is, above all, a delightful experience, and that delight is shared equally by the babbling two-year-old, the punning nine-year-old, the hip-talking high school student, and the joking or love-making adult. To capitalize on the natural pleasure in language, one need not create a classroom that is a circus or use a teaching approach that involves gimmicks and games. Alfred North Whitehead argued in *The Aims of Education* (1929) that serious learning could also involve romance and disciplined play. We think that sort of attitude should flourish in today's classrooms.

# A Philosophy of One's Own

The above premises don't exhaust our philosophy; nor are these ideas set in stone. Our philosophy has evolved over the years, and our expression of that philosophy and our lists of the essentials have become refined as we've encountered new ways of looking at our own experiences and have heard more about others' experiences.

We have been confronted at times with a resistance from some teachers to the notion of theory or philosophy. However, everyone has a philosophy, everyone operates on some theory about children, learning, or teaching. Sometimes this philosophy is not conscious or articulated, but it is there nonetheless, guiding decisions about what and how to teach. We believe that articulating your philosophy allows you to make sounder, wiser decisions and solid critical judgments about the most recent teaching fads and materials purchased by your school district. An articulated philosophy allows you to provide a strong rationale for why you do what you do in the face of questions from administrators, parents, colleagues, and your students. Most important, an articulated philosophy gives you a strong foundation for making good professional decisions as you build a curriculum in language arts that is responsive to your students.

A credo, for most of us, begins with the way we were taught (for good or ill) and evolves over many years. Here are some ways of forging and articulating yours:

- Respond to each of the items on our list. Which ideas are consistent with your own? How do your ideas differ from ours, in whole or in part? What would you add to the list as central to your philosophy?

- Create your own list, a "This I Believe" statement about teaching English language arts. Keep this in a designated place in your teaching files, or create a file on your word processor, and take it out periodically to revise and amplify as you reflect on your teaching experiences.

- Read professional literature. At the end of this book you will find a bibliography of what we consider to be the most influential books of the last thirty years (plus a few older classics). We know that it's difficult to find the time to read all the books recommended to you. However, well-written professional books can provide you with new teaching ideas, new insights about teaching and learning, and inspiration. We suggest you make a reading list of books of particular interest to you and begin your own professional library. Alternatively, you may wish to ask your school or college librarian to order books you believe should be a part of an English education professional library.

- Join professional organizations. The National Council of Teachers of English, the International Reading Association, and the National Writing Project provide a wide range of resources to support teaching English language arts. In addition to publishing professional books and journals, they sponsor national and regional conferences and support local affiliate organizations where you will find other teachers who are interested in continuing their professional development as a lifelong experience. (The addresses of these and other organizations that may be of interest to you are included in the "Resources" section at the back of the book.)

- Find colleagues who share your passion for teaching and learning. In the busy, demanding world of classroom teaching, it's important to find people who are willing to exchange ideas freely and supportively. We have found our teaching friends to be important to us as we have reflected on problems with a particular class, explored ideas for trying a new approach, or simply wanted to celebrate a day that went well.

- Establish a reading group or a teacher-researcher group to share ideas about the issues and questions raised in your teaching. Discuss questions about your students and your classroom that you would like to have answered. Sondra Perl and Nancy Wilson's ([1986] 1998) work with teachers reflects our interest in the "questions that guide a teaching life" (xiii). Reading and working with other teacher friends gives you perspective and insight.

# Faculty as Community

Teaching is often a solitary activity, but it is done in concert (or cacophony) with a group of people called "the faculty." Although you can accomplish a great deal with the classroom door closed (and, unfortunately, some teachers feel forced to do this), we think students are better served in their language growth and development if your faculty has a degree of congruence in its aims. The word we think most satisfactorily describes a good language arts faculty is *community*—a group of people who work (and sometimes play) together, who are united in a common cause, and who function under a common set of guidelines and constraints. A community of teachers will grant freedom to its members to teach as they wish, yet it will also discuss mutual concerns and seek solutions to problems.

The faculty-as-community needs to spend time discussing basic issues and fundamental questions to discover its own nature and the skills of its members. Whether or not your faculty can fully agree on answers, spend time discussing such questions as the following (if you're not yet a member of a faculty, find a group of people who share your interest in teaching English language arts—fellow students in your methods class, for example):

- What is our subject (whether we call it English, language arts, communication arts, communication skills, or just plain "literacy")? What are we responsible for?

- What knowledge, skills, and abilities do youngsters need as they progress through their schooling? What do students bring with them when they come to our classrooms? What do they need?
- What is the teacher's role in students' literacy education? What information, what experience, and what practices should teachers provide to support youngsters' growth in language?
- What are English language arts teachers doing right? Where is there room for improvement?
- What is our faculty's strength as a community? What are the talents of individual members? How can we draw on those talents to improve literacy education in our school?

In far too many schools, faculties get together so infrequently that there's no coherence, no unity. Too often, as well, faculties don't meet to discuss their own problems—the agenda is set by the principal or triggered by the latest crisis or new program. We suggest that you ask your administrator to build into the school year scheduled times for departments or teams to get together to work on curriculum and to discuss teaching issues. The following projects can help faculties generate their own professional development:

- Have a session called "This Works for Me." The price of admission: copies of a handout describing a teaching activity you're willing to give away. Make the sharing of ideas a tradition among faculty members. Create ground rules about using each other's ideas (you certainly don't want to find that next year's students have already done some of your projects), and use the exchange to talk about why activities work and to brainstorm about new ones.
- Schedule regular meetings, and rotate the faculty members responsible for the discussion topics. You might like to share responses to ideas from professional literature or to local issues of concern in education.
- Have a "Problems and Pleasures" session at which you talk over the aspects of your teaching that are most satisfying and those that present recurring problems.
- Form a teacher-researcher group. Start with an issue or question about your students or your classroom that you want to explore in more depth. Discuss with your colleagues how you might find answers to your questions. As you observe your students and read about the issue, report your discoveries to your colleagues.

- Invite language arts teachers from other schools to discuss the issues they are facing. Discuss student literacy development with teachers who teach at other levels—those your students come from, those your students go to.

- Explore the possibility of a teacher exchange with a nearby college or university. Have the college teacher come and work with your students while you work with the prospective teachers. Discuss your experiences with your school colleagues.

- Discuss materials and textbook budgets and selection processes. Explore ways you can obtain the best possible materials to use with your students.

- Learn about conferences, summer workshops, and teaching institutes for teachers. Lobby with the principal or school district to enable some of your members to attend. Have teachers who have attended conferences and workshops share their discoveries with the whole faculty.

- Encourage faculty members to learn more about their students. Poll students to discover what they find useful in school, what they learn the most from, and what they most appreciate in their courses. Do the same with parents. Have a sharing session to discuss students' and parents' views.

- Hold articulation meetings among elementary, secondary, and college faculties to discuss common concerns. Ground rule: no finger pointing or accusations. Avoid the too-common problem of those from the upper levels dictating what those from the lower levels should teach!

## Setting Priorities

We can't do everything at once; human energies and financial resources won't permit it. But we can plan—as individuals and as faculties—to establish and order our priorities and concerns so that changes come about systematically, rather than willy-nilly. The following survey can be used to create an informal rank ordering of possible techniques, approaches, and methods for teaching. It will be useful to you as an individual, to a faculty, or in a methods class to explore the discrepancies between what you consider the ideal teaching situation and what you see currently being done in classrooms. Thanks to Bob Graham, a former professor and enlightened administrator.

## A Survey of Priorities

First go through the list that follows and circle on a scale of one (high) to five (low) whether you think an item is an important part of English language arts teaching today. This is an idealized list—what you think is important regardless of whether or not it is "practical." This is your "ideals" list.

> *Example:* Teacher salaries match those of professional baseball players.

Then go through the list a second time and mark with an X whether you feel this item is widely practiced. This is your "realities" list.

> *Example:* Teacher salaries match those of professional baseball players.

After you have marked both your ideals and your realities, look for discrepancies on your list and on other people's lists. If there's a great gap between your ideal and real scores, this is an item you may want to make a high priority for discussion—and for action.

This list is by no means exhaustive, so we've left a blank at the end for you to enter items of your own.

1. Literacy is taught in all content areas, not just as part of English language arts.

   1    2    3    4    5

2. Every classroom has its own library.

   1    2    3    4    5

3. Letter grades are replaced by other forms of assessment and evaluation.

   1    2    3    4    5

4. The teaching of oral language skills (speaking and listening) receives equal attention with the teaching of written language skills (writing and reading).

   1    2    3    4    5

5. Students are required to pass standardized competency examinations at various points during their elementary and/or secondary school years.

   1    2    3    4    5

6. Literature units are organized and taught by topics or themes, e.g., "War and Peace," "Nature and Environment," "Who Am I?," "Friendship," "The Individual and Society."

1    2    3    4    5

7. Grade-level minimum objectives for literacy are established.

1    2    3    4    5

8. Students have frequent opportunities to select their own books for reading.

1    2    3    4    5

9. Creative drama and role-playing are incorporated into language arts classes.

1    2    3    4    5

10. Student writing is treated as "literature" and young writers are respected as "authors."

1    2    3    4    5

11. Personal and creative writing are taught to all students.

1    2    3    4    5

12. Students learn basic principles of literary criticism like plot, character, style, versification, and analysis.

1    2    3    4    5

13. Teachers allow students to use the dialect of their regional, racial, ethnic, or social background in speech and writing.

1    2    3    4    5

14. Literature study provides students with an understanding of their cultural heritage.

1    2    3    4    5

15. Popular culture—films, recordings, video, radio, television—is given a prominent place in the language arts curriculum.

1    2    3    4    5

16. Speakers of nonstandard dialects and other languages are discouraged from using their home language in school.

1    2    3    4    5

17. Students read a common core of classic children's and adult literature in their K–12 schooling.

1    2    3    4    5

18. Grammar is mastered in the elementary grades.

     1   2   3   4   5

19. Grammar is mastered in the junior high/middle school years.

     1   2   3   4   5

20. Grammar is mastered in the senior high school years.

     1   2   3   4   5

21. Students use spelling checkers and grammar checkers to help achieve correctness.

     1   2   3   4   5

22. Television replaces reading as the literature of our age.

     1   2   3   4   5

23. Students use the Internet to communicate with others and to learn more about the world.

     1   2   3   4   5

24. Students are encouraged to see the community—its resources and its people—as an extension of school and a resource for learning more about language and literature.

     1   2   3   4   5

25. Teachers follow a set curriculum or a set of agreed upon standards and guidelines.

     1   2   3   4   5

26. Literature instruction focuses first on students' responses.

     1   2   3   4   5

27. English language arts teachers are held accountable for the successes and failures of their students through standardized tests.

     1   2   3   4   5

28. English language arts teachers use portfolios and other self-developed record systems for demonstrating what students have learned.

     1   2   3   4   5

29. The diverse cultures and languages of students are appreciated and celebrated in English language arts classes.

     1   2   3   4   5

Others (add your own): _____

_____

     1   2   3   4   5

# Selected Readings

Perl, Sondra, and Nancy Wilson. [1986] 1998. *Through Teachers' Eyes: Portraits of Writing Teachers at Work*. Portland, ME: Calendar Island Publishers.

Smith, Frank. 1995. *Between Hope and Havoc: Essays into Human Learning and Education*. Portsmouth, NH: Heinemann.

Thomson, Jack. 1987. *Understanding Teenagers' Reading: Reading Processes and the Teaching of Literature*. Norwood, South Australia: Australian Association for the Teaching of English.

Whitehead, Alfred North. 1929. *The Aims of Education*. New York: Macmillan.

# Chapter Two

# Planning for Successful Teaching

n *Emile* (1961, first published in the eighteenth century), Jean Jacque
Rousseau describes an idyllic teaching situation in which a teacher
works one-to-one with a child, helping him (unfortunately Rousseau
didn't believe girls deserved the same attention) discover new ideas in
nature or in books. In this sort of teaching, planning is done in direct
response to a young person's needs and interests.

But because student-teacher ratios are dictated by the economics of
mass education and by contract negotiations, most of us teach students in
larger groups, occasionally as small as fifteen or twenty, more often twenty-
five to thirty-five.

Many disadvantages are inherent in this system. For one thing, a group
of twenty-five to thirty-five students is anything but ideal for easily managed
whole-class (or even small-group) discussion. For another, it becomes
extremely difficult for us to think of students as individuals, and that, in
turn, forces us to adopt common textbooks, to set generic goals and standards, and to resort to mass measures for evaluation and assessment. The
ideal of individualizing instruction—meeting students' needs as they come
up—seems far removed from the reality of classroom possibilities.

In Chapter 3 we take up the topic of individualizing, with particular
emphasis on the diversity of students we meet in schools nowadays. In
*this* chapter, we discuss some ways of designing blocks of instruction—
we call these "units"—in ways that make it possible for English language
arts teachers to enrich the dimensions of their instruction for larger-than-
Rousseau-esque numbers. By a unit, we mean a teachable "chunk," which
might be as brief as a week or two of concentrated study on a topic like
"The Environment" or as extensive as a semester-long high school course
in British literature.

## What Makes a Good Unit?

Think back through the myriad courses and classes you've taken in your
school life and identify the ones that seemed most successful. (If you're an

experienced teacher, recall some of the best units you've taught.) From your perspective as teacher and student, what made them special?

Probably the first thing that comes to mind is the instructor and his or her teaching style. Some teachers could probably teach anything from parts of speech to nuclear physics and hold our attention because of the force of their personality. And there are some teachers from whom we would (and did) learn almost anything simply because we trusted them and assumed that they had our best interests in mind.

Teaching is not solely a matter of personality and certainly should not become cultish, with students mesmerized by the teacher's magnetism. As we think about our best teachers—including Steve's fourth-grade teacher, Celia Reynolds, and Joel Gold, who taught Susan's introduction to graduate English study, as we review our experiences with them and some of our own good teaching units, we see the following common traits:

1.  *A good unit interests and engages the teacher.* We won't go to the extreme of saying "teach only what interests you," but we will argue that you should "teach what you know and love best." We've found that even when we're teaching under a set syllabus or course design, there's plenty of room for us to bring in our own particular interests—the books we like to read, the kind of writing we prefer to do. In that way, we think, students get a strong sense of the importance of what is happening in the classroom. Teaching what interests and excites you is also a way of teaching yourself.

2.  As a corollary, we'd like to offer that *a good unit allows the teacher to participate as a learner.* Recent composition theory, in particular, stresses the need for teachers to participate in the instruction they offer their students, to put pen to paper and write along with the students. We've found that our classrooms are more interesting, more spontaneous, and more energetic when we introduce fresh texts, new assignments, and previously unexplored avenues of inquiry. We are then more likely to be exploring and thinking along with our students, rather than waiting for them to give the right answer or to make the predictable observation.

3.  *A good unit deals with a topic that somehow piques curiosity or meets students' needs.* The notion that "teacher knows best" leads to instruction that fails to engage the learners. We think students often know best—or, at least, better—and have a pretty solid intuitive sense of whether or not a bit of instruction is valuable. We're not calling for easy relevance or a curriculum centered around Saturday morning cartoon characters. We do, however, feel that the curriculum has to prove itself anew with each student.

4. Thus, we believe that *a good unit involves students in making choices of topics*. More important than persuading students that a unit of work is valuable is to engage students themselves in choosing some or all of the material to be discussed. We're convinced that even the work of very young children grows stronger when they make choices, and we've been impressed by the workings of the "negotiated" curriculum (Boomer 1985), in which students are told some of the core aims of study and are allowed and encouraged to add goals of their own.

5. *A good unit offers a rich variety of materials for study*. We believe that overreliance on textbooks is both stifling and limiting. In fact, if you have any control over your materials budget, we recommend spending money on class library materials, including sets of collections for small groups, magazines, and newspapers, with a decreased emphasis on whole-class readings. However, even in schools where a common text is required, there is ample opportunity to use young adult and adult literature, periodicals, Internet sources, films, and videos to enlarge the range of authors, viewpoints, and ideas available to your students.

6. *A good unit makes its aims and expectations clear*. We've all suffered through classes in which a teacher or professor never made it clear what was wanted or required, or seemed to make assignments at random. A good unit makes its purpose and direction clear from the start. It also lets students participate in describing and evaluating their work to focus on how they have met the goals of the unit.

7. *A good unit allows individual students to shape and fulfill the goals of the unit according to their own interests and needs*. Students should be encouraged to discover ways in which the topic under study connects to their own ideas, their own goals, their own world.

8. *A good unit is organized*. At the same time, you need to be careful not to *over* organize. You want to be sure your aims and goals are clear, you have a wide variety of materials, you have devised some class activities and class projects, you have a sense of direction. But you also want to leave room for student projects, student suggestions, student materials, and spontaneous discussions.

   With those criteria in mind, we offer a seven-stage process for planning units and courses. It's a scheme we've used with both experienced and inexperienced teachers, planning units from the primary grades through college. The stages are:

1. describing the students
2. choosing topics
3. setting goals
4. selecting materials
5. designing activities
6. creating sequence and structure
7. evaluating and following up

In developing this plan, we were inspired by a presentation on planning "world famous" courses given at a national meeting by Robert Beck, an English teacher at John Swett High School in Crockett, California. We've also been strongly influenced by J. W. Patrick Creber, who, in his book *Sense and Sensitivity in Teaching English* (1965), argues powerfully for developing courses, classes, and units of work based on the needs and interests of students, rather than arbitrarily imposing the structures and knowledge of literary disciplines.

## Describing the Student

In their now-classic *Teaching As a Subversive Activity* (1969), Neil Postman and Charles Weingartner observe that teachers spend tremendous effort creating the perfect course syllabus, and then the wrong students come through the door. The longer you teach, of course, the easier it is to predict the general sorts of interests and experiences your students will bring with them to your classroom. And as the school year progresses, you come to learn more and more about your students. There is always the danger, however, that students will behave as "generic" students (Fox 1995), leaving their interests, concerns, talents, and special perspectives at the door to become like everyone else. So, though the experienced teacher may be able to describe the "typical" or "stereotypical" student, it seems worth the effort to know the potential contributions, the "specialness" of each particular group and the individuals who come into your class.

What do you know about your students' likes, dislikes, and interests? What can you learn about their reading, writing, listening, and speaking backgrounds? What kinds of writing can you expect from them? School records can supply some information, as can teachers' lounge gossip, but we recommend proceeding cautiously with both of those sources. We think it's terribly important to make your own judgments about your students.

Further, we think it's important to avoid all statements that begin with the phrase "Kids nowadays are/are not." Too often, we fear, such generalizations about young people tend to be negative, often portraying children as less capable, ambitious, polite, and ethical than the generation of the pontificating adult. Marguerite Helmers (1996) has pointed out that even at the college level, the professional literature about students characterizes them as lacking, ill, and immature.

As Robert Pattison (1982) has observed, it can't be denied that today's students (and their language) are different than yesterday's; whether they are worse is not provable. Young people of any generation differ in many ways from their parents and grandparents (though they are growing up in a culture created by those same elders). It's important to put these kinds of changes into perspective and to resist grand generalizations. To collect information about your own students, you might consider doing some of the following:

---

- Establish a free-writing or journal-writing day, preferably once a week, on which students can write about anything they like. You may wish to provide some prompts: my ideal day; heroes; one change I would make in school; how I got my scar; my biggest fear; my biggest hope. But encourage students to select their own topics. Read students' work with an aim to better understanding who they are and what they care about; then look at the writing itself for evidence of language skills. This self-selected writing should not be corrected.

- Conduct a poll or survey to learn what films, television, and music appeals to your students. (Your students will enjoy this and talk about it freely, giving you a chance to assess their oral language as well. What skills do you detect as they speak on subjects close to their interests?) What does the information you collect tell you about their interests and values?

- Take your classes to the library and invite students (singly or in pairs) to identify five books they would like to see on a class reading list. In addition, ask them to establish categories of interest. Establish a free-reading day, and keep a record of the books, magazines, and other materials students read.

- Assess students' interests by having them speculate about the future. What do they expect to be doing ten, fifteen, fifty years from now? What careers interest them? What do they see as the crucial problems the world must solve in their lifetimes? How do they see themselves spending their leisure time?

- Create literacy inventories in which students can describe their interests, their skills, and their perceived needs as readers and writers. Encourage them to be reflective about their own progress and their own understanding of their work. Figure 2–1 is a sample of a survey

very helpful    somewhat helpful    not very helpful    unhelpful

1. Having the teacher's comments on my rough draft.

   _____    _____    _____    _____

2. Having the teacher's comments written on my final draft.

   _____    _____    _____    _____

3. Having an interesting topic to write about.

   _____    _____    _____    _____

4. Having oral questions from my classmates.

   _____    _____    _____    _____

5. Having oral questions from my teacher.

   _____    _____    _____    _____

6. Having mechanical and usage errors marked on my final copy.

   _____    _____    _____    _____

7. Having an opportunity to talk and freewrite before I write my first draft.

   _____    _____    _____    _____

8. Having an opportunity to revise my first draft.

   _____    _____    _____    _____

9. Starting the paper well in advance of the due date.

   _____    _____    _____    _____

10. Writing under the pressure of a deadline.

    _____    _____    _____    _____

11. Having a friend or family member read and respond to my paper.

    _____    _____    _____    _____

12. Having an "outsider" (like a tutor) read my paper.

    _____    _____    _____    _____

13. Writing in a comfortable place.

    _____    _____    _____    _____

14. Writing about a topic I care about.

    _____    _____    _____    _____

15. Having a peer group read and respond to my writing.

    _____    _____    _____    _____

**Figure 2–1 ○ What helps me write survey**

16. Reading instructions or rules in a handbook.

——————   ——————   ——————   ——————

17. Knowing how my writing will be judged.

——————   ——————   ——————   ——————

18. Knowing a lot about the topic.

——————   ——————   ——————   ——————

19. Discussing the writing of my peers.

——————   ——————   ——————   ——————

20. Reading the writing of professional writers.

——————   ——————   ——————   ——————

**Figure 2–1 ○ *(Cont.)***

in which students reflect on what they think is useful to them as writers. Ask them: What is the best book you have read (or that has been read to you)? The worst? What do you read on a regular basis? Magazines and newspapers? When and where do you like to read? What have you enjoyed writing the most?

- Learn more about what your students do outside of class. Are they interested in cars? Computers? Sports? Do they do volunteer work? Do they have jobs? Do they collect things? make things? have particular areas of expertise?

# Choosing Topics

We have a strong bias toward teaching language arts through *thematic* or *topical* units such as "Families," "The Sea," "Alienation," "Utopias," and "The Future." We greatly prefer such topics to units that center on elements of language, or rhetoric, or literary elements—the paragraph; expository writing; or character, style, and themes in the short story. A list of themes and topics that we have gleaned from the professional literature and developed for our own teaching is provided in Figure 2-2. It suggests the range of ideas and issues that can provide a framework for teaching English language arts, K-12.

| | |
|---|---|
| Celebrations and Ceremonies | Fantasy |
| Folklore | The Wilderness |
| Imaginary Worlds | Coming to America |
| Childhood | The Environment |
| War and Peace | Sports |
| Growing Up Female | Aging |
| Death and Dying | Comics and Comedy |
| The Supernatural | Multicultural America |
| City and Country | African America |
| Images of Women | Asian America |
| Nature Under Attack | Native America |
| Decisions | Hispanic/Latino America |
| Frontiers | European America |
| The Quality of Mercy | Heroes/Antiheroes |
| Careers | The American Dream |
| Love and Marriage | Legends |
| Laws, Rules, and Freedom | Rebellion |
| Survival | Beliefs |
| Science Fact and Fiction | Other Worlds |
| Traditions Around the World | International Literature |
| The Sixties | |

**Figure 2–2 ○ Unit themes and topics**

Units are often dictated by the district curriculum guide or the adopted textbook. The organization of the chapters in the textbook often creates the curriculum. Too often, however, following the order and the activities of the textbook leads to dull, canned, rote work rather than to reading and writing that helps students see connections and enjoy reading and writing.

We suggest reworking the units or chapters of the textbook in a topical way. We'd recast a section on "American Romanticism" (usually featuring Emerson, Thoreau, Hawthorne, and Whitman), for example, into a thematic unit on "Freedom and Individual Choice," with the writing of the canonical New Englanders enriched by the writing of contemporary (and often neglected) women and minorities. Rather than simply marching through the requisite poetry unit (which, we fear, puts poetry in peril by perpetuating the propensity to parse poems by poetic paraphernalia), we'd look for poems on themes and topics identified by kids as being interesting. A number of excellent collections organize poems thematically by such topics as sports, animals, nature, and things that go bump in the night. We suggest engaging students in the planning process whenever possible. Through the surveys and assessments of student interest you collect, you will learn some topics that students might like to pursue. Consider some of the following ideas for organizing thematic or topical units:

---

- Review students' interest inventories and compile a list of the themes and topics students have suggested they are interested in. Review the textbook and core curriculum (and your own interests) to see how students' interests might be included in your unit planning for the year.

- Introduce topics you will be covering during the year, and have students suggest ways their interests and concerns might become part of the units.

- After introducing upcoming units to the class, have students explore ideas in popular media and on the Internet (we discuss the possibilities and limitations of the Internet in Chapter 9) to see how contemporary materials can be integrated with traditional textbook materials. Consider newspaper and magazine articles, films, television shows, and cartoons as ways to explore ideas you will be discussing.

- Look for linking themes in the required or suggested literature in your textbook or in your curriculum. Think about ways to use the materials in your curriculum to build and connect from one unit to the next.

---

# Setting Goals

English language arts teachers are often (and sometimes rightly) faulted for having vague goals. Evidence of the lack of confidence in teachers' ability to set their own goals for their own students can be seen in the growth of the "standards" movement, in which legislators and professional teachers' organizations at both the national and state levels work to define what teachers should be doing at each grade level. Public concerns about teachers' vague objectives, such as, "to teach students the pleasure of poetry," have led to a national effort to enforce the teaching of specific objectives. Often, such efforts can actually undermine teachers' original intent when students are asked, for example, to identify the four major rhythmic patterns of poetry or to distinguish a metaphor from a simile.

Although we believe that teachers should be able to specify their goals and objectives, we see the standards and assessment movement, in some cases, taking the creation of objectives out of teachers' hands and using testing as a means of undermining and disempowering teachers. While you may be in a position where your goals must be written within the context of state or local standards, we think you can create objectives that will also be consistent with your own beliefs about what your students need and your own understanding of how young people learn and grow in their language development.

We believe that good goals and objectives answer a very simple question: Why should anyone study or learn this? Objectives can be written in many different forms, including:

- a letter to the students (and their parents) explaining what is to happen in the coming weeks
- a description of what the student will be able to do at the conclusion of this unit
- an advance copy of exams or quizzes the student will be asked to pass
- a list of the books or other materials the student will be expected to read
- a description of the writing and speaking that will be done as part of the unit
- a description of options that will be available for students with different skills, interests, and language backgrounds

In describing your goals and objectives, you will need to keep in mind a number of criteria to make sure you are on track. First, you will want to make sure that objectives are consistent with one another, that they fit into a coherent pattern, and that they are realistic and manageable in the time you have allowed. Second, you want your objectives to be consistent with a supportable philosophy of teaching language arts and with a clear understanding of how young people learn. Can you back each of your goals with an explanation of how this activity supports and develops students' language learning? Finally, you need to ask if your goals meet the real needs of your students. Here, you will need to refer back to your description of your students, the actual people who come through the door. We are concerned that many prepackaged materials seem to have goals centered more on what someone thinks kids need or ought to have than on what will actually move their language skills ahead.

# Selecting Materials

Finding materials for a course, class, or unit, is, to us, one of the most enjoyable parts of the planning process. As soon as we know what we will be teaching the next year or semester, we start looking out for materials we can use in our courses. We pore over book catalogs, look for resources at garage sales, and poke around in bookstores, especially secondhand ones. We keep our eyes open for videos, television specials, and radio programs. We look at our old collections of literature to see what we can pull out and reuse. We look for articles that are relevant as we read the newspaper and magazines. And we use the public library. We often have dozens of books checked out from the public library that our students are using in our classrooms.

As you start your unit, spend half an afternoon browsing in the bookstore and school library. Tell your librarian what your unit (or course) title is, and ask for a list of resources available within the school. You'll soon come up with a list of dozens of titles that can be of help. As you compile this bibliography, we suggest that you code items, using a symbol system such as this:

*W* = appropriate for use by the *whole class*

*S* = best with *small groups* of students

*I* = most useful for *individual* study

Some additional questions to ask about your materials list:

---

- Do you have a wide range of literature—poems, plays, stories, non-fiction?
- Are the perspectives of women, ethnic minorities, and others represented?
- Have you included works from countries around the world, not limiting yourself to the literature of the Western world?
- Are any classic works for children or young adults appropriate?
- Have you found materials from popular or contemporary culture?
- Are students being asked to deal with language from a range of media?
- Do the materials allow for various levels of language skill?

---

# Designing Unit Activities

You have a set of objectives. You have a list of materials. Now brainstorm for the substance of your course, linking your objectives and materials by developing actual reading/writing/speaking activities for your students. (The remainder of this book is dedicated to helping you generate more and more possibilities.) As before, code the activities according to their appropriateness for the whole class (W), small groups (S), or individual work (I). As you proceed:

- Create a list of writing assignments that are appropriate to this course or unit. Think of ways in which students can use different genres to explore ideas.
- Develop ways in which reading selections might be a jumping-off point for writing. Select the pieces that will be most provocative or stimulating for your students.
- Create options in assignments for students to choose reading or projects appropriate to their ability levels.
- Brainstorm a list of audiences students might write for other than the teachers.
- Consider ways that students' self-selected reading and writing might fit into your course.
- List selections from the media—film, video, TV, radio, newspapers, magazines—that can be used as starting points for activities.
- Develop some connections students might make with other subject areas—history, science, art, music, geography, technology.
- List work activities outside the classroom that students might be engaged in—field trips, volunteer work, service learning, or jobs—that are related to your course.
- Brainstorm for ways in which you can bring the world to your classroom through speakers, demonstrations, and guests.

# Creating Sequence

This is the hard part—and the fun part: getting from objective to fulfillment. Every teacher has his or her own way of preparing for a course or unit. Some like to have a day-to-day plan that they know they will have to adjust as they go along. Some like to have more structured activities at the beginning the unit and leave more time at the end for student projects and student-initiated work. Some like to build in time throughout the unit for issues and questions that come up during reading, writing, and discussion. Our general practice is to start out with a fairly specific set of plans and activities, including those in which we try to figure out the interests and needs of the students we're working with. Then the unit starts to open up, particularly through the use of small groups and individual projects. Thus, in our teaching, we're most satisfied with units that move:

- from whole-class to individualized activities
- from teacher-initiated to student-developed projects
- from core or common to individualized readings
- from basic or introductory tasks to more difficult ones
- from where we perceive the students to be to where we think they can or probably should go
- from where the students see themselves to where they want to be

Of course, any structure you design before you actually teach the unit is tentative—a scenario, a sketch—not a blueprint to be followed to the last shingle. Although some teachers feel that typing out a syllabus or unit plan is unduly restrictive, in all of our teaching, kindergarten through college, we write out at least a tentative plan so the students will have a sense of where they're going.

Figure 2–3 shows a rough sketch of a ninth-grade English course. You can see that the teacher has worked out a series of phases through which the course will progress. From this the teacher can create daily plans in two- or three- or four-week blocks, allowing for discussions and ideas that emerge as students read, write, and discuss the work of the course.

Different teachers have different organization patterns. Some like to use the blocked-out lesson-plan books available from schools or teacher stores, so they can see a two-week schedule at a glance. Some like to lay out a grid with a box for each day to see a month or more at a time. Checking the boxes keeps you on track day-by-day, while a glance at the grid gives the larger picture of scope and sequence.

# Evaluating and Following Up

We discuss evaluation in more detail in Chapter 4, where we also take up the topic of grading. We are aware that giving students grades is one of the central responsibilities of teachers. But we want to argue for a broader, more useful (to students, to parents, to administrators, to teachers) definition of what it means to evaluate. We see evaluation as an integral part of what

Part I (2 weeks). Getting acquainted. Use interest inventories to get to know students. Teacher reading aloud and student reading silently of high-interest short stories, followed by journal responses. Students begin collecting examples of language use from newspapers.

Part II (6 weeks). Personal reading and writing. Students will write at least two personal narratives about important events in their lives. Time will be provided for free reading from the classroom library, with books mostly chosen from adolescent literature. Students start file folder of common usage errors, spelling problems etc. Teacher presents lessons on "how to read a poem," "how to read a play" etc.

Part III (6 weeks). Reading and writing about the larger world. Students write two papers reacting to issues and problems they see going on around them, in school, in the state, in the world at large. Newspapers-in-education program will provide us with copies of the daily paper for four weeks. Students read at least two books from the classroom library emphasizing nonfiction + they mostly books written for adolescents.

Part IV (4 weeks). High school reading and writing. Students write one paper about a favorite subject, after reading at least one nonfiction book in that area. Instructor will help students see ways of applying their reading and writing skills in other school courses.

**Figure 2–3 ○ Sequence for English 9**

teachers—and students—do every day. In assessing students' growth and development, we need to look at the whole context of learning—our goals and objectives, students' skills and abilities, and students' level of success at performing and mastering the work of the course. Teachers need a variety of ways to communicate their sense of students' success beyond simply putting grades on tests and papers. We believe that students need to be engaged in this process as well. Students need to assess their own sense of accomplishment based on the goals of the course and their efforts to meet those goals. And finally, teachers need to be constantly reassessing themselves, using students' input to gauge the effectiveness of their efforts. In designing a broad evaluation plan, consider some of the following:

---

- Keep a teaching journal. Spend a few minutes each day jotting down your perceptions of what's happening in your classroom. The journal will allow you to keep tabs on students who interest or puzzle you, as well as give you an opportunity to focus on your efforts.

- Keep a "showcase" portfolio of your teaching. Sometimes in the rush of teaching and the frustrations of daily classroom life, you forget to focus on what's working. Keep sample lessons, photocopies of sample successful student work, photographs of displays and student projects, and any of the successful writing you did with your students.

- Have students keep portfolios of their work; "process" and showcase portfolios demonstrate both students' development (with drafts, notes, and in-process thinking) and achievements (projects, lists of readings, final drafts) (more on portfolios in Chapter 4).

- Check with students periodically to see how things are working for them. When they hand in compositions, ask them to add a note about what they like and don't like about the paper. At the end of a class period, ask them to summarize what they have learned that day or week. Have them do weekly "sign-offs" telling you how they feel about the week's work, raising questions and issues they'd like answered or addressed.

- Create criteria for grading papers or projects collaboratively with your students. In a class discussion on grading, ask students to develop the list of things you should consider when grading and how each aspect of the assignment should be valued in importance.

- Work with students to create test items that address what they consider to be the important work they have been doing.

- At the end of a unit, write along with your students a course- and self-evaluation that looks at the unit's strongest and weakest points and what might be done differently the next time.

---

In addition to getting students to think about their own success and the success of the course through evaluation, we think it's important to think of follow-up activities that extend reflection beyond this particular unit or course. We like engaging students in discussions of "what next?" since it encourages them to offer suggestions for subsequent activities. Moreover, we think that it's important for students leaving our class at the end of the year or the end of the semester to think about how this course or this unit fits into the rest of their school career. What might they expect from the next teacher? What skills have they learned in your course that they can take elsewhere? How can they use their learning from your class—knowledge from specific books, reading strategies, writing processes, and insights about how to study or work—in other aspects of their school career and life? We believe that asking students to make these connections provides a model for how they might think of their learning as being part of a bigger picture.

# A Footnote on Lesson Planning

The seven-step unit plan we have described provides you with a skeleton or outline, but it does not detail day-to-day teaching. The term "lesson plan" is anathema to many teachers, and a lot of old pros claim they never use one. We're old pros, too, and happily confess that we still write lesson plans, feeling that it's important to go into class having a guide down on paper. (We also confess that our lesson plans are shorter and a good deal less formal than they were in our early days of teaching.)

For new teachers and experienced veterans both, we suggest a lesson-planning form that is a microcosm of the six-step plan, beginning with objectives and moving toward evaluation. Given our earlier discussion of unit planning, we think the lesson plan given in Figure 2–4 is self-explanatory.

1. Objectives

   In two or three sentences, describe the major objectives of the lesson: what the students will read, discuss, write, and think about—and why. Focus on what students will actually accomplish in the lesson. Your objectives may also show how this lesson builds on whatever preceded it.

**Figure 2–4 ◦ A short form for lesson planning**

2. Materials

   List the basic resources: texts, media, speakers. Don't forget pencils, scissors, markers, and glue, if they'll be needed for student projects.

3. Procedures

   Outline what you plan to do in as much detail as is required for clarity and your own understanding. Don't lock yourself into a script. Provide space for student response.

4. Evaluation and Follow-Up

   Note how you propose to assess the unit and the students. Some of this may be observation, some may be written response, and some may be based on specific criteria for projects, writing, and even tests. Use the evaluation part of your planning to think about how this unit fits into the bigger picture of what you are trying to accomplish with students and where you will go next.

5. In Retrospect

   Complete this part after the unit. Using student feedback and your own journal or observations, take a few minutes to write up your own reactions. How did it go? What would you change if you were doing the same lesson tomorrow?

6. In Prospect

   What have you and your students learned from this experience? How can it be applied in the future—for them? for you?

**Figure 2–4** ∘ *(Cont.)*

# Selected Readings

Boomer, Garth. 1985. *Negotiating the Curriculum*. Sydney: Ashton Scholastic.

Creber, J. W. Patrick. 1965. *Sense and Sensitivity in Teaching English*. London: University of London. Reprinted by the Exeter Curriculum Study Centre, St. Luke's, College of Education, Exeter, U.K.

Fox, Tom. 1995. *The Social Uses of Writing*. Carbondale: Southern Illinois University Press.

Helmers, Marguerite. 1996. *Writing Students*. Carbondale: Southern Illinois University Press.

Henderson, James G. 1996. *Reflective Teaching: The Study of Your Constructive Practices*. 2d ed. Englewood Cliffs, NJ: Merrill.

Postman, Neil and Charles Weingartner, 1969. *Teaching As a Subversive Activity*. New York: Delacorte Press.

# Chapter Three

# Diversifying and Individualizing

There's little disagreement among English language arts teachers about the need to meet students' individual needs and interests. "Meeting kids' needs" is virtually a cliché in our profession. We know that students come to us with varying backgrounds and skills in language. Some seem to have been born speaking fluent, articulate, socioeconomically "correct" language. Others struggle with language, particular the forms that are generally accepted and promoted by the schools. We realize, too, that unlike some subjects and disciplines in which goals are common for all students and the sequence of instruction is clear, language study is by its very nature less precise and predictable.

Yet when it comes to creating a classroom that's responsive to these varying individual interests, learning styles, language abilities, reading levels, listening and speaking competencies, and writing skills, overwhelmed teachers often prefer a less effective—but less chaotic and more time honored—"shotgun" approach: teaching a bit of everything, aiming in the general direction of the class, and hoping that most of the students are hit by one linguistic pellet or another.

Further, individualizing is made difficult by large classes. Paying attention to diversity would be a lot simpler if we could see kids one at a time or in small groups. Even getting to know the strengths and interests of our students is difficult in classes with thirty-five students. And when one has five classes of thirty-five, the task seems nearly impossible.

Nevertheless, individualizing is possible even under less-than-ideal conditions. If you're truly committed to the philosophy of "teaching kids where they are" and if you're willing to explore alternative ways of structuring and organizing the class—everything from text-selection to how you spend your time in the classroom—there are a number of approaches and strategies that can work for you.

# Characteristics of the Individualized Classroom

1. *Your role as a teacher is widely varied.* Sometimes you will be at the center of the classroom, providing instruction or directions for a project in which the whole class is involved. At other times you will act as a resource person, moving from student to student, group to group, helping students make decisions about how they want to approach their work. You may also act as a librarian, assisting students in finding materials; this requires that you know a wider range of literature than the usual classics. You must be alert to techniques and approaches that will involve many different kinds of students. Which kids seem to need highly structured activities rather than independent projects? Which students function best in small groups? Which ones are loners who prefer to be by themselves? Are there students whose language background prevents them from participating fully in class or in groups? Are there kids who are sufficiently bored or alienated by school that they need particular attention to get back on track?

2. *The roles of students vary and often are different from classroom to classroom.* Students often become accustomed to lockstep assignments about which they don't have to make very many decisions. Independence for the learner is an important component of the individualized classroom, and students often must receive instruction before they can work successfully. In fact, they sometimes rebel, initially, when forced to figure out things for themselves. They don't know what's important to learn, because they haven't been asked to think about it before. Students may not have worked in small groups, and they may not have experienced self-selected projects. Rather than lamenting these problems, you as an individualizing teacher must see this learner dependency as an opportunity to help students function in a wider range of learning/self-teaching ways.

3. *The individualized classroom requires a variety of ways of assessing students' progress and keeping records.* Perhaps the biggest objection we've heard to the individualized classroom centers on record-keeping. "It's tough to monitor thirty kids doing the same thing. How am I supposed to keep track of the same bunch doing thirty different things at once?" Although there are no easy answers to this objection, individualized classrooms have been around long enough that we know some concrete ways of doing the record-keeping and of having students be responsible for doing it themselves. And, in fact, expecting students to be accountable for their

own work, their own progress, and their own demonstration of accomplishment is one useful outcome of individualized classrooms.

4. *Individualization requires a lot of materials and organization.* A second common objection we hear involves the raw amount of material required: more books, more audio and video recordings, an enormous range of reading materials, access to Internet sources, and a great diversity of activities. It's understandably easier to select a chapter from the text and give everybody the same assignment. When you are aware, however, that some students don't do the assignment, some try but don't get it, and some do it but find it boring, you become worried that too many students may not be learning what you hope to teach. And when you are aware that the world is full of useful and engaging materials, many of them available in your school or community at very low cost, then you start considering the advantages of individualizing. The trick is, first, to have the commitment to individualize and, second, to become aggressive in moving your classroom beyond the limitations of the textbook.

5. *Individualized classrooms require flexible use of furniture and space.* Wait. We'll modify that to say that, at best, individualized classrooms are furnished helpfully. We've dreamed about an ideal classroom for years: one with a variety of comfortable chairs and tables, a publishing center, a computer center, an art center, small-group meeting space, a well-stocked media section, and places where students can be alone to concentrate on their reading and writing. Yet our own teaching has more often than not been in barren conventional classrooms, including some with desks bolted to the floor. And too often, unfortunately, teachers have to move from room to room to teach, leaving them no possibilities to create a classroom environment, not to mention organize their materials in a useful way for students. Despite those limitations, we find it possible to individualize.

In this chapter, we offer some ways of getting started in creating an individualized classroom (keeping in mind the reality that most of you will *not* teach in idyllic conditions with unlimited supplies). Then we review some of the ways of structuring and organizing the individualized classroom, and conclude with a potpourri of ideas for introducing even greater range and diversity into your English language arts classroom.

## Some First Steps

It's important to remember that individualizing takes time. Don't try to individualize all your classes at once, and don't try to do it every day of the year. Further, don't abandon the cause when your early attempts to reach difficult students fail or when kids sit around doing nothing rather than thanking you through action for the opportunity to take control of their own learning. Here are some ways to get started gradually:

- Set up a corner or cabinet in your classroom to be used by students who have completed their regular classwork. Stock it with magazines, current newspapers, a paperback book rack, a file of crossword puzzles, and some word games.
- Establish free-reading and free-writing days, times when the only assignment is for students to engage themselves productively in *their* choice of language activities. Many teachers who start this sort of program eventually use the approach for entire classes. If "free" bothers you or sounds too unstructured, call these "reading/writing workshops."
- Use workshop or free-reading/writing days for conferences. Talk with students individually about their favorite assignments, books, or projects. Help them with reading and writing assignments. Discuss what they might like to do in the future.
- Identify the most-difficult or least-motivated students in your class and concentrate on bringing in books they might especially enjoy.
- Expand the number of options you give in assignments. If you've been giving students one topic to write about, let them have a choice of three. If everybody has been reading the same novel, experiment with offering two or three choices.
- Get students started creating and being responsible for their English language arts portfolio. Keep the folders in a box or crate in the classroom. Make it the students' responsibility to include (organized) copies of written work completed for the class, along with lists of the books, stories, and poems they've read. Get your students used to bringing their portfolios when you hold conferences.
- Begin a journal-writing project that allows students to pursue self-selected topics. Once students are in the habit of writing in their journals for ten minutes every day on topics they wish to pursue, they begin to discover what they are interested in and to use writing for their own purposes. Use this information about their interests to create student-centered assignments.
- Assign more small-group work. Only when you get yourself away from center stage can true individualizing take place. As students work in groups, you'll find that you are freed to begin working with

them one-on-one. Moreover, as more responsibility is placed on students for directing their own activities, they will learn to work independently without your constant direction.

- Use your responses to student writing as an opportunity to get to know students and help develop their direction and goals, rather than as an opportunity to correct their language. Your response to students' work can help them see where they may go next.

- Use student-group interactive journals as another means of placing emphasis on student collaboration. Set up these journals as working documents in which students can respond to one another about ideas for group projects, the literature they are reading, collaborative presentations, etc.

# A Catalog of Structures for Individualizing Instruction

## The Project Method

This technique dates back to the 1920s, when progressive education was experimenting with new approaches. The class (or group of students), with the assistance of the teacher, selects a topic or project for study. Projects can range from the handy/practical (building birdhouses, planting a community garden) to the abstract and/or political (getting out the vote, lobbying for better after-school care). Literary, historical, even philosophical topics can be investigated as well. The individualizing comes about as students break the project or task into manageable portions for individual or small-group work.

Geoffrey Summerfield wrote what is perhaps the best book on topic selection, *Topics in English* (1965, now unfortunately out of print). His topics for work with junior high-aged children include "Reptiles," "Fire and Ice," "The Antarctic," and "Home and Family." For each topic he lists literature for the teacher to read aloud to the students, literature for individual reading, and ideas for individual study. The projects he suggests range from "hands-on" research (such as observing a snake in a terrarium and reporting on its habits) to imaginative writing (a short story about being terrified by a snake). If you can find a copy of Summerfield's book, read it.

Project teaching has been an important part of elementary school teaching in Great Britain, Australia, and New Zealand. It has never really caught on in the United States. More's the pity, we say.

## Teaching by Themes

A variation of the project method better-known in the United States involves teaching by themes. (The unit design we present in Chapter 2 reveals our interest in this style of teaching, which we rely on heavily in both our school and college classes.) The steps in thematic teaching are these:

1. *Choose a theme or topic to provide focus for the class.* (A list of sample themes is provided in Figure 2–2.)
2. *Identify core or common readings for the whole class.* This might be a required novel, but more often common readings are short—stories, poems, plays, essays—either read aloud by the teacher or found in classroom anthologies or texts.
3. *Create possibilities for individual and/or small-group reading or writing on the theme.* Frequently these can grow from initial discussion of the core readings, so students themselves are identifying fiction, nonfiction, poetry, and drama they would like to read and the writing they would like to complete.
4. *Provide time for individual and small-group work.* This allows time for you to act as coach, resource person, tutor, and cheerleader.
5. *Provide time for coming together and sharing reading and writing.* This creates opportunities for students to demonstrate their expertise and to learn from one another.

The pattern, then, is one of starting from a common point, branching out into individual work, and returning to the center.

## The Workshop Approach

The enormous growth in teaching writing "as process" in the United States has helped teachers learn about the workshop approach to teaching. Of course, the workshop is an old and respected model for teaching in many fields and disciplines, from theater to woodshop. It is student-centered and hands-on, and places the teacher in a tutor/tutee or master/apprentice relationship with students.

In the writing workshop, writers work on their own papers, developing their work from idea to draft to final copy. Students sometimes work in small groups or in pairs, but they spend much of their time alone. Movement from writing to talking and back to writing is fluid and based on student needs. The teacher checks with individual students to see how she or he may be of help, confers with individuals and groups who request it and answers questions or nudges students who are stuck.

The writing workshop approach seems so comfortable and productive that many teachers have launched their own reading workshops or reading/writing workshops in which students read on their own, share their responses with peers and teachers, and write about what they have read. Nancie Atwell's book *In the Middle* (1998) describes the workshop approach in considerable detail for middle school classes, and most of her strategies can be adapted at higher and lower levels.

The essence of the workshop method is to abandon the notion of a common curriculum. The teacher helps students identify topics to write about through interest inventories and journal writing and assists them in finding books to read in the library, from book carts brought to the room, or from a classroom library the teacher has built up over time. Students work at their own pace, as long as they are productive, and the teacher, freed from the common or core curriculum, has plenty of time for individual conferences and assistance.

Of course, a pure workshop approach—five days a week, 180 days a year—may seem excessive, and using workshops can be combined with other approaches. Many teachers are comfortable doing common activities two or three days a week and conducting class workshops the rest of the time.

Some teachers have reservations about workshop teaching—it seems unstructured and doesn't guarantee common learnings. We invite you to consider that, properly carried out, a workshop guarantees that kids will concentrate on self-selected reading and writing topics much of the time they are in the language arts class, developing the skills and ideas they are ready to work on. Given the amount of time spent over the years flogging students through grammar, spelling, organization, and literature-appreciation lessons, we see the hands-on, time-on-task focus of workshops as being decidedly superior.

## Small-Group Work and Student Collaboration

A key to individualized learning is for you as the teacher to abandon the traditional role of lecturer–information dispenser and become a kind of classroom manager: one who guides students into language and encourages them to take responsibility for their learning. Having kids learn from each other is a very effective way of accomplishing this change of role. Some possibilities:

- Cross-age teaching. Many schools have experimented with using students to work with children of other ages. Second graders read to kindergartners. Tenth-grade students read to senior citizens. Middle school kids put on a puppet show or readers' theater performance for fourth graders. College education students teach senior high writing. In these settings, "teachers" seem to learn as much as or more than "students."

- Peer tutoring. Equals can learn a great deal from one another. Although some teachers worry about "shared ignorance," peer tutoring more frequently turns out to be a sharing of growth. As tutor and tutee articulate questions and answers and work on problem-solving, both are sharpening their language and thinking. Students can help each other with reading, writing, and literature, raising questions and focusing on potential solutions. They can respond to and edit one another's writing, talk through interpretations of literature, suggest strategies when they are stuck in their reading, and answer one another's questions about spelling or usage.

- Small-group work. Group work is a mainstay of individualized teaching. Instead of asking questions about the meaning of a poem, give it to a small group and ask them to present their ideas about it. Create writer-response groups in which students give one another feedback on their drafts. Use groups to subdivide and explore thematic topics and prepare class projects; ask groups to locate reading material for others in the class; allow students to prepare and dramatize scripts; and have students prepare group readings of their own writing. Group work is most productive when students have some choice in the kind of work they do and when they will be accountable for an end product or result.

- Using student assistants. Using students as teacher aides involves them more deeply in the real activities of teaching and learning, especially when their work is meaningful rather than just handling routine classroom tasks like filing papers or tidying the classroom. We know of an elementary school in Canada where aides helped the librarian put together collections of reading materials for in-class libraries that circulated in the classrooms. Fourth-grade aides in Michigan put together tape-recorded book reviews so that children choosing new books could listen to a taped commentary by a peer before confirming a selection.

- Sharing skills. We are continually astonished by the range of skills and knowledge that our students bring to our classes, and we often ask them "What do you know about that people never ask you about in school?" We discover kids who are skilled in sports, crafts, and hobbies; students who are involved in community service and clubs; and, not infrequently, students who like to read and write on the sly, outside the watchful eyes of teachers. Have your students share their skills and interests. In doing so, they'll create a great deal of interesting and lively language.

## Learning Centers

In learning or activity centers, *materials* do the work of structuring and individualizing. You may use activity centers as a part of a reading/writing workshop, as places where students may work with their small groups, as centers for working on individual projects, and as resources for students who have finished whole-class assignments. You may also devote one or two days a week to activities in which students make use of learning centers. You may wish to gear your learning centers to a particular unit the class is working on, or you may create learning centers that provide alternatives to regular ongoing classwork.

A key to successful learning centers is to have plenty of interesting ideas and materials available for students. In addition, you will want to keep the center organized so that students can easily find materials they would like to use. (You may wish to have teams responsible for tidying the learning center, letting you know when supplies are low, changing the decor, and even adding their own ideas to the reading and writing suggestions.) Make sure that you provide instructions for students to be able to work on their own. Some possibilities for centers include:

- Reading (with a rich supply of books, magazines, and a daily newspaper). Students who need quiet to read might find the reading center a nice escape.

- Responding. In addition to a place where a group of students can sit to discuss their reading and writing, there might be available here posters with good questions to ask writers and to use as the basis for response to books. (Having students generate new questions and make the posters is a good center activity.)

- Writing. This is a great place to put a computer or two. Having lap boards, scratch paper (the backs of computer drafts), and writing utensils available puts writing at kids' fingertips.

- Editing/copyediting. Set up this center with lots of reference books, dictionaries, and tips and reminders for polishing writing.

- Graphics. A learning center is a good place for a computer with desktop publishing and drawing/drafting programs. Also make available attractive paper, cardstock, glue, staples, and tape for bookmaking, with instructions for various kinds of binding.

- Listening. Include recorded literature done by students and professionals with tape or CD players with earphones, so that more than one student can listen at a time without disrupting others.
- Language games. Include *Scrabble*, crosswords, hangman, and word searches, as well as materials for kids to create puzzles for one another.

---

A learning center approach obviously requires a permanent classroom of your own, something not always available to secondary school teachers. As an alternative, create a mobile learning center through the use of activity cards. Do these on 8½-by-11-inch pieces of poster board, with glued-on graphics, instructions, and photographs. Or, create a series of index cards that suggest writing, dramatic ideas, art ideas, or study questions.

Each activity card contains a task or assignment, plus instructions on how to complete it. Whether or not you have a permanent classroom, you might construct sets of cards for particular units you're teaching. At appropriate points, open up your box of cards and allow students to select the ones on which they want to work. You'll achieve instant individualization. In addition, you can have students add their own ideas for reading, writing, speaking, and listening, and extend the range of possibilities for future students.

With the aid of a computer, you can simplify your work by filing away activity ideas in a database or hypertext program, adding to your collection year by year, sorting through the ideas electronically, and printing out fresh copies of the activity cards you need for a given class.

## Contract Learning

In contract learning, students design or "contract for" the work they will complete in order to satisfy a class requirement. Contracts can be written for just about any component of a language arts class: reading, literature, writing, drama, speech. Generally a contract, designed by the student and approved by the teacher, will include:

1. *the topic or title*, plus a one-sentence description of what's to be done
2. *the student's aims* in completing the contract: what does he or she want to learn?
3. *a specific plan*: books to be read, writing to be completed, scripts to be created
4. *a timetable* for completion of the project

5. *a set of criteria for evaluation,* showing both teacher and student whether the contract has been fulfilled

Malcolm Knowles's book *Using Learning Contracts* (1986) provides a particularly comprehensive look at the design of contracts, although his focus is primarily on adult education and fields other than language arts. You can learn a great deal by analogy, however, from the contracts his students have designed in fields such as nursing, psychology, and higher education. (We also discuss contracts as a useful method of *grading* in the next chapter.)

Related to the contract system is the more traditional *independent study,* in which students develop an entire course of study and complete the project work on their own, perhaps checking in with a teacher from time-to-time. The Washoe County (Nevada) School District does this through the awarding of travel credits. Students who are vacationing with their parents (or accompanying them on business), study the place they are visiting to learn its history, culture, and art. They may visit historic places, museums, or libraries. They may read newspapers and literature of the place; write essays, stories, or poetry; and take photographs or collect postcards. A final product may include a scrapbook, a series of writings, an album, or a combination of these. We think this is an especially interesting and valuable activity for immigrant children who make visits to their homeland, or for students who have artifacts, photos, and memories of their native country.

We believe that there's a great deal of potential in contracts and independent study. First, such work begun early in students' careers can go a long way toward making them independent and responsible for their own learning. Second, students have more opportunity to pursue the learning they find to be vital. Finally, students can make much greater use of their own knowledge, their own histories, and their own cultures and bring them into the classroom in a way that instructs other members of the learning community and places value on diversity.

# Putting It All Together

There's no fixed or obligatory pattern for individualizing class instruction. The very word suggests flexibility rather than a master plan. As we suggest in Chapter 2, our own teaching usually begins with common or core activities that set the tone and content of the unit. We then increase the amount of small-group work in the class, helping students become more and more skilled at working independently of their teacher. As we help students work together productively in groups, we also encourage them to think about individual projects, topics, or readings, sometimes as spin-offs from whole-class or small-group activities, at other times simply growing from the students' own interests. We then draw this all back together through reports, presentations, and performances based on small-group or individual work. This pattern, incorporating the various approaches to individualization discussed in this chapter, is presented in Figure 3–1. We believe that if we want to help our students become self-directed and independent, we must help them practice the decision-making, self-selected projects, and choice that independent learners engage in.

# Additional Ideas for Individualizing and Diversifying

- Search through the holdings of your school or district media center for materials that will add diversity to your teaching.
- Systematically videotape programs that make connections with your teaching.
- Work with your school librarian to build up the children's and young adult collections in the school. Read *The English Journal, The Journal of Reading, The Reading Teacher, Language Arts,* and other professional publications to look for titles that your library should acquire.
- Invite parents to read and review books for you. (This is also a useful way to head off censorship problems.) Parents might also volunteer to go to your local public library and look up appropriate titles and call numbers to help students find individualized reading.
- Use the Internet to find an incredibly dazzling array of materials—from educational to governmental to corporate to private resources—your students can draw on. Teach students to "consider the source" when evaluating materials from cyberspace.
- Review CD-ROMs on a variety of topics to see what might be appropriate to the work your students are doing. Ask your librarian to order these for the media center. CD-ROMs provide the multimedia experience that students have become accustomed to in their multisensory worlds.
- Campaign to get a paperback bookstore established in your school, with the proceeds to be used to help build the range of resources available in your school.
- Start a class newsletter, with most of the work being done by the students, as a regular publishing venture. Send this home to describe the varied events going on in your class.

**Whole Class**

Announcements, Requirements, Common Readings
Discussion of Central Theme, Brainstorming for Projects
Lectures (as needed), Whole-Class Discussion
Common Writing Assignments, Films and Videos

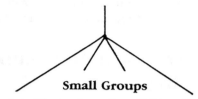

**Small Groups**

Literature Discussions, Peer Editing, Scripting
Investigating Theme Subtopics, Planning Presentations
Reading Special-Interest Books
Working in Activity Centers

**Individual Work**

Contract Work, Independent Study, Individualized Reading
Special-Interest Writing, Completing Activity Cards
Tutoring and Being Tutored, Reading/Writing Center
Student-Teacher Conferences
Solo Work in Activity Centers
Personal Evaluation, Record Keeping, and Assessment

**Whole Class**

Shared Writing, Book Reviews and Reports
Small-Group Reports and Presentations
Individual Reports and Presentations
Discussion and Evaluation of Whole-Class Performance

**Figure 3–1 ○ Patterns of individualizing class instruction**

- Find the address of your state council for the arts and humanities and learn about its "writers in the schools" program. Find out what other educational opportunities state agencies offer schools.

- Find a book on sources of free and inexpensive things (most bookstores carry several such titles). Get students started on a letter-writing campaign for free pamphlets, brochures, and posters that would be of use in your teaching. Also write to the U.S. government asking for its consumer catalog, which lists many free and inexpensive materials you'll find helpful in a variety of ways. The address is: Consumer Information Center, Pueblo, CO 81009. You can reach them by e-mail at catalog.pueblo@gsa.gov. Their website is www.pueblo.gsa.gov.

- At the public library, you will find brochures related to local, regional, state, and national concerns for health, consumerism, and services. See if any are related to projects your students are working on.

- Explore school-business partnerships. Many businesses are eager to help with supplies, speakers, and even classroom volunteers.

- Campaign for a schoolwide reading/writing center, where kids with particular problems can get help.

- Explore service-learning opportunities for your students. Students learn about the community, practice volunteerism, and gain skills by helping with parks improvement, food distribution, and recreation needs in the places they live.

- Tap the expertise of your students' parents. Find out what those parents have as special skills and invite them to come into your classroom to meet with the students.

- Develop a list of interviewees (friends, neighbors, relatives, and parents) who students might draw on as they pursue individual topics.

- Look for volunteers to come into your class on a regular basis: parents, university students, senior citizens. Use these folks to help you break down the class into smaller and smaller groups.

# Selected Readings

Allen, Janet. 1995. *It's Never Too Late: Leading Adolescents to Lifelong Literacy*. Portsmouth, NH: Heinemann.
Atwell, Nancie. 1998. *In the Middle: New Understandings About Writing, Reading, and Learning*. 2d ed. Portsmouth, NH: Heinemann.
Knowles, Malcolm S. 1986. *Using Learning Contracts*. San Francisco: Jossey-Bass.
Summerfield, Geoffrey. 1965. *Topics in English*. London: Batsford.

# Chapter Four

# Assessment, Evaluation, and Grading

Teachers are often afflicted by the "end-of-term blues." Not only do they have papers and projects stacked up to read, but they must translate student work into a grade as well. Students must be sorted and categorized to find their place on an A, B, C or E, G, F or 4.0–0.0 or 100–0 scale. The problem is one of reducing the complexity of a student's growth and development to a single abstract symbol. Should we grade on interest and involvement? Cooperation? Overall growth? Competency? Work effort? Actual output? What do we do about the student who comes with few language skills and works hard throughout the term, but who still performs less well than peers? Or the student who is very competent to begin with and produces uninvolved but acceptable work all term?

Regardless of the problems experienced by the teacher in reaching the final grade, we know too well the reactions of students and parents. The As and 4.0s are prized, the Bs and 3.0s are seen as measures of second-rateness, and the Cs and 2.0s are interpreted as indicators of outright mediocrity. Grades often divert attention from true language development; they induce false competitiveness in students; and they force students and teachers to focus on narrow, "countable" aims and objectives.

In the field of English language arts, grades are extraordinarily subjective. Assemble a dozen English teachers and ask them to come up with a concrete list of criteria for "good" writing, or ask them to place letter grades on some themes read in common. The assigning of grades and criteria will vary widely. This is not to suggest that we language arts teachers don't know what we're doing. Literacy is such a complex affair that the range and value of what we read and write is highly nuanced. Although most specialists can agree in general on the traits of excellent work, we quarrel and debate on the finer points.

Educators, psychologists, and learning theorists can present strong evidence of the ill effects grading has on students. Yet grading is deeply entrenched in the educational system. Students and parents claim they need grades, that they "want to know where things stand," even when that knowledge can place students, teachers, and parents at odds with each other, even when students begin to narrowly define themselves based on grades. College admissions offices rely on grades as a predictor of success, and some potential employers look closely at students' grades as one clue to their value as employees. Even some educators seem to place undue emphasis on students' past records to predict their success (or failure). So the education mill continues to grind out grades.

What is the response of the humanistic teacher who finds grading harmful or arbitrary? What kind of evaluation system can we construct that will be genuinely helpful to student learners and still provide the sort of information demanded by the public and the school system itself?

We will anchor our discussion by noting some important distinctions among the three terms that head this chapter: *assessment*, *evaluation*, and *grading*. Too often, we find, grading is taken as a blanket term for the other two, which are, in fact, much broader concepts.

# Assessment

*Assessment* is the most comprehensive of the terms in our lexicon. It involves a wide range of estimates and measures and is a description of what *is happening* rather than what *has happened*. Assessment generally tries to avoid judgmental statements of *good* or *bad, weak* or *strong, success* or *failure*. Rather, in assessment we try to compile information—as much as we can manage—that provides a snapshot (or hologram) of what our students are accomplishing.

Even though language growth is difficult to measure, there are a number of ways you can assess achievement. You might begin by getting a sense of the status of the class, assessing in global terms how your students are doing as a group. You might assess the whole class by:

1. keeping track of the number of books your students read in a term

2. observing whether or not your students complete a writing plan, drafting and revising their work, and editing and publishing final copies

3. noting what's accomplished in small-group discussions, listening to the quality of the discussions, seeing leadership emerge, and observing students efforts to stay on task

4. focusing on the quality and level of participation in whole-class discussions

5. tracking students' growing independence as they come to rely more on one another and on reference materials than on you

6. observing the ways in which students use their time in class during reading/writing workshops and times for independent work

7. keeping track of the number of books or other pieces students publish in your class

8. observing attitudes toward and instances of error and how students solve writing, spelling, and editing problems

Developing an inquiring attitude toward how the class in general is doing will help you keep your goals in mind and keep you on track. You can assess, through these general observations, whether your class is moving in the direction you want them to go. However, we want to collect information that will give us more detailed and more informative data about how individuals in our classes are doing. Sometimes we are aware that a class is going very well—students are productive and engaged—for *most* students. Then we notice that not everyone is participating or some are doing so in perfunctory ways. Among the most fruitful forms of assessment that we have used to collect information about students' achievement are:

---

- Logs. Instead of simply jotting down letters and numbers in a grade book, keep a log of student accomplishments, an annotated list of what students have done and when they did it. A computer database program can be helpful here, allowing you to log considerable amounts of information and then sort through it and print out appropriate excerpts. A loose-leaf binder on your desk, with one page allotted to each student and the pages arranged alphabetically, will allow you to jot quick notes as you observe. Additionally, you can ask students to write daily or weekly progress reports on what they've been doing in class. When parents or principals ask about what's been going on in your class, show them the log.

- Portfolios. A portfolio is a carefully prepared collection of student work that demonstrates that class goals have been accomplished or shows a representative range of student work. Portfolios can be used for a variety of purposes:

  o Process portfolio. Students save drafts, notes, peer comments on their work, teacher responses, marked-up papers, and versions of papers. Students who work on word processors should print out drafts of their papers as they revise. Both teacher and student can get a sense of how writing grows and improves and how the student works.

  o Works-in-progress portfolio. Students frequently have ideas for pieces they'd like to write, but don't complete, or they get taken with another idea and set in-progress pieces aside. We encourage

students to save everything and come back to their in-progress pieces later.

- ○ Showcase portfolio. These are the pieces the students consider their best work, the pieces they want to share, and the pieces they present for evaluation and grading. We use the showcase portfolio as a way for students to do their own self-assessments, too, detailing their progress as writers.

- ○ Reading portfolio. Students keep a record of the fiction, poetry, drama, and nonfiction they have read and their responses to it. Copies of group work or individual projects may also be kept in the reading portfolio.

We insist that students be responsible for their own portfolios, keeping track of all of their work and making it manageable and accessible to teachers and other readers. Some states have adopted the portfolio as a means of assessing student progress, and in England, portfolios have also been explored as an alternative to the one-shot sit-down exam. In some U.S. colleges, entering students can present a portfolio of their work instead of taking placement exams. While we welcome alternatives to standardized exams, most portfolio scholarship insists that the best use of portfolios involves student ownership and student decision-making about the contents.

- • Classroom observation. Perhaps the most traditional form of assessment (yet the one least easily documented) is your day-to-day observations of students. You must be very cautious and self-critical in using your own observations. Students' records, reputations, and facades can often establish expectations that interfere with our ability to observe fairly. Teachers also need to be looking for potential, for ways to bring everyone into the literacy circle. Discover students' actual behaviors and habits to see how you might take them to the next step. Watch students in discussion groups, watch them while they're drafting a new piece of writing, interview them in conferences, watch them read silently, study their performances in dramas and role-plays, and watch how they use the resources of the classroom—materials, other students, and you.

- • Teacher questions. Too often characterizations of students are made without the students' input. We think that students should be asked to take more of a part in self-description and self-definition. Some questions that collect students' ideas are: How's your writing going? Which piece in your portfolio is most successful? How do you think your improvisational performance went? How is your preparation coming along for your showcase portfolio? How is your reading

group working out? Open-ended questions allow students to characterize their work.

- Teacher-researchers. An important development in recent years has been the recognition that teachers can conduct research to answer their own questions. The teacher-researcher concept simply systemizes classroom observations. You needn't have a degree in statistics or a high-powered computer to collect data on what your students are doing and to acquire valuable knowledge about how learners perform. The general pattern for classroom research is to:

  ○ Identify a question that you want to answer. (What kinds of writing problems do students solve in peer groups? How do ESL students participate in small-group discussions? What sort of writing do my fifth graders like the best? What sorts of questions help college-bound students analyze the literature they read?)

  ○ Collect data that will answer your question. Most teacher researchers will collect several kinds of data. They may look at student portfolios, student logs, their own teaching journals, and standardized test scores. They may also interview students; offer pre- and postunit questionnaires on attitudes; observe, audiotape, or videotape small-group work; read students' self-assessments of work; and conduct whole-class discussions about the topic.

  ○ Reflect on this information and draw conclusions. Share appropriate information with the class (be careful, of course, not to betray private information). The fact that you care enough about their work to do research can have a tremendous impact on students' sense of their value and the importance you place on their learning. Moreover, your insights about how they work might help them.

The results of teacher research are always limited to the particular group of students you are working with at a particular time, and you must be very cautious to not overinterpret your data, claim too much for it, or generalize too grandly on the basis of limited data. In addition, you must guard against tunnel vision; that is, seeing only what you expected or wanted in the first place. In the process of conducting research, you guarantee that you have created a solid assessment base for any evaluation or grading that follows.

- Standardized tests. Despite their frequent misuse, standardized tests do have a role in assessment. Before employing such tests, however, you probably need to educate students, parents, and other teachers about their proper interpretation. At their best, standardized tests merely provide norms and information bases; they are easily misin-

terpreted and misunderstood. One of the most insidious effects of testing has been the reporting of schools as "inferior" on the basis of standardized test scores. Both students and teachers suffer from the stigma that can result from test scores being used to define their accomplishments or their commitment. Frequently, low test scores reflect the low socioeconomic status of the test-takers, which too often leads to the mistaken assumption that poor people are inadequate rather than to an understanding that the more likely cause of low scores is that low-scoring schools and families have much less access to the enrichment resources enjoyed by the privileged.

# Evaluation

The distinction that we want to insert here is that assessment *documents*, while evaluation, well, *evaluates*. Evaluation adds judgments and criteria to the process.

We sympathize with members of the public who say, "People want to know where they stand. They want to know how well they're doing." Yet often the criticism people receive is decidedly unhelpful. None of us likes to be hollered at, to receive scathing criticism, or to have our work held up to contempt or ridicule. Although most of us prized our As and worried about our Bs and Cs, we probably didn't find our grades especially informative in telling us anything about how we were doing in any significant sense. We are increasingly convinced that internal evaluation or self-assessment is at least as powerful as—and probably more powerful than—external evaluation. Even the kindest and most humane of evaluations isn't much help if it simply holds up a yardstick, rather than explaining the units of measure.

At the heart of any evaluation scheme is a careful and articulate statement of criteria. Our students tell us horror stories of trying to figure out what criteria professors are using, usually resulting in them "trying to guess what he wanted." It's a useful exercise and a service to students for you as a teacher to state exactly what you value and what you see as important: the criteria or other measures you intend to apply. (We like the idea of giving students a copy of the examination on the first day of class, along with an explanation of how it will be evaluated.)

Among the forms of evaluation we have found most effective are:

- Self-evaluation at all points in a reading, writing, listening, or speaking project: at the beginning (to help students set goals, to activate prior knowledge, and to establish major ideas) and in the middle (to assess progress and to make sure students are comprehending), as well as at the end. A useful schema we have used for self-evaluation asks students to:

- ○ Describe what they have done: what they have written, what they have read, how they went about completing the assignment.
- ○ Evaluate their work. Did this turn out as they wanted it to? What parts were most successful? Which were least satisfactory?
- ○ Predict what they feel they will need to do next time to produce even stronger work.

- Peer evaluation, where students gather to assess and evaluate (not grade) one another's work. Peer evaluation is discussed in considerably more detail in Chapter 8 on the composing process. In addition, small groups can provide "status of the group" reports that keep you apprised of any problems in the group and any snags students have hit, either in the group process or in accomplishing the task.

- Student-developed criteria. Many of our colleagues have had excellent success with having students develop their own criteria for evaluating one another's writing. Developing criteria helps students become aware of what's important in performance and gives them practice in applying it as they respond to one another's work. One of our writing teacher friends has students develop a new set of criteria for each writing project, demonstrating that different kinds of writing call for somewhat different skills and approaches.

- "Twenty-six letter grading" (the written evaluation), where we write out assessments of a student's work. Does this work seem to reflect the student's full capacity? Does it meet the basic requirements of the class? What are the strong and weak points of this work as presented? Where are the areas for improvement? What specific things ought the student to work on next time? We find that the written evaluation, when separated from the single-letter grade, is perceived not only as nonthreatening, but as directly helpful by students. It is, of course, time-consuming for the teacher. We have found it useful to use the student's self-evaluation as an opportunity for dialogue, responding to the student's observations with observations of our own.

- Teacher conferencing, where face-to-face evaluation provides much richer dialogue than written notes. Conferences may last from three to ten minutes, with the teacher simply stopping by a student's desk to comment on work in progress, or the teacher may conduct longer conferences near the end of an extensive project.

- Portfolio evaluation, where we assess students' work collected over time and discuss its perceived strengths and weaknesses, areas for improvement, and possibilities for new directions.

- Gut feelings on the part of students and teachers that, yeah, this has it or, thud, something just doesn't seem to be right here.
- Testing, both short answer and essay, especially when there are particular facts and concepts to be measured.

# Grading

Tales of bizarre and macabre grading practices abound in our trade. Teachers have allegedly tossed papers down a flight of stairs and awarded grades based on the step on which a paper landed. There are also those who grade religiously "on the curve," statistically distributing grades so that for every A there is an F, for every B a D, and the majority wind up with Cs. And what about those amazingly precise graders (92.75) (A-/B+)!

Grading is the moment of truth, when assessment and evaluation must be condensed into a symbol. In our experience, grading is far less threatening if a proper foundation has been laid—if criteria for evaluation are clear, if there has been lots of assessment and feedback along the way, and if students have been involved in self-evaluation.

Still, if evaluation in language arts is ultimately so subjective, how do we go about grading fairly? We'll confess that we have never discovered a system that we find altogether satisfactory. (If you come up with a perfect grading scheme, we surely hope you'll tell us about it.)

Among some of the better possibilities:

- Self-grading. If students have been given the responsibility of assessing and evaluating themselves throughout the term, it seems sensible and fair that they should have some or even all of the responsibility for the final grade. We have, on occasion, had students recommend grades for themselves and have found that, on the whole, kids do a responsible and reasonable job of settling on a grade. Some teachers we know use a system of *matched* grades, in which student and teacher come up with a grade independently and split the difference.
- Portfolio grading. Students have a great deal of choice in presenting work they would like to have evaluated. What's included, however, represents the best of the work that students have been developing all term, usually with advice and feedback from teacher and peers. Many teachers have students include a "metacognitive" piece introducing the portfolio, justifying its contents, and evaluating the pieces included, perhaps based on criteria established at the beginning of the term or developed during the process.

- Minimum plus. In this system, the teacher sets minimum standards for a passing grade and additional work to be done for higher levels. For a C, a student might complete certain core reading and writing; for a B, she reads additional books; for an A, he undertakes some original writing as well.

- Point systems. Here various tasks are assigned point values: Reading a book carries, say, ten points; writing an essay carries fifteen. Ranges are set up for A, B, and C work, and students store up points in grade book heaven as the class progresses.

- Analytic scales. Here the work for a class is broken into categories: class reading, writing, oral language, drama, etc. The teacher ranks student performance on a scale of one to ten; for example:

Drama Work

| Low | 1 | 2 | 3 | 4 | 5 | 6 | 7 | 8 | 9 | 10 | High |
|-----|---|---|---|---|---|---|---|---|---|----|------|

  The various categories can also be weighted so that, for example, reading is thirty percent of the grade, drama ten percent, writing forty percent.

- Contract grading. In the previous chapter, we suggested that contracts provide an especially effective way to individualize student work. They also offer what seems to us an especially equitable way of grading. Like the point system and minimum plus, contract grades award productivity—the more you do, the higher your grade. However, as we note in that chapter, contracts require the student to specify aims and goals, the criteria by which the work will be assessed and evaluated, a timetable for proceeding, and checkpoints along the way.

# Toward Pass/Fail Systems of Grading

A few schools and colleges have done away with letter or other symbol grades in favor of pass/fail or credit/no-credit systems. In our ideal world, such a scheme would be standard practice, rewarding students for meeting class requirements skillfully and well without inducing the competitiveness and anxiety of conventional grading. Pass/fail grading does not result in any lowering of standards, for students can all be held to high levels of achievement. (There need be no "gentlemen's C" in a pass/fail system.) Furthermore, this sort of evaluation allows grading, evaluation, and assessment to be fully and smoothly integrated, maximizing the effectiveness of the whole process.

Too often, we see grades being used in school as "carrots" and "sticks" to get students to behave in certain ways. The result of this is that many, many students work solely in response to the punishments and rewards associated with extrinsic goals. For students to embrace learning for their own intrinsic purposes, they need to have choice—choice in what they would like to learn, choice in how they would like their work to be viewed, and participation in the evaluation process. Teachers who want to help students become independent, self-sufficient, joyful users of language need to discover ways to create evaluation systems that are consistent with their instructional goals.

# A Note on Mass Testing

The use of mass testing or standardized testing instruments by schools, school districts, states, and even national authorities and agencies has increased steadily in the past several decades. A common response to complaints about the quality of education is to institute yet another examination. The most recent manifestation of political pressure has come in the form of the "standards" movement, which seeks to institute higher standards in a number of core curriculum areas and then enforce those higher standards through the use of tests. Some states are threatening school districts with high-stakes proficiency tests that result in students who don't pass being retained. High school graduation exams are being instituted in more and more districts. There is even a recurring discussion about national examinations linked to a set of national curriculum standards.

Having had considerable experience with mass assessment measures, particularly at the state level, we remain dubious about the value of such measures. Indeed, we think much of the effort and money that has been put into mass testing in recent years would have been more profitably directed toward professional development programs for teachers, curriculum development, and purchases of materials—books and magazines, computers and software—for schools.

Professional organizations and prominent leaders in language arts education have issued frequent warnings and resolutions about the misuse of mass test data, yet misinterpretations of test scores are common, especially among the media and the public. Every major announcement of test scores is almost invariably greeted with a new round of criticism of the schools, the teachers, and sometimes even the American way of life, even though the relationship between test scores, school quality, and performance in life is tenuous at best.

At our most cynical, we view such measures as being primarily political in aim and purpose. It's easier to test students than to provide them with adequately funded schools. It's simpler to complain about performance as measured by a set of digits than it is to understand the deep and complex problems of educating diverse youngsters in today's world. Further, strong evidence suggests that mass tests favor white majority students and serve to disqualify and discourage the children of minorities from some educational opportunities.

Furthermore, tests, with their emphasis on norms and rank-ordering of children, fail to account for what we know about human development and language learning. Children develop language differently. Children learn at different rates and accomplish skills at different times in their development. Moreover, children whose native language is not English need time and many rich language opportunities to develop English proficiency. Children whose parents don't have time to provide extensive educational opportunities outside of school need opportunities for more language experience in school. Standardized tests, however, rank all children of the same age/grade level regardless of their educational advantages or disadvantages and in total ignorance of the tremendous growth they may be experiencing.

Yet the tests persist and are likely to increase in number during the shelf life of this book. Teachers (in particular new teachers, who may not yet have tenure) need to attend to the tests, and in fairness to kids, we do owe it to them to help them score as high as possible.

Some possible strategies for dealing with mass testing:

- Learn what is on the tests your students will take. We're astonished by the number of teachers who justify the teaching of grammar by claiming, "They need to know it for the SAT." In fact, knowledge of formal grammar was removed from the Scholastic Aptitude Test in 1948. It is important to know what your students will (and will not) need to know.

- Study your curriculum and your teaching plans carefully to see how they already cover basic test matters. Any decent reading and writing program—in particular one that has students read and write often—will naturally cover a great deal of what appears on virtually any nationally standardized examination. Be prepared to highlight your coverage for the benefit of students, parents, and administrators.

- Cautiously add additional elements to your program to make certain you fully cover required items. We say "cautiously" because you don't want to let your class be shaped by the test, and you do not want to insert items that are foreign or even contradictory to your own philosophy or to accepted research.

- Help students prepare to take the test. If sample test items are available, run a few practice sessions shortly before the test. This will help your kids feel more comfortable in the testing situation. We also recommend that you look for commercial test preparation books. Our experience shows that such books contain accurate test items and give students a solid indication of what to expect. (A few teachers argue that prepping students for tests is unprofessional or even unethical. We believe that to give students actual answers to test questions would, of course, be highly improper. But we also believe it is not only professional but highly desirable to share public knowledge about tests with your students. Indeed, it's a disservice to them *not* to.)

- Know in your heart that a full, rich language arts program is, in the long run, a better course in literacy than a curriculum based on the demands of tests and test makers. Have confidence that if you get your students reading and writing, if you get them to play with language and feel comfortable with it, if you help them assess their work and understand their own strengths and weaknesses, they will do as well as possible on tests, probably outstripping peers whose teachers teach only to the test or allow their programs to be constricted by tests.

## Selected Readings

Calkins, Lucy, Kate Montgomery, and Donna Santman. 1998. *A Teacher's Guide to Standardized Reading Tests*. Portsmouth, NH: Heinemann.

Graves, Donald H., and Bonnie S. Sunstein. 1992. *Portfolio Portraits*. Portsmouth, NH: Heinemann.

Sunstein, Bonnie S., and Julie B. Cheville, eds. 1995. *Assessing Portfolios: A Portfolio*. Iowa English Bulletin. (Available through the National Council of Teachers of English.)

Tchudi, Stephen, ed. 1997. *Alternatives to Grading Student Writing*. Urbana, IL: National Council of Teachers of English.

Tierney, Robert J, Mark A. Carter, and Laura E. Desai. 1991. *Portfolio Assessment in the Reading-Writing Classroom*. Norwood, MA: Christopher-Gordon.

# Summary and Troubleshooting

# Dear Abby Fidditch

In concluding this section on curriculum and class planning, we let an old friend do some talking for us. "Abby Fidditch" is an unwillingly unemployed former language arts teacher who lost her job when the voters in her district defeated their fourth school bond issue, shortly after the auto assembly plant closed and put three thousand parents out of work. Abby has taught in one-room schoolhouses and giant urban high schools; she has taught *Hamlet* and *Charlotte's Web*, old grammar and new grammar, smart kids and smart alecks. Many of her former colleagues write to her from time to time for advice, and in her imposed leisure, she replies. We hope you'll find these letters and her answers helpful.

• • •

Dear Abby Fidditch,

My school district recently initiated a new testing program in writing called "trait scoring." There are six traits—voice, topic, development, organization, vocabulary, and conventions—and students get points in each category that add up to their total score. Now, we talk about all of these things as we are working on writing in my eighth-grade classroom, but I never isolate them to teach separately. My department chair gave an inservice and said that's what we need to get good scores. What do you think? Yours truly,

Fragmented

o   o   o

Dear Frag,

I'm with you. If what we're trying to do with our young writers is show them how real writers work, then breaking down their work in this way for the purpose of tests seems a distortion. I've never known a writer who sets out to write something that's "well organized" or "has a good vocabulary," although these, of course, are among the range of considerations one has when one writes. Carry on in your writing workshop evaluating writing holistically with these usual concerns integrated into your practice, and your eighth graders will do just fine.

Abby

•  •  •

Dear Abby,

Our whole staff is totally depressed. The local paper just published the last test score results for our school district, and our "at risk" (the new term is "at hope") school ended up next to the bottom. The article next to the test results called us an ineffective school and politicians were quoted as saying we'd better get higher scores next time or else! Abby, I've never known a staff that works harder or a group of kids that cares more. Lots of our kids are just learning English, and several of our kids are homeless. We're working on a lot of fronts here, and we're doing a pretty darn good job. How can we get people to understand?

Down and Out

o   o   o

Dear D and O,

I can certainly identify. When I taught in a one-room school in the Midwest, half my kids would disappear during harvest and planting seasons. Unfortunately, those are the times when testing came around, and needless to say my kids' heads were somewhere else.

But I think there are some things teachers can do to improve public perceptions of their and their students' work. First, write letters to the editor. Don't whine about the disadvantages (though you should make some mention of them), but share your students' accomplishments. Try to get information, from both tests and your own records, about how your students have grown, and make that information public. Enlist the aid of your local and national professional organization in lobbying for alternatives to standardized tests that measure growth rather than establish norms.

Your job of changing public perception is not an easy one, but teachers need to stand up for themselves and for their kids.

Abby

•  •  •

Dear Abby,

I am feeling very isolated in my high school English department faculty. I'm the only one who goes to conferences or reads about new ideas. Everyone else is either apathetic or downright hostile when I suggest new ways of doing things or new ideas for books or materials. How can I get some things going with colleagues who just don't seem to care?

A Dangling Modifier

o   o   o

Dear DM,

I can certainly understand your frustration. I was once a member of a faculty who would talk to one another only when they went bowling. Our curriculum was spare, to say the least.

But there are some ways I found to stir things up and to get people talking. I told the bowler/teachers that we needed a parental relations program to communicate more successfully what we were doing. When we began to talk with one another about that, we began to agree (and disagree) on some key points in the curriculum.

I also found it was very important for me to restrain my criticism of fellow teachers. I have had to stifle my objections on many occasions, but I have learned as well that people like to be asked what they're doing, if they think you won't be critical of them.

It's also important for teachers (especially new ones) to seek out kindred spirits and to work with them. Once, a couple of colleagues and I formed a small group to try to figure out why some of our kids simply never completed their assignments. As we talked with kids about what they needed, we found ways to adjust our assignments for these kids. Word got around about that, and some teachers came to us to help them with similar problems and to ask for our advice.

You'll probably never unify your faculty completely, but you can at least cooperate and support people who see things more or less the same way you do. Though a unified faculty is a positive goal, in some schools you may just have to find one or two people who view school and kids the way you do (and they may not be in your department!).

Abby

•   •   •

Dear Pedagogical Poetaster,

How do you cope with the problem of imposed standards and objectives? It's all well and good for *The English Language Arts Handbook* to talk about teacher autonomy and designing your own units and imaginative grading systems and all that, but I teach in a district that has jumped on the standards bandwagon, and these standards focus on grammar, spelling, and vocabulary skills. We will also be getting a district competency test administered every year, and teachers whose kids don't do well will be called on the carpet. I think the standards and tests are rather trivial, but I have to worry about my students (and my own you-know-what).

Over-Standardized

o   o   o

Dear Over,

You seem to hit the nail on the head when you say that the standards and tests are "trivial." The people who wrote them were probably sincere, but they have taken a narrow view of the language arts.

Tempting as it is to cover your you-know-what, don't let the skills list dominate your teaching. Integrate the required list with your own objectives. You teach basic skills by the hundreds every time you enter the classroom. In the course of an ordinary composition or reading assignment, you probably cover most of the skills on the list. Develop the habit of noticing how your own teaching covers the standards. Then jot down some notes to show how you have done the work.

I strongly believe that high standards are very important to kids' growth and development. It's important that you not let the demands and objectives prevent you and your students from achieving all that you and they possibly can.

Abby

• • •

Dear Superteach,

I'm really being driven crazy by the idea of individualized learning. I know I need to do it. The kids in my class differ enormously in abilities, and about a third of them are non-native speakers of English. But how on earth do I manage the materials, the projects, the different schedules? I read these professional books where the teachers seem to succeed with every kid. Sign me,

Overwhelmed by Individuals

o o o

Dear Overwhelmed,

Slow and easy does it, I say.

For me the best routes into individualizing were free-reading periods and in-class writing. Both are pedagogically sound uses of time, but they also have the advantage of getting everybody quietly busy while you figure out what you're doing. I brought lots of reading material into my classroom, everything from comic books to serious literature, and I had students write in their journals daily, at first just a few minutes, eventually up to half the class period.

Those two strategies allowed me to have conferences with individual students and to get a variety of activities going on in the classroom. After my students became accustomed to the routines, I started moving into more complicated work with thematic units, a greater variety of literature, and writing beyond the journals.

I was also inspired by a teacher in my building who said she made a checklist of kids she *wasn't* reaching. In a tough class, that might be twenty-five people in September. She kept on keepin' on: bringing in books, trying writing ideas, and casting about for activities to reach each one of those kids. By June she would report that she had the list whittled down to maybe a half-dozen. She never claimed or expected to reach every last one of her students. In my book, she was the real Superteach.

Just Plain Abby

• • •

Dear Letter Woman,

What do you do about grades? Some kids in my classroom will do something only if they are going to get a grade on it. Other kids won't do anything, even if I tell them that if they miss assignments I will fail them. So, grades seem to be the primary motivation for some and of no use at all for those kids who have stopped playing the game. I've tried a number of schemes in *The English Language Arts Handbook*, but I'm still struggling with how to assess, evaluate, and, *yuk*, grade.

Unglued and Ungraded

o   o   o

Dear Double U,

I haven't an easy solution to offer you. I've struggled with grading all my pedagogical life, and I uneasily admit that I often had to spend as much time working on the grading scheme as I did on my syllabus. But I did find a way to ease my conscience.

First, I realized that the grading scheme was not of my making, not of my imposition. I don't want it, like it, or need it. My employers do. So I eliminated some of my own agonizing by focusing on the fact that I was not responsible.

Second, I set about to neutralize what I saw as the negative effects of grading systems. Toward the end of my teaching days, I did most of my work with contract teaching, where kids would elect a grade and work for it. This was not a perfect system. The grades were often pretty high, but I think that was because kids had so much more choice and could complete projects they were interested in. There were still those kids who did work only for the grade, but they did do the work and, I believe, learned something in the process. But mostly, contract grading let me talk with kids as partners rather than as enemies.

Third, even when I used other systems of grading, I worked hard to help the students understand and even set the criteria for grading. Then I told them my job was to help them do as well as possible (and thus earn as high a grade as possible), but I tried to place the emphasis on the value of their work and develop pride in work that was *theirs*, rather than acting as the Goddess of the Ideal Answer judging them from on high.

Abby with an A
(Well, OK, maybe a B+, but no lower)

• • •

Dear Behavioral Modifier,

Why is it that nobody has much to say about the most pressing of teacher problems: discipline. You can't plan and teach and evaluate creatively unless you can keep the class under control, and everybody knows that's harder and harder these days. So what about it? What about the trouble-makers, disrupters, and malcontents we real-world teachers face day after day?

Just Plain Tired

o  o  o

Dear Elixir of Youth,

Let me tell you what I learned indirectly from a methods class at Grimm University: The rules people give you about discipline almost invariably don't apply very well to particular classes. "Don't smile for the first six weeks," they told me in college. I smiled by accident and found a class of kids smiling back. "Start tough, then lighten up," somebody advised. I started tough and when I tried to lighten up, the kids were so afraid they wouldn't talk. There are guidelines and limits, of course, but I've found that with discipline problems I can only work with kids one at a time, try-ing to be fair on the one hand and true to my values on the other.

I am also firmly convinced that discipline problems grow in proportion to the irrelevance of the curriculum. If you want discipline problems, try teaching them Henry James. If you want to calm a class down, get them reading and writing about their own world. It's not a magic cure, of course. Some kids are so alienated that they can't see that school has any-thing to offer. I've had some of those kids, but usually, when I've shown kids that I was interested in their lives and experiences and interests, they've responded with some good, sometimes even astonishing, work.

No Hero, Just a Kid-Booster,
Abby

# t · w · o

# Ideas for Teaching Reading and Literature

In a world exploding almost daily with new electronic forms of communication, information, and entertainment—constant updates in everything from the Internet, to cell phones and pagers, to CD-ROMs reproducing historical documents, films, and encyclopedias (with new forms always on the horizon)—reading is still central to most people as they weave their ways through their daily lives. Not only do we encounter environmental print at every turn—from menus to labels on consumer items to stop signs to e-mail—but we still get much of our daily information—whether it be through newspapers or the Internet—by reading it. And though much of our entertainment comes in the form of TV, film, and video, bookstores (especially the major chains) continue to thrive. Moreover, the route to jobs and continuing education continues to be through people's ability to read.

Just what constitutes reading—and how people learn to do it—remains somewhat contentious. Though reading test proponents and some public officials continue to see literacy as simple decoding of print and as basic comprehension—"just the facts," reading research and theory over the past thirty years has emphasized the centrality of the reader—the reader's prior knowledge, the reader's experience in and understanding of the world. The ground-breaking work of Kenneth and Yetta Goodman (1987, 1988) and Frank Smith (1971, 1985, 1988, 1995) has demonstrated how readers actively use their language and experience to make sense of the text. Louise Rosenblatt (1978, 1983) and Alan Purves (Purves, Rogers, and Soter 1990) have written about the transactional, response-centered approach, which empowers readers to make sense of texts for themselves. Recent theory looks at the social and cultural implications of readers and reading, asking how students' gender, ethnicity, and class position them to read and understand in particular ways (Corcoran, Hayhoe, and Pradl 1994).

All of this research can guide us in making decisions about how to manage readers and reading in our classrooms. If we place readers (rather than skills, information, or required texts) at the center of the reading process, we can more easily answer the questions such as: Are we teachers of reading or basic skills? Should our focus be on "great" literature, or literature for children and adolescents, or the "relevant" literature of popular culture? What is the role of nonfiction and informational reading in our English language arts classes? What do we do about kids who are not reading at grade level? What do we do about non-native speakers of English? What skills do students need before they begin to read? And, most important, how do we influence young people to become lifelong, committed readers?

As we consider that last question, it becomes clear that we need to be teachers of literature *and* reading (including skills or strategies); we need to introduce popular *and* traditional literature; we need to provide a range of texts, from picture books to how-to volumes to encyclopedias (in books and on CDs) to literary texts. And, again, we need to be knowledgeable about our students, about reading theory, and about the resources available to promote lifelong reading for *all* students who come through the door.

Our philosophy of reading centers on four main aims for a classroom that emphasizes reading and literature:

1. *Get them reading*. Nothing happens until students make contact with print. People learn to read when print is an important part of their worlds. Although print is readily available to everyone, even in an increasingly nonprint world, print has to be an important aspect of their lives in order for students to become fluent and enthusiastic readers. You can't control what happens at home, but you have a good deal of control over what happens at school. Fill your classroom with print of all sorts—books, magazines, newspapers, brochures, and pamphlets, as well as student-produced versions of all of the above. Cover the walls with posters and student-made writing, and change the display frequently, so there's always something new to learn from print.

2. *Treat reading as a meaning-making activity.* Rather than telling students what their reading means, ask them to tell you—whether through a new poster on your wall, a student paper written in class, an assigned poem or short story, or a newspaper article. It is students' beginning responses that they (and we as teachers) will build on to develop deeper and more sophisticated responses.

3. *Treat reading as a social and communal activity.* Although some may see reading as a solitary activity, much of the meaning readers create comes from sharing their responses with others and talking about their understandings. Such exchanges of ideas about what they've read help students develop their critical skills and their ability to evaluate their reading.

4. *Help students recognize that reading and literature are not remote from life, but are an expression of it.* Virtually every student who goes through the public school system has twelve years in which a major focus of their school lives is reading, and yet many, many students fail to consider reading an important part of their lives after they've completed school. Too few return to books for pleasure; many are more likely to use TV for information and entertainment. We think this is a sad commentary on our teaching of reading and literature. We believe that there are ways of teaching literature in school that will demonstrate for students the satisfaction and usefulness of literature and have more potential for creating lifelong readers.

We believe that a good reading and literature program draws on young people's natural curiosity and interest, elevating reading from an arid classroom study and helping it become a critical part of young people's lives.

# Chapter Five

# The First "R"

Reading—that famous first "R"—has surely gotten more attention from teachers, parents, the public, and politicians than any other subject or skill in the school curriculum. From kindergarten through graduate school, the ability to read is seen as central to students' success. Reading (along with writing and math, which are tied in a close second) is seen as the skill on which success hinges after completing school. The inability to read—illiteracy—is considered the blackest mark of a person's failure in school and the greatest failure in the American school system.

Statistics on illiteracy are notoriously unreliable, yet one regularly hears that there are in the neighborhood of twenty-five million "functional illiterates" in the United States, people incapable of operating successfully in a print-oriented society. Responding to that concern, dozens of programs have been developed—both in and out of school—that promise to teach people to read.

Everybody from the school board president to the parent of the kid next door has theories about the reading "crisis." The press, for its part, tosses about statistics freely (a single issue of one newspaper cited figures of forty and twenty-five million functional illiterates in two separate articles, neither figure documented by anything more than secondhand evidence or some authority's best guess.) Even worse, the media and the public search for scapegoats for the reading problem. In their frustration and lack of understanding of how children learn, politicians, too often aided by school administrators and teachers, establish new and higher standards and devise more tests hoping to change teachers' and students' performance by willing (or threatening) them to be better. Unfortunately, in many cases, the standards and the tests simply reinforce practices that have proven to be misguided and ineffective.

Despite the public uproar, the inflated statistics, and the scapegoating, it must be acknowledged that there is a grave reading problem. By almost any standards, too many children and adults either can't read or don't want to read, and until the day we are all equipped with Dick Tracy–style wrist televisions and videophones, there will be a need for people to learn to read. Moreover, those of us who love to read want to share the pleasure and satisfaction that come with being able to live in the world of books.

Although there are myriad causes for children's failure to learn to read, the problem can be traced, we believe, to some basic ideas about how people learn to read. One of these, that children learn to read from parts-to-whole, has its roots in practices as old as reading itself (Moustafa 1997). The method that addresses this idea—teaching children decoding subskills—assumes that reading is simply a process of decoding or translating print into oral (or silent) language. The programmatic emphasis is on getting students to sound out or pronounce words on a page, with the assumption that if students know how to say the words, they know what they mean. Parts-to-whole practices (starting with the alphabet, learning sounds, and learning how those sounds make words) and whole-word approaches (teaching children to identify common words) may seem intuitively sensible, but a good deal of research over the past forty years demonstrates that emphasis on decoding and on reproduction of surface structures may not only *not* be the best way to instruct readers, but may, in fact, create reading problems.

Overemphasis on sounding out misleads students about what it means to read. The emphasis in reading should not be to teach children to decode to sound (or to silent language), but to model for children how to make sense of the print on a page. Decoding to sound is a small part of what it means to read, yet many children learning to read believe that is what they are supposed to be doing. They struggle to *say* the word correctly rather than to *figure out* the meaning of what they are reading.

The alternative to decoding is an approach that focuses on "whole language." This paradigm views reading not as a mechanical process in which words are figured out and then added up to mean something, but as a cognitive process, a thinking process. Readers are seen not as passive—as simply translating words into meaning—but as active—as meaning-makers. Based on a considerable body of research, it argues that reading is something learned, rather than taught. People master reading when they need to get meaning from a page, have some clues about how the reading system works, and are put to work in a setting where they can make meaning for themselves with coaching and tutoring as needed. The *whole* in whole language has multiple meanings: It refers to the notion that reading is learned as a *whole* process (as opposed to bits and pieces of language); that one must make *whole* meanings from *whole* or complete texts; and that one must treat the language arts as a *whole*, with children reading their own writing as well as texts, with writing being generated in response to reading, and with oral language instruction underlying integrated work in reading and writing.

Readers bring their own life histories to reading. Reading researchers have dubbed readers' knowledge and experience (that they bring to all new experience, not just reading) "schema theory." In addition, all readers come to reading with a language system. Young children—five- and six-year-olds first coming to school—have a well-developed sense of syntax (the structure of the language). All of these are brought into play as children read. When children encounter a text, they use all of their knowledge and experience to understand what they are reading. First of all, they pay attention to context. Based on their experience, they consider what the print is likely to say. For example, when you ask children to read a sign, they read the entire context: Is this a gas station, a clothing store, a street sign? What are the pictures that surround it? What clues are there about what this might say? Children also use their knowledge of how the language works. Upon encountering a sentence like "New Beanie Babies can be purchased at your local shopping center," children who are encouraged to make sense of print but do not know the word "purchased" will know that a verb goes there (even if they don't know what a verb is). In addition, children drawing on their own experiences to make meaning of a sentence such as the one above will draw on their "sight-words" like *Beanie Babies,* their knowledge of how syntax works, their knowledge of sound/letter correspondences, and their knowledge of what happens to Beanie Babies to understand the print.

The public and media periodically voice concern about the decline of phonics instruction, but the fact remains that even today an exorbitant amount of school time is spent teaching children sound/letter correspondences rather than helping them read for meaning. Elaborate programs have been constructed to teach letters and sounds, including such gambits as letter-shaped puppets and toys and celebrations of a "letter of the week." Spelling and vocabulary continue the decoding emphasis, based on the assumption that if we teach unfamiliar words in isolation, somehow reading and comprehension will result.

Programs that focus solely on decoding or mastering phonics rules can severely hamper the development of broad, flexible reading and thinking abilities. Moreover, phonics rules are so complex and there are so many exceptions to the rules (Weaver 1999), that anyone trying to make sense of print by using phonics will only become more confused. Unfortunately, however, struggling readers—ironically, often those who try hardest to follow the teacher's direction to sound things out—often end up in remedial programs where they are taught even more decoding skills and spend little time in real reading activity, the kind of engagement with whole texts and contexts that allows them to make meaning.

We suggest that all students—beginning readers, struggling readers, developing readers, and successful readers—be engaged in reading activities that emphasize students' role as meaning makers:

- Allow students to choose what they read. Students are more likely to gain meaning from reading if they are interested, if the topic is one they know something about, or if they have a purpose for reading.
- Use real books. Use the classroom, school, and public libraries to provide fiction, nonfiction, plays, and poems for students at all levels—children, young adults, and adults.
- Model what successful readers do. Successful readers frequently stop reading works they are not enjoying, skim sections that don't interest them, skip over parts they already know, read selectively, think about what's going to happen next, predict the ending, etc.
- Emphasize reading as communication rather than as skills to be mastered. Encourage students to guess at words they don't know, then keep reading.
- Encourage students to become active and critical thinkers, responding to and evaluating what they've read. Encourage the notion of writers as people with whom one can disagree.
- Encourage nongeneric responses. Encourage students from other cultures and with other perspectives to articulate their points of view.
- Value affective and aesthetic responses, not just the comprehension of black-and-white facts on a page.

# Initial Reading Instruction

The topic of initial reading instruction is too complex to address in detail here, and a number of excellent professional books take up the issue of beginning readers in language arts classrooms. However, we include some general guidelines about what it means to present reading as a whole language activity rather than as a study of subskills and workbook activities. A number of practices in the teaching of initial reading make use of children's schema, knowledge of the language, and desire to make meaning.

One practice that has proven to have a tremendous impact on children's literacy development is the reading/writing workshop. Supporters of this approach believe that children's reading and writing are developed in tandem, and that in practicing their writing, children learn about reading. Teachers in the reading/writing workshop assume that children come to school already aware of the world of print, as a result of their contact with "environmental print"—the language they see on labels, signs, newspapers, magazines, pamphlets, and television. Teachers ask children to begin writing right away, using "invented spelling," spelling the words as best they can.

Some children come to school knowing the whole alphabet, some the letters in their names; some have had reading and writing experience at home, some have had little experience "playing" with print. However, most children are willing to see themselves as writers, and will "write." At first, their letters, words, and sentences may be highly individualistic and idiosyncratic, but gradually, as teachers "read" children's writing with them, as teachers share books with children, and as children begin to attend more to the print in their environment, their letters, words, and sentences become more and more conventional.

What happens in the reading/writing workshop can be best described using the venerable "osmosis" metaphor: People absorb language from the concentrated language experiences that surround them. The great drive people have to understand print, which is based in their need to know about the world around them, helps them detect the regularities (and eventually the irregularities) in print. It's the same mechanism that allows us to pluck meaning from the babble/babel that surrounds us when we're infants—the intense desire to be a part of things, to create meaningful experience. When nonreaders and nonwriters encounter print regularly, when they try their hands at spelling, when they read some of their own writing and the writing of others, the systems mutually reinforce one another.

The reading/writing workshop is supported, of course, by lots of reading. The teacher shares books regularly with children, reading stories of various kinds out loud. She also brings reading buddies—third-, fourth-, and fifth-grade students—into her classroom to share with children one-on-one. She invites parents into the classroom to read with small groups and to listen to children's stories. She calls attention to interesting words, interesting ideas, and interesting sounds of the language. In addition, she uses other approaches to provide children with information they can use to see how the language works.

The "language experience" approach (Van Allen 1976) has been used for years to help both beginning readers and non-native speakers of English start with reading that is understandable and predictable. In this approach, beginning readers and writers dictate stories to an adult, who, in turn, helps the children learn to read from their own writing. The ingenious aspects of this approach are that it is *always* meaning-centered (since the child is creating the story from his or her own experience); that it grows from oral language competence (which develops in advance of reading and writing); and that it teaches children to recognize the words they use most frequently in their day-to-day conversation. We believe that the language experience approach is an excellent complement to the reading/writing workshop, because it models conventional spelling while giving children opportunities to experiment with their own spelling; it allows children who have lots to say the opportunity to create stories of some length and complexity without the arduous task involved in writing the stories themselves. Students who come from different cultures and who have a variety of life experiences can express their worlds in their language.

In addition, class-authored books can be written on chart paper and posted in the classroom so that children can come back to them again and again. Their knowledge of what the books say allows them to begin to recognize particular words and to see the relationships between sounds and letters. They continue, in the language-rich classroom, to make the generalizations they need to test out their ideas on new texts.

Other teacher practices help children learn the "rules" of reading. Reading and rereading predictable and pattern books also helps children connect what they hear with what they see. The use of big books—oversized books with large print—helps teachers share reading with the whole class. The teacher begins by reading the book to the children and pointing to the words. Gradually children begin "reading," too, as they memorize the story, first reading with the teacher and then reading on their own.

In fact, many children learn to read at home, before they begin school, pretty much this way. Sitting with their parents, they "read" and reread books. Parents may point out particular words or may encourage a child to share in the reading of the story with words he or she knows. Children who have lots of opportunities to see print, to relate print to what they hear, and to participate in "reading" become readers easily. Recognizing this, teachers have adopted some of the methods in which children learn naturally.

Busy teachers can get help in providing their students with more reading opportunities. Older students and parent readers can provide one-to-one or small-group opportunities to share reading. However, children can also be aided by electronics. Many books come in taped versions, which lets a child listen to the tape while looking at the book. In addition, new CD-ROM interactive stories allow children to read books on their own, but to click on words they don't know and get help.

When nonreaders and nonwriters encounter print regularly, when they try their hand at spelling, and when they read some of their own writing and the writing of others, the systems reinforce one another. Reading and writing are learned as wholes in a complex process that sometimes seem miraculous. Reading is a miracle, but we know some ways to support it in the schools:

- Fill the classroom with books. Allow children plenty of time to look at books and to talk about books, and allow them to bring books from home.

- Read to students frequently and lovingly. Share big books and picture books in small and large groups; read "chapter" books that may be too hard for your students to read alone but that provide them with opportunities to hear more kinds of stories and interesting language.

- Allow children to write. Even if their first letters and words aren't decipherable, children are exploring their conception of how the language works. Take the time to figure out and talk to them about what they've written.

- Make available wordless picture books, which allow the nonreader to make meaning and tell stories by looking at and interpreting pictures. Ask children to tell stories to one another as they "read" the pictures.

- Encourage children to respond to books. Talk about the books you read to them and the books they are hearing at home. Ask them what their favorite books are and why.

- Encourage plenty of talk. Demonstrate the relationships between books and life by talking about students' reading and their experiences in relation to one another.

- Engage in storytelling. Tell stories to children and ask them to tell stories to the class and to one another.

---

In short, the whole language approach focuses on immersing kids in reading and making reading meaningful and inviting.

Of course, as inviting and noncontroversial as that may sound, the approach has not received global acceptance. Challenges to the whole language approach come from parents and others who were taught phonics and who believe that learning the rules was what taught them to read. (We see this as a mistaken view of cause and effect. Like all curious people, they probably learned to read because they were curious meaning-makers.) Moreover, the literature-rich classroom has been attacked by some members of the public because they object to the schools "teaching values" (and, of course, much of literature focuses on values); they don't like "overly realistic" stories (about true-to-life events); and they object to "witchcraft" and violence (mostly in folk and fairy tales).

These controversies in education—the clash between the public's and the professionals' views—are likely to continue. Teachers need to do the best they can at maintaining professional standards while educating parents and other members of the public about contemporary educational information.

# Working with Struggling Readers, Nonreaders, and Kids Who Hate to Read

Regardless of the outcome of the whole language wars, which we expect to continue for many years to come, the fact remains that at any grade level you will encounter many students who can be identified by the heading above. There will be students who don't and won't read the assigned material, students who cannot read well, students who "read" but fail to comprehend, and students who take every word they read literally. You'll have students who lack confidence in their ability, children who are blocked by a fear of making mistakes, and kids who are highly skilled at masking their reading problems.

Recent work in reading suggests ways to help students who struggle with reading and who find the process baffling and inscrutable. Rather than continuing to teach students discrete subskills, reading researchers and teachers have turned to proficient readers to learn what good readers do and to develop classroom strategies and practices that employ good readers' behaviors. Ellin Oliver Keene and Susan Zimmerman (1997) summarize those strategies in developing their reading workshops. Good readers:

1. Activate prior knowledge before, after, and during reading; they use their knowledge (schema theory) to understand the text.

2. Decide what they think the most important ideas and themes are in a text, so they can focus on what's important and screen out peripheral issues.

3. Create visuals to extend and deepen their sense of the meaning of the text.

4. Interpret the text as they read, drawing inferences and conclusions, and making judgments and predictions.

5. Re-create the whole text as they read, synthesizing the information as they encounter it and placing it into a whole.

6. Rethink and rework the text when comprehension breaks down and something doesn't make sense; they reread, skip ahead, figure out from context, or use some other strategy to figure out meaning.

That proficient readers use these procedures to understand points to reading as a meaning-making and active process. Students must interact with the text in order for it to make sense. Students who see themselves as passive, then, as simply making the words into language (oral or silent), will gain neither meaning nor satisfaction from the text. Students must be helped to see themselves as central to the reading process and to know that they think as they read.

The following strategies will help struggling readers and nonreaders conceive of the process of reading as one in which they are meaning-makers, and will help give them ownership over their reading.

---

- Develop the reading/writing workshop, where students have many opportunities to talk about what they read and write with you and with one another. Devote a good deal of time to this student-centered activity, in which students are able to choose their own reading materials.

- Create a classroom environment that reflects the importance of reading. Provide a variety of reading material—magazines, newspapers, paperback fiction, nonfiction, and poetry—and make it easily accessible. Figure 5–1 shows one such center, with bookcases, magazine racks, spinner racks for paperbacks, and comfortable places to sit.

- Balance whole-class reading with individualized reading. There may be some books, stories, poems, or plays you want everyone to read. Whole-class reading gives students opportunities to share their understandings and explain how they arrived at them. However, students will be more likely to find success and enjoyment in books that are appropriate for them. Use the interest inventories in Chapters 2 and 3 as a starting point in helping students choose books.

- Draw on the expertise of the school librarian. She or he knows a great deal about what's available and will be willing to help match students and books.

- Teach students strategies that remind them to be active as readers. Give them strategies for predicting (What's going to happen next?), for connecting (How is this like my life? Have I heard or read other books like this? How does this fit with my understanding of the world?), and for figuring out the entire context (What do the pictures tell me? What does the cover tell me? What do I know about the author? What type of book is this—fiction? nonfiction?)

- Discuss useless or misguiding "rules" that students may have been taught about reading. We frequently encounter students who think they must read every word on the page, who believe that you should not glance back at something you might have missed, who believe that if they don't know what a word means they should stop and look it up, and who think that if they can't pronounce a word they can't read it. Students should be encouraged to guess, to reread if they are not comprehending, to look forward to see if their lack of

**Figure 5–1 ∘ A classroom reading center**

comprehension will be solved later, and to skip words they don't know to see if they can understand the meaning from the context.

- Read to your students. We believe that no students are too old or too sophisticated to be read to. As adults, we still enjoy hearing stories read on the radio or by visiting writers. Being read to is especially important to struggling readers or nonreaders, because it gives them experience with the language of print and develops their schema, providing support for when they read on their own. In addition, there's nothing like a good book to motivate one to read.

- Use tapes, films, and records. Use audiovisual materials before, during, or after reading. Filmed versions of novels and stories may differ somewhat from the original, but offer points for discussion. Above all, they give students a visual frame for reading. Tapes and records of authors or actors reading works can reveal the pleasure of books and help students develop an ear for the voice, sound, and rhythm of literature.

- Do book talks. Since you're a reader yourself, you can give a great boost to reading simply by talking about good books you've read and sharing your own responses and reactions.

- Conduct prereading discussions. Talking about a book or story before students begin to read it creates context. Begin by talking about the title: What do they think the book will be about? Read the first couple of pages together. Where and when does the book take place? (Historical or fantasy settings can throw an inexperienced reader. Is there some prior knowledge the youngster needs to read further?) Who seem to be the characters of importance? (The introduction of lots of names at one time can confuse readers. How can they sort them out?) What does the topic seem to be? (Getting an idea of what the characters are up to from the beginning gives the reader something to go on.) Helping students get oriented in the first few pages of a book can be extremely important in their ability to keep going.

- Use picture books. In the last several years, there has been a proliferation of picture books for older readers. These books in no way condescend to more-sophisticated thinkers, and the humor of many of them appeals to adolescents. We have found Susan Benedict and Lenore Carlisle's *Beyond Words: Picture Books for Older Readers and Writers* (1992) extremely useful for finding and using books with older readers. Contributors to *Beyond Words* use picture books to explore the creative process, and look at thematic issues as models for storytelling and bookmaking and as sources for research in the content areas. In addition, the illustrations in picture books provide context and help readers fill in and develop meaning from the text.

## Using Writing to Teach Reading

The reading/writing classroom has been enthusiastically adopted by many teachers of English language arts because the two are naturally pedagogically intertwined. As students write and revise, they read their own work and the work of other students. As they read writers they admire, students get ideas for their own writing—for both style and topics. As they share their writing with one another, ideas are sparked for new things students might try. The reading/writing classroom helps students see themselves as authors—they come up with topics, they draft, they revise, they share their work with others, they get their best writing into a final format in which it can be shared with others—and the mystery of the distant writer becomes lessened. Students know that writers make choices to have an impact on their readers, and they learn that they can shape their language to make an impact too.

Some ideas for a reading/writing workshop:

- Create a classroom newspaper or newsletter. As the students work on this document, they will naturally engage one another in fine-tuning their reading skills. As an alternative, create a class computer bulletin board or an online newspaper, where students can type in ideas and stories, respond to one another, and read the large volume of writing that often results.

- Have students create a webpage that demonstrates the ideas and issues in your classroom. Let them explore the world of webpages and other online information. (More later on critical reading/thinking.)

- Write collective or collaborative stories. Similar to the "language experience" collaborative story we discussed in the initial reading section, the collaborative story allows students to negotiate to decide what they want in their stories. Stronger readers and writers can be of great help to students who feel less confident by acting as scribes. Students also enjoy the "add-a-line" story, in which each student adds to the story after reading only the last line that was added. Though this often proves to be a goofy story, students seem to find them highly amusing. The teacher can use the opportunity to talk about how stories are constructed in order to build in foreshadowing and prediction that guide readers.

- Write serials, in which different members of the class (or of small groups) take responsibility for installments in the continuing adventure of a character.

- Create editing partnerships and groups. (More on this in our composition chapters.) Teaching students to respond to one another's texts and to read and share with one another is a powerful way of teaching reading.

- "Publish" students' writing in a variety of ways. Establish an "author's chair" in your classroom, so students can read finished work to the rest of the class. Create periodic class anthologies for students to reproduce their best works. Have students' showcase portfolios available for parents and administrators to read. Create a readers' hallway in your school where students' writing can be posted. (Teachers we know who have done this say that they have had no problems with vandalism; students' work is respected.) Keep a continuous rotating display of students' work up in your own classroom, so everyone's work is honored.

## Need-to-Know Reading

Too often our classrooms are dominated by teachers' goals only. Of course, our knowledge about the goals and aims of an English language arts classroom and about students' development is extremely important in shaping the curriculum, but as we have repeatedly said, students' own goals and values have an enormous influence on their motivation and growth. We think the English language arts classroom should make a place for students to read about things they want to know. Our increasingly diverse schools need to support learners from various cultures and backgrounds who have a range of goals for their futures. We think that focusing on students' own interests can be a means to support the teaching of reading, as in some of the following cases:

- The Internet: As more and more schools are getting connected to the Internet and more and more classrooms are gaining access to computers, the Internet is becoming a more-available source for all students for both communication and information. As students join chat rooms, engage in e-mail discussions, and seek information on the Internet, they will be reading for their own purposes. (This access also gives teachers of the language arts a great deal to talk about. We discuss aspects of the issues of Internet use and abuse in Chapters 9 and 12.)

- The Community: Creating lifelong readers involves developing behaviors in school that we hope will continue into students' lives after school. Reading the daily newspaper and other local publications helps students learn about their community and perhaps see ways they can contribute. Have them focus on areas that are of interest to them, then share those interests with the rest of the class.

- Practicalities: Students are often making big decisions about their lives that involve reading. High school students are looking for part-time jobs, thinking forward to full-time jobs when they finish high school, weighing decisions about college, and buying cars. Younger kids make a lot of consumer decisions as well about toys, games, and sports equipment. Sponsor some "decision" days in which you and your students bring in reading material (catalogs, flyers, booklets, and advertising information) that focuses on their out-of-school interests.

- Entertainment: Have students talk about how they use reading to learn about their own forms of entertainment—music, film and television, and sports. Although they may get much of their information from TV and radio, ask them to look at print related to their interests—CD covers; magazines with information about music and musicians; film and video guides; sports statistics and sports records; and news articles about actors, musicians, and athletes.

## Reading in the Content Areas

The concept of reading in every subject area is one that English language arts teachers should support and encourage. We can't afford to restrict reading to the language arts period in the elementary grades or to English class at the secondary level. Although the organization of different fields and disciplines—science, social studies, math, art—requires some different reading strategies, the need for readers to make meaning as they read is still a central concern.

Prereading strategies are especially important when students are encountering new material. Before they begin to read, help students remember what they've read previously in the text and what they already know; point out how the text is organized and key features of the text (headings, boldface type, italics, boxed information); define key terms or point out key passages; and raise questions that will be answered in the text.

During reading, students can test their comprehension by stopping from time to time to check if they have questions about what they are reading and to predict what will come next. Teachers can support this questioning and predicting by creating a selective reading guide to help students fulfill the goal of the reading assignment, focus on relevant content in their reading, and use appropriate strategies (Dornan, Rosen, and Wilson 1997).

Often, teachers use tests to see if students have learned material from texts. However, tests may only reflect superficial knowledge gleaned from reading. Having students engage in discussions or write about what they understand from their reading may give teachers a clearer sense of students' construction of meaning. In addition, having students apply their learning by putting it into another form—a story or a poem, a chart or a game—provides them with opportunities for greater assimilation of their knowledge.

Knowing what proficient readers do when they encounter new material is useful for novice readers. Helping students become aware of reading strategies will help solve some of the reading problems they encounter with disciplinary texts. We think, however, that English language arts teachers can be helpful in promoting other possibilities for reading in the content areas:

- Hold a faculty meeting on the problems students have reading various kinds of texts. What are the common elements? How do problems in the disciplines vary? If you're a specialized teacher in a high school, encourage teachers of other disciplines to work on those problems in their own classes (they are in a better position to do that than you are). If you're in a self-contained elementary classroom, you're ideally positioned to focus on reading skills throughout the day.

- Get your school to move beyond textbooks in teaching content areas. Nonfiction books for children, young adults, and adults are often much livelier and more accessible to school-age readers than are the tomes we give them for texts. At the least, encourage other teachers to supplement text chapters with interdisciplinary reading libraries.

- Use and encourage the use of video in the disciplines. The areas of social studies and science are especially rich with videos on subjects of interest in nature, the environment, the history of scientific discoveries, new directions in science, biographies of famous historical figures in all disciplines, and important eras in world and American history. These videos are lively and filled with interesting images and relevant details about and interpretations of the subject by experts in the fields.

- Make your own teaching cross disciplines or team teach with another person. Much reading is naturally interdisciplinary. Books on anthropology touch on social issues and problems. Books on science deal with issues crucial to humanity. Literature talks about life, death, love, hate, warfare, ethics, race, gender, history, and science fact and fantasy. Capitalize on this natural interdisciplinarity to strengthen students' reading skills and build their schema.

## Reading for Non-Native and Dialect Speakers

In our theories of literacy development, we have emphasized that students' learning grows from their own knowledge and experience. All learners use what they already know to learn new things. All learners have acquired language structures, knowledge of words, and information about the world. All too frequently, however, students who speak a different dialect or a different language are treated as if they come to school as a *tabula rasa*, a blank slate. Even as other students read whole, meaningful texts, students who come from different linguistic backgrounds are given subskill activities and drills in workbooks that ask them to master sound/letter correspondences and word study.

We discuss the issue of dialects in greater detail in Chapter 11. However, we would like to address the issue of reading here. Speakers whose native language is not English and those who use a dialect of English are likely to have grammatical features and pronunciation features that differ from what is considered "standard" English. For dialect speakers, these grammatical and phonetic features are a part of a regularized language system. For non-native speakers, the grammar and phonetic features of their native language interfere with their immediate ability to master our different system in English. For example, in Spanish, direct and indirect object pronouns precede the verb (instead of saying "I gave him the book," you would say "I him gave the book"). Word order is but one way in which English differs from other languages. Students mastering English have much more to do than simply learn a bunch of words in their new language.

These features, however, need not interfere with comprehension in a reading approach that does not emphasize word calling or exact reproduction of what is on the page. Dialect speakers easily learn to read if they are asked to make meaning of what is on the page. Just as speakers of "standard" English can read and understand the dialects used in literature (including such books as *Huckleberry Finn* or *Their Eyes Were Watching God*), speakers of dialects can read literature written in "standard" English. In addition, non-native speakers learn to both understand and read English by being immersed in situations where language is used meaningfully and for real communication purposes. Students eager to learn new words in English may create their own dictionaries and phrase books to help them remember key words, but their greatest learning occurs when they are in situations where language matters. The suggestions we gave for initial readers and struggling readers apply to non-native English speakers and speakers of dialects.

# Multiethnic and Multicultural Literature

We strongly support the greater inclusion of ethnic, minority, women's, and international literature in the English language arts classroom. We put ourselves in the camp of the pluralists who want to see the range of cultural materials expanded in the schools, and we are strongly opposed to the "cultural literacy" movement, which argues for focusing instruction on the classic literature of the Western world.

We support greater diversity for a variety of reasons. First of all, our classrooms are becoming much more culturally diverse. Though many have rejected the metaphor of the melting pot (preferring metaphors like "salad" or "stew," in which the ingredients maintain their identities even as they are mixed), it is certainly true that we continue to be one of the most diverse countries in the world, with large groups of people who have immigrated from Asia, South and Central America, and the Caribbean being significant portions of our population. In addition, Native Americans and African Americans continue to make significant contributions to the life of our country. We believe that the literature in our classrooms should reflect the entire culture of our country, not just one element. In addition, students in our classrooms who participate in this diversity of culture should be able to read about their cultural heritage. In the case of women's literature, we believe that girls too seldom encounter literature that allows them to reflect on and consider their own lives and their own possibilities.

Second, we believe that reading about other cultures and other ways of looking at the world is extremely valuable for students in expanding their knowledge and understanding. We believe that literature, by offering students vicarious experiences, has the potential to sensitize students to other ways of valuing and seeing the world. Too frequently, we hear about racist and sexist comments or even harassment in our schools and in our communities. If literature has any utilitarian function it might be this: to awaken students to the humanity of people who are not like them.

Thirty years ago, many teachers responded to the need for multicultural literature by creating special courses and units: Afro-American Literature, Hispanic Literature, Women's Literature. These courses served an important purpose, but we think there is a need to move further: Schools need to integrate multicultural literature throughout all classes and courses. We cannot afford to isolate or ghettoize the literature of ethnic minorities or women. Multicultural reading ought to be happening every day in every class.

Unfortunately, few teachers have been trained in this area. Colleges have introduced some multicultural literature, but by no means has the professorate been able to integrate such literature throughout the curriculum. You need to seek your own, then, but fortunately there are many sources of help:

- Read the professional journals. In particular, *The English Journal, The Journal of Reading, The Reading Teacher, Language Arts*, and *The Horn Book* regularly publish good columns introducing new multiethnic and multicultural materials.

- Check for bibliographies in school and public libraries, where there are many excellent sources both in the reference section and in circulating material.

- Consult teachers of women's and ethnic literature for suggestions about what titles and other materials would be useful and relevant for your class.

- Teach thematically. Thematic/topical teaching maximizes the possibility of introducing diverse literatures. Such themes as "Equality," "Family," "Generations," "Pioneers," and "Decisions" are common to virtually all cultures and literatures.

Figure 5–2 provides a checklist for you consider when you are selecting books for your teaching.

# Reading Resources

We have hinted strongly about a major tenet of our philosophy of teaching reading: If you put kids in contact with relevant and interesting reading materials, *reading happens*. There is growing evidence, in fact, that a great many reading skills are picked up by people in the process of reading itself, as they struggle with and solve reading problems. For this to happen, however, you need to have a rich variety of reading materials available. Yet as school budgets continue to be restrained and restricted, it becomes difficult for teachers to stock the classroom with such materials.

Here are some ideas for increasing the range of materials available in your classroom:

- Attend rummage sales, garage sales, and auctions as a source of cheap used paperbacks, old magazines and comics, and other interesting materials.

- Write or visit county, state, and federal government offices for free pamphlets and booklets. Often, the public library will have a rack of these free materials.

1. Have I included literature that challenges my students' values as well as literature that reinforces them?

2. Have I made available literature that represents the ethnic backgrounds of the students in my class?

3. Have I included literature that shows people and life-styles that are new to my students?

4. Have I been attentive to male and female representation in the literature I have chosen?

5. Have I been careful to counter stereotypical views of people, values, and life-styles with more precise, detailed, and authentic views?

6. Have I chosen literature that emphasizes similarities and universal qualities as well as differences and unique qualities?

7. Have I focused on the work's literary merits as well as its social and political merits?

8. Have I been sensitive to stereotypes that might be damaging or hurtful to students who are in the minority in the class or school (be they Anglo, African American, Asian, male, or female)?

9. Have I provided a richness of alternatives so that students may have choices in their reading?

10. Have I provided opportunities for discussing images of people, their values, and their life-styles as they are presented in literature?

**Figure 5–2** ○ **Checklist for selecting multicultural literature**

- Enlist students and parents in the effort to increase the range of reading materials. Parents are often willing to contribute old books, as well as magazines and newspapers, to your classroom library.

- When making decisions about the departmental or school budget, explore the possibility of buying single copies of good literature rather than sinking large sums into multiple copies and classroom sets. (We've been discouraged to learn that many excellent teachers have been forced to accept the anthology that the school district adopted, only to have it sit unused in the closet as the teachers use reading materials more relevant and interesting to their students.)

- Explore the mail-order book clubs as a way of enticing kids to buy their own books. Or establish a paperback bookstore in the school and stock it with fetching titles.

- Build up your school's recorded literature collection by surveying catalogs and making recommendations to the media center director.

- Get to know your school and public librarians and find out about their book acquisition procedures. In our experience, librarians are discouraged by teacher apathy in requesting books. Identify the books you want available for your professional reading and send the list to the librarian. Even in financial hard times, you're likely to see the collection shaped to your needs and interests.

- Check out your limit of books at your school or public library and take the books to your classroom to use for thematic units or students' special interests.

# Selected Readings

Benedict, Susan, and Lenore Carlisle. 1992. *Beyond Words: Picture Books for Older Readers and Writers*. Portsmouth, NH: Heinemann.

Dornan, Reade, Lois Matz Rosen, and Marilyn Wilson. 1997. *Multiple Voices, Multiple Texts: Reading in the Secondary Content Areas*. Portsmouth, NH: Boynton/Cook Publishers.

Edelsky, Carole, Bess Altwerger, and Barbara Flores. 1991. *Whole Language: What's the Difference*? Portsmouth, NH: Heinemann.

Keene, Ellin Oliver, and Susan Zimmerman. 1997. *Mosaic of Thought: Teaching Comprehension in a Reader's Workshop*. Portsmouth, NH: Heinemann.

Moustafa, Margaret. 1997. *Beyond Traditional Phonics: Research Discoveries and Reading Instruction*. Portsmouth, NH: Heinemann.

Taylor, Denny. 1998. *Beginning to Read and the Spin Doctors of Science: The Political Campaign to Change America's Mind about How Children Learn to Read*. Urbana, IL: National Council of Teachers of English.

Van Allen, Roach. 1976. *Language Experiences in Communication*. Boston: Houghton Mifflin.

# Chapter Six

# Reading and Responding

I n her classic book *Literature as Exploration*, first published in 1938, Louise Rosenblatt speaks of reading as a "performing art." Not only does literature perform for us, she observes, but we learn to "perform" upon texts, creating our own interpretations. As students mature, as they go from initial readers to child readers to young adult readers, their ability to perform on texts becomes more sophisticated. Rosenblatt's "transactional" approach argues that the literary experience exists as an interaction between the text—the black marks on the page—and the reader, who performs on the text.

For many years, New Criticism (launched in the same year as Louise Rosenblatt's book with the publication of Cleanth Brooks' *Understanding Poetry*) received a good deal more attention in critical circles and in education, and literary study in the schools was dominated by the view that the text was central and that the reader needed to read carefully to ferret out the meaning contained in the text. Often this led to teacher-dominated literary studies in which teachers—the superior readers—would tell students what the literature they were reading meant.

In recent years, however, transactional (or reader-response) theory has received enormous support. Reading theorists (emphasizing the effects of prior knowledge on understanding and interpreting) and academics (exploring a much greater range of approaches to reading and suggesting there may be as many texts as there are readers) have cited the work of Louise Rosenblatt as important in reshaping our understanding of the relationship between reader and text.

A response-centered approach makes four assumptions about the relationship between literature and the reader:

1. *Experience with literature is personal.* A student's reaction to a book or story or poem is based on a complex set of past experiences. How students respond depends, to a considerable extent, on who they are, what they have experienced, and what they have read previously and recently. If we want students to be moved by literature and to be responsive to it, we must help young people find literature

appropriate to their emotional development, their age, their interests, their needs, and their reading level.

2. *Engagement with literature is a natural process.* We don't have to trick kids into reading and reacting to good books. Nor do we need clever, cute activities to elicit their responses. The most productive experiences with literature (as with life) are fundamentally absorbing. In working with students we need to be careful to support and nurture engagement, not get in its way.

3. *People read different literature for different purposes.* We need to be knowledgeable about ideas and issues; we read out of curiosity; we read to enter new worlds; we read to find ourselves and learn about others. Recognizing this, teachers should encourage students to explore a range of literature, not just standard school texts and anthologies.

4. *Students' reactions to what they read are based on both their purpose for reading and on the nature of their involvement with the text.* The basics of the plot interest one student. Another is fascinated by a particular character. Another wants to learn more about the place. Yet another is fascinated by the art or illustrations in a book. Rather than forcing children to pay attention to the formal elements that textbooks often emphasize, we need to allow for a variety of interests and patterns of engagement.

Recent critical theory has opened up new ways for us to help students think about their responses to literature, and to help teachers address the issue of greater diversity in their classrooms. Much of the canonical literature taught in English classrooms creates difficulty for students who come from diverse cultures and language backgrounds. Because of very different understandings—different histories, myths, archetypes, symbols—students from minority cultures may have difficulty identifying with the products of mainstream American culture.

Introducing the literature of minority groups can create its own problems when, as frequently happens, white teachers have to "teach" students of color the literature of their own culture. In addition, majority students may resist or find it difficult to engage with the literature of minority cultures; boys may feel alienated from literature that focuses on women's experiences; and minority students from different cultures may find one another's cultures baffling. We believe that such diversity of literary experience is valuable for both minority and majority students (whatever the majorities and minorities in your classroom may be), extending their awareness and understanding.

Cultural theories of literature suggest that the meaning of literary texts is created as a result of interaction between the reader, the text, and the community. Explorations of the social, political, cultural, and historical backgrounds of the literature they read allows students to find a "way in" to literature that may seem alien or inaccessible. Moreover, reading literature from diverse cultures helps students not only celebrate our multicultural society but challenge assumptions about privilege, knowledge, and power. Focusing on class, race, and gender issues in reading helps students account for multiple ways of reading and understanding the text.

In a culturally oriented approach to reading and responding to literature, both students and teachers engage in reading as a community activity, and teachers need to:

- Find literature that reflects the culture and experience of the students in their classes. Although minority literature has had difficulty finding its way into classrooms, there is a good deal of high-quality, award-winning literature—children, adolescent, and adult—that belongs there. Teachers need to know their students (refer to Chapters 2 and 3 for ideas on surveying your students) and to explore the literature of the cultures of the students in their schools.

- Read and discuss classic or traditional texts with attention to the ways in which they construct both minority groups and the majority. It's important to recognize, too, that while women have an edge in numbers, they are underrepresented as writers and spokespeople. What we know of women in literature is often from the point of view of men.

- Explore ways to help their students talk about *difference*. Students in diverse classrooms may find it tension-producing to discuss issues related to one another's cultures. Teachers need to provide models of ways in which students can talk without being hurtful or embarrassed. Help students find a way into the discussion without making them spokespeople for their culture. Students can easily be silenced and feel marginalized, even in discussions about their own culture. Great sensitivity is required to lead discussions of race, gender, and class.

- Help students recognize stereotypes. Both literature and history texts abound with stereotypes of "the other"—African Americans, Native Americans, Latinos, and Asians. Making available literature that represents the views of minorities allows minority students to construct themselves rather than being described by the majority.

- Learn more about the cultures and values of the students they teach. The role of the teacher is especially demanding in a multicultural classroom. The teacher needs to be able to recognize his or her own biases while helping students articulate their own understandings.

And the teacher needs to nurture all voices—even those that are resistant and challenging.

---

# Approaches to Literature in the Classroom

Our own teaching in secondary schools started in standard fashion: We would present a text to the class, tell a little about the author or period, then lead a discussion that largely followed the lines of the New Criticism—teasing out the meaning and focusing on the formal elements of the text. Those discussions often found us answering most of our own questions or carrying on a dialogue with one or two students while the rest of the class hid their heads in books. Later, as we explored response theory, that pattern changed. Although we still spend some time talking with the whole class, a much larger portion of our time is spent organizing and listening to small-group and individual reading programs and discussions. So we have come to see the literature/reading classroom operating with a balance among whole-class discussions, small-group explorations, and individualized reading.

## Shared Experiences

Traditionally, classroom experience with literature has meant a professor or teacher presenting a view of the meaning of the text through lecture or pseudo-Socratic dialogue. The contemporary word *sharing* is not euphemistic; it isn't a cover-up for some sort of sentimentalized chitchat about literature. Rather, *sharing* describes a class and teacher exploring books, with all readers invited to contribute to the discussion. A genuine response can sometimes be quite heated; it can lead to anger and tears. We also find the common class experience to be a useful way to help students learn to "perform" for themselves by seeing how other people engage with and respond to literature.

Because of the tremendous diversity of interests and reading levels in most secondary classrooms, we believe that novels and other long works (biographies and other nonfiction) are best left to individualized reading. We suggest the following alternative approaches to common class readings:

---

- Use short selections—children's books, poems, one-act plays, and short stories—that can be read and responded to in one or two class periods. We find this preferable to working through a long novel that some students have no interest in and must be dragged through, but that others read in two days.

- Show creative videos and films related to topics and themes you're exploring in the class, then follow those with selected short readings.
- Assign TV shows (both pop and educational) related to classroom topics; follow with reading and discussion.
- Treat students' writing as literature to share with the class. Give it the same respect you would professional writing.
- Back up shared readings with recordings of authors reading their own work or actors doing dramatic readings. Or, have your students present and tape readings to share with the whole class and add to your classroom audio library.
- Have students present oral readings of the common text, then discuss how various presentations shape the meaning.
- Discuss your own reading, not only literature, but newspaper and magazine articles and "escape" reading. Invite your students to share their outside reading as well.
- Use bulletin boards to post poems, articles, student writing, and excerpts from plays and novels.

## The Discussion of Literature

We know how difficult it is to get a discussion going when you have thirty or more students in a class. We've had the experience of feeling pleased by what we thought was a lively interchange, only to realize later that less than half the class participated. And we hate to recall how many times we've carefully prepared discussion questions only to have students sit like porcupines, quills out, when we invite them to talk. But despite our wounds, we still value those community exchanges, and we have a few bits of advice to offer:

- Treat reading as a process. Elicit responses from students before reading (What do you think this will be about? What does the title tell you?); at early stages of the reading (What catches your attention in the first few lines? Pages? What do you think will happen next?); as they engage with the characters (Who do you like best? Least? Why?); in responding to the world of the book (When and where is this taking place? What is the impact of this place on the characters and action?); and in thinking about the significance of the piece (How does this piece relate to your own world? What did you discover from this reading? How do you see things differently? What ideas or issues does this piece explore?)

- Preface group discussions with oral reading. Read (or invite willing students to read) large chunks of literature aloud to the class to make certain the students have experienced it (even if they have supposedly read the literature for homework).

- Allow plenty of time for gut reactions. Good literature often elicits a strong emotional response from students. They need an opportunity to say what they *feel* as they are articulating their ideas about what they *think* (and, of course, the two are connected).

- Preface discussions with writing—five minutes or so for students to jot down their responses and reactions. Even if you have assigned a journal or another piece of writing for class that day, asking students to write in class moves them back into thinking about the literature.

- Ask honest questions. Don't ask, "Who can tell me the symbolic significance of the porcupine in this book?" when you already have an answer in mind. The best kinds of questions seem to be those that ask for student engagement: What did you think of this book? How did you like the main character? Have you ever done anything like this yourself? What about that porcupine?

- Let "literary matters" emerge through students' responses. Instead of plunging into the discussion with a question about plot or character, let students discuss their reactions to books. Introduce the "language" of formal matters (plot, theme, character, setting, etc.) as the discussion develops.

- Model ways of talking about literature by talking about your own response—the questions, ideas, and feelings that occurred to you as you read. As you raise questions that are of interest to you, ask students to add their own questions and tentative notions about what's going on in the text.

- Ask questions that help students develop an awareness of themselves as readers (and writers) responding to writers. What do you think of the way the writer handled this material? What kind of person do you think the author is? How do you think your own values and opinions affected your response to the world this author set up? Were there ways in which you resisted this depiction of the world? How did the responses of others in the class affect your ideas and feelings about the piece? To whom would you recommend this piece and why?

## Group Experiences

We use small-group work extensively when we teach literature. Sometimes our students will discuss reactions to a story or poem or book that
everyone in the class has read; at other times we have groups work on different selections. In both cases, group experiences with literature allow
for a wide range of responses from people whose values and opinions may
be very different from one another's. Exchanges with people who have
different views of the world, and thus different interpretations of the texts,
not only help students grow as readers, they help people grow in self-
awareness and awareness of others as well.

A major advantage of small-group work is that students can be given
choices in their reading at the same time they are part of a community of
readers. Teachers need to model ways of talking about literature, so that
students can operate increasingly independently in small groups. When
students are working in their groups, the teacher is available to circulate
among groups to help those who are stuck or confused about how to proceed. However, it is important that the teacher encourage students' self-
reliance in their reading and responding.

Some alternative approaches to group experiences with literature:

- Within a thematic unit, allow groups of students to choose what they
  wish to read and discuss in their groups from a broad range of fiction,
  nonfiction, and poetry.

- To start students out in group work, provide them with some questions you might ask if you were conducting a whole-class discussion
  of a literary work. Ask them to add to and delete from that list according to their own interests.

- Ask students to respond to literature without guidance from you.
  Have students tape-record the discussions to listen to later. How do
  their discussions and responses to literature change over time?

- Have small groups introduce the selections they are reading to the
  rest of the class. They may do this by creating oral readings, introducing characters by reading selections from the text that illuminate
  these characters, creating a readers' theater presentation of the text,
  introducing themes and motifs in the text, and describing the twists
  and turns of the plot.

- Let small groups develop as reading clubs, focused on favorite
  authors, genres, or thematic ideas.

- Ask reading clubs to create thematic units for the class based on their
  own readings and their own expertise developed in a particular area.

Encourage them to use class anthologies, library materials, and the classroom library to build their units.

- Let groups specialize in an author, learning all about the work and life of their writer and reporting back to the class.

- Make writing an important part of group work. Have them write back and forth to one another about their reading. Create a group journal in which everyone writes an entry a week responding the ideas of others in the journal. If your students have access to e-mail, encourage them to write back and forth online.

- Use reading groups for college-bound students to read classics considered important for college. Have groups share summaries, interpretations, and evaluations.

## Individual Reading

Individual reading is at the heart of the teaching process. After all, what we want to accomplish in the literature/reading program is to lead students toward individual competence. We advocate giving kids lots of time in school to pursue their individual reading, particularly given the competition for their out-of-school time and attention. To foster the individualized reading program:

- By hook, crook, or school budget, build up your classroom library. Research shows that much of the teaching of reading involves getting the right books into young people's hands (the magnetism of literature will take care of the rest). The closer the books are to the kids, the more likely it is that they will read.

- Explore and exploit your community and school libraries. In addition to bringing in books to meet students' interests, help students learn to make effective use of the library themselves, so that book repositories no longer exist as the stereotypical bibliodungeon for baffled students.

- Do frequent book talks to publicize books available for individualized reading. Have students do book talks as well to sell titles they've recently read and enjoyed. Invite the school librarian in to tell students what's new in the library.

- Encourage students to use the Internet to find out about what people are reading, what's new in literature, and what discussions are taking place about literary matters. Webpages allow students to read magazines, explore virtual libraries, and find subjects of particular interest to them. Have individual students find sites that might be of interest to others and share them with the whole class.

- Hold frequent individualized conferences with students to discuss their reading. Ask questions that extend and expand students' thinking about their reading. Suggest new books based on their interests.

- Set aside a reading/conversation corner where students can discuss books they are reading. Encourage talking about books as a "natural" conversation, rather than just a schoolish activity.

- Sponsor regular classroom times devoted to reading. You may wish to demonstrate the value you place on reading by devoting a whole week early in the school year to students' silent reading. Or, you may provide one day a week in class on which students may read on their own and talk about their reading. (We've heard teachers say they simply don't have time with all they have to cover in the curriculum. We can only respond by asking what's more important than encouraging and developing independent, self-motivated readers?)

# Extending the Range of Response

A good English/language arts class will include a combination of reading experiences. It will provide large-group sharing of diverse responses to individual works, small-group explorations of common or group-selected texts, and plenty of time for individual reading and response. It will also encourage students to perform on texts in a variety of ways. Options for response must allow for different kinds of students and many types of reading materials. The suggestions that follow allow you to vary the ways in which students synthesize their reactions to reading.

## Talk and Drama

A good book, poem, play, or story often leads naturally to substantial talk. "Substantial talk" does not mean a heavy emphasis on the formal features of literature. We've been interested, in talking with our own students, in how easily they can talk about their responses to a film they've seen—why they found certain characters appealing or unappealing; why they found the plot to be implausible; what scenes they thought advanced the story or misled them; what they thought the filmmaker's point was. However, in the same sorts of discussions about literature, they seem much more reluctant to speak, much less certain that their insights have value. Perhaps reading and talking about literature has been made too artificial for them; perhaps they have had teachers who have told them what the literature means; perhaps overemphasis has been placed on formal elements (plot, theme, setting) at the expense of students' own ideas about the impact and meaning of what they've read. Whatever the cause, many students seem alienated from literary experience. We believe that student-centered, natural talk about literature—in whole-class, small-group, and one-to-one discussions—can provide students with ownership of their literary experiences.

In addition, literature is naturally dramatic, and a powerful piece of literature can be focused through the use of classroom drama. Drama can allow students to participate in the story, to view it from the inside out. You can have students:

- Do improvisations based on key scenes from a story, perhaps exploring alternative endings or different possibilities for characters' actions. Frequently, students will express skepticism or disapproval of a character's behavior or the direction a plot takes. Have them play alternative scenes to explore what might have happened.

- Extend or create scenes that are presented sketchily or are alluded to but not shown "on stage." Filling in these gaps in stories gives students an opportunity to explore both plot and character in more depth.

- Prepare a readers' theater production of a work. Have students find scenes that are primarily dialogue and rewrite them into a script, assigning narration and description to a narrator. Have them act out scenes with the script in hand, without sets. Minimal props or pieces of costume can be used to suggest (rather than re-create) the characters.

- Have students who like to read and who read dramatically create audiotapes of their favorite poems or stories to add to your classroom audio collection and be made available to other students.

- Videotape students' readers' theater productions. Or, create more elaborate productions of dramatizations of poems, plays, stories, or scenes from novels. Allow students to create the scripts, sets, and costumes for their dramas. Have them direct and film their productions.

- Act out plays. Plays are meant to be a performing art, and their full impact is realized when they are staged.

## Writing Activities

The reading/writing connection allows students to explore their responses to literature in a variety of ways. The traditional expository essay allows students to argue their interpretations of a literary piece, but other sorts of writing give them other ways into literature. Having students do informal writing in a journal gives them a chance to figure out what they think and feel. In addition, they can use the journal to think about themselves as readers, noting their reading process as well as responding to the literature. Using writing before, during, and after reading helps students become active readers.

In addition, participating in the authoring process demonstrates to students that writing a novel, play, poem, or story is a matter of making choices. Students can learn a great deal about how literature "works"—about characters, themes, ideas, style—by writing imaginatively. In addition, students enjoy writing that allows them to become the characters or the author of a piece of literature. Let students explore literature through writing in some of the following ways:

- Rewrite the ending of a story or novel to explore other ways the characters might have ended up or other twists the plot might have taken.

- Write a sequel to a story, novel, or play, describing the characters or actions that follow "The End." Have students compare their different conceptions of what might happen next.

- Write and exchange letters between characters from different books. Allow students to explain how their common interests and concerns reflect on the issues and themes of the literature.

- Adapt a short story into a play. Students can explore ways to integrate narrative and description into dialogue and stage direction.

- Describe how they would film a scene from a novel, story, play, or poem. Where would they set the piece? Who would they cast?

- Write a poem or song based on the mood, images, or feelings created by a story. Or, write a poem or song that explores the themes or issues of a character's life.

- Write a journal from one character's point of view, describing their reactions to and feelings about the events of the story.

- Rewrite a scene from another character's point of view. Students can explore the impact of first- and third-person (and various omniscient narrators') points of view by imaging how different characters would conceive of the events.

## Media Activities

Our students live in an increasingly nonverbal world. Film, television, multimedia CDs (audio, video, graphics, animation), magazines, and the Internet provide a range of ways for young people to experience the world. Allow them to draw on their audiovisual experience and interests to express their responses to literature. Have your students:

- Design a multimedia CD-ROM to provide an introduction to the literary theme they have explored. Have them include audio and visual clips, as well as pieces of text that characterize the literature they have read.

- Design a webpage to introduce Internet surfers to a piece of literature. Encourage them to include information about the author, a summary of the literary piece, and pieces of writing that students in the class have created in response to the literature. (Use writing that emphasizes students' imaginative writing.) If you have computer experts in your class or in your school, have them create your webpage.

- Explore Internet sources in which they can share their ideas about literature with others. Help your students explore e-mail, electronic bulletin boards, and listservs to begin or join ongoing conversations about literature. Find resources in this ever-changing world through magazines and newsletters that focus on Internet teaching.

- Create music audiotapes that capture the mood of the poems or stories they are reading. Have them create a music tape for a novel.

- Translate a poem or story into a music video. (The 1997 movie version of *Romeo and Juliet* might provide a model for the translation process. Though not approved of by all English teachers, it certainly attracted a lot of teenage interest while remaining true to Shakespeare's language.)

- Make book jackets, magazine spreads, or advertising posters that will attract a book buyer. Have students create different versions for different magazines—*Rolling Stone, Newsweek, Ebony, GQ, Seventeen,* emphasizing the interests of each audience.

- Draw maps based on stories, both literal maps of the settings and figurative maps of the relationships among characters and events.

- Illustrate favorite poems or stories (including their own).

- Create a live multimedia introduction to a thematic unit.

# Critical and Evaluative Reading

One of the charges often leveled against a response-centered program is that it fails to develop students' abilities to evaluate what they read, to tell good from bad. "If students simply react," goes this argument, "how will they ever come to know that some books are better than others, and that any old reaction to a book just won't do?"

All of us want our students to appreciate good literature. Without being snobbish, we can say that some books stand the test of time better than others (see the next chapter), that some are fuller and richer examples of the writer's art and craft than others. We don't want our kids to pick dreck over substance, easy reads over those that challenge the mind. Moreover, we don't want students to dismiss books just because they can't "identify" with the characters or the situation. The response-centered approach doesn't ignore such matters; rather, it tries to promote growth in critical reading from within the student rather than to enforce it from without.

How can we nurture the growth of artistic, aesthetic, and critical awareness? We think the following principles are important to keep in mind:

1. *Both students and teachers have "taste," but their tastes are often very different.* It may seem to you that what students appreciate is stereotypic, even simplistic. (And even the most sophisticated of us enjoy a range of types of literature—from "escape" to "challenging.") It's important to recognize, however, that from kindergarten (and before) children are establishing their own identities and trying to establish their relationships with the world in which they live. They're looking for answers, and they respond to literature that seems to offer them answers. Students' gender, class, and ethnicity will also have an impact on what they value. Some of their questions may be about their direct experiences, and some may be very pro-found indeed. To undercut their choices and their taste is to under-rate the power of literature to enrich their lives.

2. *Tastes change as people change.* This is true for adults as well as young people. How have your values shifted in the past five or ten years? What do you care for today that was undreamt-of in your phi-losophy a few years back? We've observed that as long as people are in an environment that offers them new experiences, they expand and enlarge their interests. We worry that too often kids are "chal-lenged" prematurely with books designed to improve their taste. The result is often that they quit reading and their growth comes to a halt. A response-centered program offers students new opportunities for experience and enlarges their horizons gradually. We have a lot of confidence in young people and believe in letting natural growth in reading take place.

3. *Growth in awareness comes as a result of building on previous lit-erary experiences.* It's important to consider the cumulative effects of reading on growth. A good experience with one book helps pave the way for success with the next. Enjoyment of a simple book creates a foundation for something a bit more complex. Thus we emphasize the importance of exposure to a wide range of literature in a response-centered program, coupled with opportunities for students to react to a text on their own terms within a community of readers.

Here are some activities we use to catalyze and promote this natural growth in students' critical abilities:

---

- Read a novel aloud to the class over a period of several weeks, perhaps a chapter a day, perhaps as little as ten minutes a day. As you read, present your observations about the book and invite students to exchange viewpoints. In this way you model ways of responding and give students opportunities to respond as well. Discussion of the book is natural and conversational, and you and your students can learn about how the other thinks.

- Ask open-ended questions, then probe for explanations. Don't begin with formal evaluation of a work. Let students' unexpurgated likes and dislikes emerge first; then nudge students to back up their responses with illustrations from the text. Encourage them to read from the text as part of their illustration.

- Celebrate tangents. The most fruitful discussions we've had with both young and older students have grown through side trips and excursions we could not have anticipated. These are not digressions, and you're much too savvy to let the kids deliberately derail your train of thought. Tangents are a form of critical response, one to be understood rather than avoided.

- Avoid teaching literary terminology in advance (this is especially difficult in secondary school, where many of the textbooks are organized by formal elements). We know that terms like *plot, theme, character, narration, irony, symbol, setting, imagery, dialogue, metaphor*, and *rhythm* are useful in many ways in discussing literature. However, mastery of terminology is not a substitute for or an easy route to literary evaluation. We introduce literary terminology in class discussions as it seems helpful in encouraging students to discuss their own reactions. Ah, you liked the way the characters talk? Yes, the *dialogue* is effective. You thought the comparison of love to fire and ice was neat? That *metaphor* is an interesting one, isn't it? We're constantly made aware of how often opportunities to present this enabling terminology come up in class.

- Encourage comparisons of literary works. Help students link their past reading to the present by talking about books previously read by the class or by inviting students to draw their individual reading into class discussions. Students will also compare texts to their filmed versions or to other films that have similar characters, plots, or issues.

- Allow students to work out interpretations on their own. Give students plenty of chances to talk in small groups or in pairs about the things that are being read by the whole class or by individuals. Encourage students to bring to bear their notions of the world (rather than the official, generic institutional response) to make sense of the text. Students often come up with very interesting interpretations that can challenge other students in the class.

- Use writing extensively. Have students keep response journals as they read; let them write reaction papers during and after reading or listening to pieces being read. In place of the traditional book report, let them engage in imaginative writing. Let them write postcard reviews on index cards to keep in a class file. Ask the school librarian to devote a library bulletin board to student reviews of books. Start a book review newsletter in which your class recommends good titles to other classes or grades in the school.

- Try to curb your anxiety about "coverage." In-depth reading, responding, and writing take time. In order to develop thoughtful responses, students need time to think and write. On the other hand, don't hold back avid readers by keeping everyone on the same schedule. Balance whole-class and individualized reading so that every student is working to his or her capacity.

Finally, you should never underestimate the power of a book, poem, story, or play to teach itself. Literature does enculturate students, enlarging their range of experiences, refining their tastes and sensibilities. It also helps them explore the diversity of the world and has the potential for creating more-tolerant, more-flexible human beings. Good books can often do these things without the domination of the teacher. But it's also clear that some books benefit from the help provided by good supportive English language arts teachers in order to work their best magic.

# Selected Readings

Corcoran, Bill, Mike Hayhoe, and Gordon M. Pradl. 1994. *Knowledge in the Making: Challenging the Text in the Classroom*. Portsmouth, NH: Heinemann.

Purves, Allen C., Theresa Rogers, and Anna O. Soter. 1990. *How Porcupines Make Love II: Teaching a Response-Centered Curriculum*. New York: Longman.

Rosenblatt, Louise. [1938] 1995. *Literature as Exploration*. New York: Modern Language Association.

———. 1978. *The Reader, the Text and the Poem: The Transactional Theory of the Literary Work*. Carbondale, IL: Southern Illinois University Press.

Wilhelm, Jeffrey D. 1997. *"You Gotta BE the Book": Teaching Engaged and Reflective Reading with Adolescents*. New York: Teachers College Press.

# Chapter Seven

# The Classics, Popular Culture, and Cultural Literacy

During our teaching careers we have observed a number of efforts to create a narrowly conceived traditional core curriculum with a narrow definition of the skills and knowledge students should have. With his book *Cultural Literacy* (1987), E. D. Hirsch launched an enormous controversy in the teaching of arts and sciences. Drawing on some of the research we cite in the previous two chapters, Hirsch observed that readers bring prior knowledge and past experience to bear on reading an unfamiliar text. If students have a paucity of knowledge, he argued, they will have difficulty appreciating the standard classic works that form the core of a culture. Hirsch argued that youngsters are not "culturally literate," and argued for increased teaching of core or common elements of the culture. He confidently subtitled his book *What Every American Needs to Know.*

Over the years there have been a number of advocates for a core curriculum, often initiated by political groups and governmental agencies. These advocates argue for central concepts, standards, and information that all children should learn. In an era when schools are widely perceived to be failing, those who advocate core curricula have received continued strong public response. Core curriculum advocates supply support for those who would like to reduce "nonessential" offerings in schools and get back to a basic, core curriculum with a heavy emphasis on traditional mathematics, science, history, and literature.

Many opponents of a narrowly conceived core curriculum are concerned on a number of fronts. They see the Hirsch cultural literacy list as elitist and racist (most core reading centers on the work of white male writers). In addition, in an era in which North America is increasing in diversity and the world has shrunk so that we are in immediate relationship with one another throughout the globe, many see the need for a greater emphasis on learning about the cultures, ideas, languages, and literacies of other people and places. And finally, the narrow focus on a core curriculum ignores the tremendous need for students to become more conscious and critical of the world in which they live—the world of television, video, film, newspapers, magazines, audio recordings, and the Internet.

We've never heard anybody argue against the value of classic books, and most people would agree that at some point in their lives, students probably ought to encounter them. And there hasn't in recent years been any appreciable withering-away of interest in the common culture. In secondary schools, especially, despite the wealth of alternatives, students spend extraordinary amounts of time with conventional literature anthologies, plodding through such hoary classics as Jonathan Edwards' "Sinners in the Hands of an Angry God" and William Cullen Bryant's "Thanatopsis."

In this chapter we argue for a middle ground, or, perhaps better, for a comprehensive view of "cultural literacy" that gives the classics their due but recognizes that we are living in the twenty-first century—not the nineteenth or even the twentieth!—and that the nature of culture has changed. Specifically:

1. *All children are "literate" in a culture already.* By "literate" we mean that they live in a culture and are negotiating it, for the most part successfully. It may be a culture dominated by television, family, siblings, and peers. It may be the culture of an all-white Boston suburb or a racially mixed blue-collar neighborhood in Sacramento, but it is a culture, and it is complex and rich.

2. *People become literate in new or different cultures in response to opportunities and exposure.* By "exposure" we do not mean a guided tour through anthologies like *Skipping Through American Literature* or *The Pomp and Circumstance of BritLit.* Rather, people become enculturated as their personal interests, ideas, motivations, and opportunities expand. Memorizing bits of cultural knowledge will neither enculturate minority (or majority) children nor pop them free from their present culture and into the "mainstream" (which, in the United States, at least, we defy Hirsch or anybody else to define and describe accurately).

3. *Cultural literacy is personal and plural.* Although one can compile lists of commonly read works, it's a grievous error to assume that there is a monolithic "cultural literacy." People's knowledge of the culture is unique and idiosyncratic. It is personal, based on their needs, interests, and circumstances.

4. *Classic and popular culture are both part of a continuum, not contradictory or opposites.* In fact, even the word *continuum* may be inappropriate, since it implies a one-dimensional scale with the classics at one end and popcult at the other. A better metaphor might be the earth's atmosphere: It contains a mix of oxygen, nitrogen, auto

exhaust, mouthwash fumes, and other gases we don't want to think about. It's a jumble of molecules. Most teachers would like to enrich the air with the oxygen of what we see as good or better books for kids. We'd like to cut down on some of the noxious fumes of, say, literature that is exploitative, excessively violent, or written to manipulate kids rather than to inform them. But we can improve the air quality only by getting kids out into the fresh country air of reading, not by locking them in a musty library stocked only with the classics.

In this chapter, then, we begin with popular culture, showing that it is more than "pop and pulp," more than assigning TV shows that kids would watch anyway. After we explore some ways of using these materials in a variety of elementary and secondary school classrooms, we go on to discuss the classics, here directing our remarks mostly to secondary school teachers (though by no means forgetting that the classics and young people's cultural literacy include elementary favorites like *Mother Goose, Cinderella, Snow White, Alice in Wonderland*, and *Charlotte's Web*).

# Popular Culture in the Classroom

The world we live in is rich with multimedia, multimessage experiences that demand our attention and our dollars. Some of the products of popular culture are passing fads and fancies, flashing into the center of our attention for a few weeks or months and then disappearing with barely a trace. Others become cultural icons, sometimes even shaping the ways in which the mainstream culture understands itself. And still others become significant to subcultures and speak to particular groups of people. The world of popular culture includes actors, playwrights, film writers, cartoon characters, rock musicians, jazz musicians, blues musicians, politicians, gangsters, consumer products, games and toys, visual artists, athletes, poets, heroes, and more. The study of these, as serious scholars of popular culture tell us, provides us with important clues about people's beliefs, values, traditions, and identities.

Popular culture in the United States reflects the richness of the American experience in its entertainments, diversions, and aesthetic experiences, and includes all of us in some contexts. But popular culture isn't exclusively American. As our British readers would be quick to remind us, England's popular culture is much older than ours and includes folks named William Shakespeare, Charles Dickens, the Brontë sisters, and Arthur Conan Doyle. The popular culture traditions in Australia, New Zealand, and Canada are perhaps a bit shorter than ours in the United

States, but they are filled with interesting characters and personalities and art, from convict poetry to Footrot Flats, from *The Thorn Birds* to hockey players.

Although popular culture, by definition, appeals to a large number of people, it is not necessarily inferior or mediocre in quality. We think that the study of popular arts and culture, both of today and of previous periods in history, can be a rewarding and significant English language arts experience for several reasons:

1. *The study of popular culture enriches students' understanding of their country and its history.* The fiction and poetry, magazines and newspapers, radio and television programs, and movies and plays that we enjoy provide insight into our tastes, values, and beliefs. They reflect who we are, where we have been, and what we have believed to be beautiful, ethical, and important. Through a study of popular culture, students can begin to answer questions: What is peculiar or unique about our culture? How have we changed through history? What traits and beliefs have endured? How have we come to be what we are today?

2. *The study of popular culture helps students understand their own values and tastes better.* Students can examine their own interests and compare them to the interests of their peers, their parents, and people in other times. They can look into the ways in which the things they like have impact on values and tastes. Moreover, students can explore what's behind the images that are projected. In addition to seeing how popular culture is created, they can look into its commercial and economic roots to see how it is "sold."

3. *Popular culture is diverse and rich.* While recognizing that products of popular culture are a commercial commodity, students can also appreciate the expertise and artistry involved in creating these consumer arts. There's plenty to learn as students look into how a film is made, how a cartoon is produced, or how music is created.

4. *Popular culture is everywhere.* The experiences of popular culture—from television to radio to film and video to the Internet—have become so much a part of our experience that they are almost like the air we breathe. Students of varying interests and skills will be able to find something they would like to explore in greater depth. And they will be able to find it at great ease and relatively inexpensively. Moreover, examining what seems "natural" to students develops their critical awareness and opens their eyes to ideas, messages, and perceptions that they had taken at face value.

To show the potential of these materials, we want to review three approaches to popular culture: historical, genre, and thematic. In choosing such apparently "literary" modes of organization, we show how popular culture can be meshed with traditional study. In fact, we think that popular culture, as well as being worthy of study in its own right, can be integrated into nearly any discussion of literature and language in your classroom, from kindergarten through graduate school. Moreover, since popular culture is such an extensive and ubiquitous aspect of students' lives, we believe it is crucial in students' language and thinking development to turn an analytical eye to it.

## The Historical Approach

- As part of your study of a particular period in literature, have students look at the popular culture of the period. What did the Puritans do for fun? What music, sports, and art appealed to Americans of the North and South during the Civil War? What made the Twenties "Roaring"? Use a range of sources, from the Internet to facsimile materials from the period to coffee-table books, to explore these periods.

- Team up with a social studies teacher to explore the literature, politics, and popular culture of an important decade or period in American history—Reconstruction, World War I, the Twenties, the Depression, World War II, the Vietnam War. How did literature and the popular arts reflect the concerns of the time?

- Have students select one author whose culture they are interested in studying. What were the fashions, the pastimes, the entertainments, and the sources for news during Shakespeare's life? What was Shakespeare's role in the popular culture? What was a day like for Charles Dickens and other Londoners in nineteenth-century England? How did people live in New England during Emily Dickinson's lifetime? What was popular in New York during Zora Neale Hurston's life there?

- Choose a single important day in twentieth-century history and have students study the cultural milieu of that time. Have students examine newspapers and magazines (available at most reasonably large community libraries) and discuss the news of the day, trends in fashion, popular songs and other music, theatrical entertainment, and radio and television offerings.

- Have students reproduce or imitate a popular art form from an earlier era. They can write dime novels, create vaudeville shows, write and draw cartoons, create radio dramas, or invent television advertisements. Or, have them write a short story or play that reflects the interests of a historical period they are studying, using the information they have learned about the culture of that period.

- Let students create monologues for historical figures from periods they have studied. The person may be real (an author, a musician, a politician) or a fictitious composite based on what the student has learned about the teenage girls, middle-aged men, or grandmothers of that period.

- Have students view the popular media to explore images, expectations, and treatment of groups and their place in the social hierarchy during periods of social upheaval. What were the roles and expectations for women at the turn of the twentieth century? How did African Americans fare in the south during Reconstruction? How were European immigrant groups viewed during the Depression? Or, engage students in exploring the changing constructions of women, immigrant groups, and poor people during different periods in history.

- Have students interview their parents and grandparents about how they entertained themselves. What did they read? What did they listen to on the radio? What films, television programs, and comics and cartoons entertained them? What did they do on Saturday night? From this, have your students create a popular-culture time line that shows the entertainment of three generations.

- If you're lucky enough to work in a multicultural, multiethnic school, have students share the differing popular cultures of different cultures. Compare parents' and grandparents' favorites in music, reading, and films. If parents or grandparents grew up in a different country, have them describe how the entertainment in their native country differs from the entertainment in the U.S.

- Have a treasure hunt in which students search attics, basements, and closets at home for books, magazines, newspapers, or other memorabilia saved by their families. What has survived? Why? What does it say about values?

- Visit garage sales, rummage sales, and secondhand stores to pick up old children's and young adult books. Create a popular-culture library for your students to read, analyze, and discuss these "survivors." Do the same with old textbooks. How has what's emphasized in schools changed over the years? How has it stayed the same?

- Have students bring in family collections of school yearbooks and picture albums. What can they learn about the values, interests, and fads of those times by studying the photographs and inscriptions?

## The Genre Approach

Popular culture clearly follows trends and formulas. One successful television show spawns a dozen like it; a best-selling novel is followed by myriad imitations; popular futuristic, fantasy, and action thrillers are followed by sequels and clones. As students look for the common elements that make up a formula, they are engaging in critical, analytical thinking that aids them as both students and consumers. The critical eye students use can be applied to traditional literature study, as well as being used to heighten students' awareness of the culture in which they live.

- Teach a "best-seller" unit. The reference librarian can help you find the lists of best-sellers, or look in old *New York Times Literary Supplements*. How long have best-sellers been tracked? How many of them are still available in the public library? How do they change from generation to generation? What common elements do they have? Have students do a general survey and then read books to look for more specific elements of popular literature.

- Teach a Newbery/Caldecott unit to explore what has been popular in children's literature over the years. What themes, styles, and authors have been popular over the years? How has the field of children's literature changed? How has it stayed the same?

- Engage students in exploring a particular popular fiction genre—the western, the detective story, the romance, science fiction. To what extent do the novels conform to a formula? To what extent do they deviate from the formula? Which authors and series are most formulaic? Which are most inventive? Have different groups of students work with different genres, then share their ideas about formulas *across* genres. What do they discover?

- Have students do the same thing with genres in film. What genres in film are most popular now? What were most popular ten years ago? Twenty years ago? Thirty years ago? Have students look at old magazines and newspapers to discover what was popular. Show classics from those periods to see what has survived and why.

- Help students compare television, film, and popular literature. What do they have in common? How does each medium affect the others? What books are made into films? What films come out in book form?

- Allow your students to explore the various genres on television and to understand the appeal of that programming for its audience. Some genres to consider: the soap opera, the talk show, the situation comedy, the prime-time drama, the adult cartoon, the kids' cartoon, the music video, and the children's show.

- With your students, examine lists of Academy Awards and the various categories in which movies have won prizes. Watch some award winners and analyze the ways in which what is stylish in movies has changed.

- Hold a Walt Disney Film Festival and figure out the formulas for the classic cartoons and the family escape films produced so successfully by Disney.

- Have groups of students do histories of music: rock 'n' roll, blues, jazz, hip-hop, rap. What are their roots? How have they changed over the years? What has created the change? Students will find a great deal to read, as well as a great deal to listen to, as they work on music.

- Let students choose a media figure to research: a musician, an actor, an athlete, a popular writer, a cartoonist. How has that person become successful? How long did it take them to make their mark? How long have they been (or how long did they remain) in the spotlight?

## The Thematic Approach

We are partial to the thematic approach, because it asks students to look at ideas and issues over time and across space, to make connections, and to be analytical about what they see. Nowhere is this kind of analytical approach more important than with popular culture. Because popular culture is so close to our day-to-day experience, we seldom stop to examine it. Students develop the habit of watching certain television shows, films, and cartoons; playing video games; listening to music; seeing zillions of advertisements; taking in gazillions of images without stopping to explore what those images say about America's values, priorities, and position in the world. We believe that helping students use language to explore the world in which they live is a central responsibility of the English classroom. To that end, we suggest that students:

- Look at gender issues in the media. What are men's and women's roles in soap operas? Who has what kind of power? How do different genders wield their power? What are women depicted doing in television ads? How are women treated in rock 'n' roll? Have groups of students explore single genres in popular culture: the adventure film, the situation comedy, rap music, the women's magazine ad. Or, they may wish to do historical studies to see how things have changed over the years.

- Explore race and ethnicity in popular culture. Television and film are especially rich media to see how people from other cultures or U.S. minority groups have been constructed. For example, historical study of prime-time television programming will show changes in the role of African Americans over the past fifty years.

- Study the American hero. How has the hero changed over the years? What did the American hero do in the 1920s? In the 1930s, 1940s, 1950s, and so on? How did the events of American life affect what people thought of as heroic?

- Examine the notion of beauty. Students can look at classic films, television programs, magazines, and newspapers to see how what has been considered beautiful has changed.

- Explore technology and its impact on American popular culture. This is an especially good project for students who are interested in science. How have advances in television (the videotape; the CD-ROM) changed people and the media?

- Explore violence in film, television, comics, and music. Have students explore research (available in the popular media) on the impact of violence on children's behavior and write about their own observations of violence in young people.

- Research humor. This is another good unit for historical study, but it is also a good unit for study across cultures, generations, and gender. Do men and women find different things to be humorous? Do African American comics pitch a different sort of humor than Asian or white comics? What do kids find funny that their parents don't, and vice versa?

- Explore class in the media. What classes are represented on television? How can you tell? In what ways are the lives of working-class people depicted as being different from those of rich people? Are poor people ever represented in television? How? What do we see of the various classes in films? What is the impact of class on the lives of the people in films and television programs?

# A Warning Concerning Monoculturalism and Popular Culture

Throughout this book we argue for a curriculum that is pluralistic and multicultural. In a sense, the study of popular culture attempts to bring a wider range of materials into the curriculum. But popular culture can also be narrowly interpreted as being the culture of the majority; after all, film-makers, TV producers, journalists, and writers generally play for the largest possible market. In the United States, television has made some efforts to center shows on minority interests, yet, as your students will discover (if they pursue one of the activities suggested in the previous section), the life of a minority person on television is far removed from the lives of many people. It's extremely important, then, that "popular culture" not be interpreted simply as the culture of the majority.

As we stated earlier, every child is a part of a culture, and that culture is a *popular*—that is, *living*—culture. Some of the following activities can help ensure that popular culture studies become and remain genuinely pluralistic:

- Through reading reviews and summaries in professional publications, educational publishers' catalogs, and Internet sources, learn about best-selling writers from other countries. Bring their books to the classroom or put them on individualized reading lists. Do the same for children's literature published in other countries.

- Study the popular culture of a country far removed from our own. What is happening in art, music, literature, and television in Mexico? China? Japan? Ecuador? Egypt? Kenya? Peru? Russia? Lithuania?

- Remember that folkways are a part of popular culture. Have your students read the folktales of majorities and minorities and have them listen to folk music from many different cultures. If you have students from different countries, approach them to see what they would be willing to share from their own cultures.

- Subscribe to a newspaper with good international coverage and keep your bulletin board filled with clippings that help reveal the cultures of other countries (and not just the latest McDonald's to open in China).

- Have students study how international and intercultural problems are handled and discussed in science fiction. How does this differ from what they see in today's world?

- Regularly assign the watching of documentary programs (on public television or other educational channels) that show popular culture in countries other than our own.

# The Wide, Wide World

The wide world of the Internet has made exploration of the sort we have been discussing above both easier and more difficult. It is easier in the sense that resources for the study of popular culture are available—in texts, in images, and in sound—to any classroom or media center that has Internet access and allows students to make use of that access. As we write, more and more schools are seeing Internet access as essential to students' educations and even schools that have financial problems are finding ways to make some access available to everyone. Other worries—such as students having access to materials that are inappropriate to children and adolescents—have led to schemes for policing access while kids are on the Internet. Parents and guardians are signing waivers allowing their children to explore the Internet at school. And more and more families are seeing computer access as being as important a source of family information and entertainment as television.

The world of the Internet makes study more difficult in that it is a virtual dumping ground for anyone and everyone who wants to put themselves out there in the ether. Anybody can create a webpage and make it available. You can even access our teenage son (though we don't advise it) as you are surfing the web. Sorting through the junk—to say nothing of protecting children from pornography and violence—requires some expertise and experience. Otherwise students waste a lot of time trying to find worthwhile material that they can actually use and that they can actually call "research." Moreover, evaluating the truth of the material discovered presents problems. Since there is no screening of what goes up on the web, students may find materials that are just people's opinions, or worse, that distort the truth in an effort to sway people to a certain social or political agenda.

Of course, print media represent a wide range of opinions, biases, and distortions as well. Hard copy, however, has usually gone through editors and other readers prior to reaching the public. In addition, authorship of books, magazines, and newspapers and their sources is usually known. It's somewhat easier with a book, then, to consider the source than it is with material on the web, where, occasionally, no author is identified. It is perhaps for that very reason, however, that teachers should integrate research on the web with other sorts of research in their classrooms—to help students learn to make judgments and evaluate what they find.

Moreover, through the use of newsgroups, students can engage in and "overhear" dialogue about the issues they are interested in. Although a website may provide a means of accessing it by e-mail in order to ask questions, such sites usually present the opportunity to converse with only one person. Newsgroups, however, may engage people all over the world in conversations on topics of common interest. Students may post questions about a topic that they want to know more about, and they may get dozens of responses (depending on how interested people are in the question). Newsgroups, then, can act as sources for "interviews" with people who may be experts and who share an interest in a topic. If students need further clarification of the answers they receive, they can go back and post additional questions.

In addition to the availability of this wide-open world of the web and newsgroups on the Internet, there are more confined, perhaps easier, ways to help students find information on specific topics through the use of educational Internet services.

To help your students get the most out of their research on the Internet, you should:

---

- Find out which computers in your school are connected to the Internet and what type of access you have. Many schools have computers in their library, media center, or classrooms that have been networked and have direct access to the Internet. Netscape, Pine Mail, and Mosaic may be immediately available by clicking on icons. If your school is not networked, you can set up a computer in your classroom by using a modem, a phone line, and an online provider such as America Online, CompuServe, or NETCOM. Recognizing the importance of helping students get connected, many schools are finding resources to provide students with this opportunity.

- If your school has computers housed in one place, such as a lab or media center, find out when they are available to students and how you may schedule students for Internet time. Where computer time is at a premium, students may have to work before or after school or during lunch hours. After you know your students' topics and research needs, help set up computer times to accommodate their schedules.

- To help students zero in on their topics more efficiently, provide them with resources such as *The Internet Yellow Pages* or the *Whole Internet User's Guide and Catalog*. These sources provide students with addresses organized topically.

- Teach students to use search engines effectively. Alert them to the fact that different engines will yield different results, and help them structure a search to make it specific or general enough to capture what they're trying to find.

- If students have access to computers to do their work, have them download and print out research from the Internet to read and study later. This saves valuable time for those waiting to do their Internet research.

- Have your students do critical comparisons of the information they find on the Internet. What's junk? What's worthwhile? How do they decide what information they can trust? What can they figure out about the source of the material they have found? What points of view are represented? What are the various ways in which ideas are presented? What is the role of graphics and visual information?

# And Then There Are the Classics

For openers, it follows that among the classics we include literature (and arts) from many different countries and cultures. In Chapter 5 we review some basic resources and starting points for the teacher who doesn't feel familiar with a wide range of literatures. To recap: Read the professional journals, look through catalogs and book lists published by the various teacher organizations and educational publishers, and talk with your school and local librarians. It may take some digging, but you'll find international classics available.

But what is a classic, anyway?

When we think about a classic car, a classic style in clothing, a classic piece of music (as opposed to a *classical* piece), a classic movie, or a classic comic book, we think of the old standards, the ideas, artistic creations, and material objects that have stuck around, the ones that have staying power. We believe that classic literature is literature that has staying power, literature that continues to arouse emotion, provoke thinking, and address important ideas. The classics of literature for children, young adults, and adults need no apologists or defenders; they don't need to be artificially propped up by being forced or obligatory reading in school curricula.

Yet many of the standard classics of world literature seem to leave young people cold. In particular, there seems to be a conflict at the secondary level between the great books many *hope* students will read and the books they actually *will* read. Many of the promoters of core curricula and standard reading lists regard this lack of interest among young people as representing some sort of decay in education and in the minds of young people. We think there's a far easier explanation.

The simple fact is that the language, values, mores, and manners of *Hamlet, The Scarlet Letter, Uncle Tom's Cabin, Great Expectations, The Grapes of Wrath*, the *Odyssey*, or *The Rubaiyat* are often confusing to and remote from the lives of young people who live in contemporary cities and suburbs, who work at McDonald's for spending money, who watch and enjoy contemporary television and film. Understanding classic literature comes relatively late to most young people, and their engagement often occurs when they have chosen a book out of a particular interest. Though teachers and parents want their children to be exposed to the best that culture and literature have to offer, early pressure to read books that are too difficult often destroys students' interest in reading and the possibility they will *ever* read the classics. The authors of the classics don't need to be artificially supported by English language arts teachers, and they don't need to have us kill off their potential readers in our zeal to enculturate.

## Weaving in the Classics

The heart of teaching the classics is, we think, getting kids to enter into new worlds and to see the relationships between the ideas, characters, and events of those new worlds and those in their own world: to somehow connect to the world of the literature they read. We've all seen teacher-centered classrooms in which the teacher told students what the poem or story meant. In addition, we've seen classrooms where the elements of literature took precedence over students' experience with their reading. This won't do, of course. What we must do is help students perform on literature, entering the world of the texts, linking them with their own ideas and experiences, and forging interpretations and responses to what they read.

This can be done with single texts, although, as we've said, we prefer reading books that are a part of a unit organized topically or thematically. This provides the opportunity to integrate popular culture with the classics, to integrate young adult and children's literature with adult literature, to look at films as well as to read books. A unit for high school students on "Love and Romance," for example, can include adolescent fiction and contemporary fiction, and such novels as Charlotte Brontë's *Jane Eyre*, Emily Brontë's *Wuthering Heights*, Thomas Hardy's *Jude the Obscure*, Leo Tolstoy's *Anna Karenina*, Kate Chopin's *The Awakening*, and Zora Neal Hurston's *Their Eyes Were Watching God*. Plays for the same unit could include Shakespeare's *Romeo and Juliet*, O'Neill's *Desire Under the Elms*, Ibsen's *A Doll's House*, and Beth Henley's *Crimes of the Heart*. Sir Walter Scott's *Lady of the Lake* might be woven in, along with Greek myths of Cupid and Eros, Chinese tales of courtship, and even Biblical stories, including the tale of the Garden of Eden (if your school censors will allow that bit of suggestive literature).

A thematic unit on "Values and the Individual" might include works as diverse as Conrad's *Lord Jim*, Dostoevsky's *Crime and Punishment*, Thoreau's *Walden*, Twain's *Huckleberry Finn*, Wendy Wasserstein's *The Heidi Chronicles*, Maya Angelou's *I Know Why the Caged Bird Sings*, Whitman's *Leaves of Grass*, and poetry collections by Nikki Giovanni and Marge Piercy. That's a pretty heavy reading list, of course, and we present it simply to show that works from the common core of Western culture can easily be included thematically alongside more contemporary literature. From that list, you can easily go on to add materials from popular culture, international literature, and contemporary books written for young adults. Moreover, you can provide options for students according to their interests and sophistication as readers—providing some opportunities for individualized and small-group reading of books selected by the students.

Whatever the pattern you choose and whatever the literature, it's important to recall that reading (like writing) is more than a collection of decoding skills, and involves far more than digging out the meanings intended by the author. The reading of a classic, like the reading of any book, needs to be prepared for, supported when underway, and followed up onto ensure that engagement has taken place.

## Prereading Activities

- Pose for discussion some of the ideas and issues that the reading explores. Anticipate some of the questions the students will ask. Discuss with students what they already know about the topics or time period their reading covers.

- Discuss the title of the book. What does it mean? What do students anticipate the book to be about? If there's a cover, or information about the book on the back or the leaves, how does it shape students' expectations about what will happen?

- Use film versions—cautiously—to preview a story. Rather than showing the whole movie, we suggest that you get the video and show a few key scenes that will prepare the way for better reading and heighten students' curiosity.

- Spend some time providing necessary historical background if the book is far removed from your students' lives in time or place. However, be cautious about overkill here. A light overview is often sufficient to set the stage; the book itself will often supply the details of history or geography necessary for comprehension.

- If the history is complex, begin a time line of the period, showing the major events and allowing students to write in key events from the book as they occur.

- Read a key description from the book. Ask students to visualize the place being described. You may wish them to create a visual representation to help them "see" the place.

- Bring in picture books that show the country where the story takes place.

- Read some sections out loud to give students a sense of the language, so they can begin to hear the sound of the book and its worlds. Preview crucial difficult vocabulary. (Here again, we caution against overdoing the vocabulary work or turning a potentially rewarding encounter with a classic into a mere vocabulary lesson. Encourage students to figure out most unfamiliar words from context.)

- Create an improvisational drama in which students role-play issues and problems that come up in the book, such as conflicts over love, values, religion, and politics.

- As students begin to read, have them describe their way into the world of the book to one another. If the beginning is complex or challenging, let them talk about what they think is going on and how they figured that out.

- Show enthusiasm, interest, and excitement as you get students underway in their reading. Drop little hints that will heighten their curiosity about what's going to happen.

## Activities During Reading

- Have students keep a reading log, a running record of their reactions (How do I feel about characters and events?); projections (What's going to happen next? How will this problem be solved? What's going to become of this character?); imaginings (How would I react in this situation? What if something like this happened in my town or school?); and reflections (How does this relate to the world as I know it? How does it relate to what I value and am interested in?).

- Let students select from a list of major characters in the book and keep an imaginary diary for the character they choose, recording responses to major events and to twists and turns in the plot.

- Pause regularly and have students write their reactions to the book, including their frustrations and lack of comprehension. Use these to help students who are getting offtrack or losing interest.

- Have students keep lists of questions as they proceed: questions about the author and his or her approach, questions about character and motivation, and questions about the time and place of the novel. Have kids raise their questions in class and invite others to provide some ideas (without spoiling surprises in the story).

- Invite students to sketch, draw, or diagram key scenes. Have them re-create key places visually with maps or floor plans.

- Bring in speakers to talk about aspects of the world of the book—art historians, geographers, period historians, theater directors.

- Have students do dramatic readings or readers' theater presentations of key scenes. Have students prepare these rather than just having class members take turns reading. Let them practice so they can put some pizzazz in their reading.

## Follow-Up Activities

- Allow students to become the characters. Have them dress the part and present dramatic monologues to the class from the characters' points of view.

- Discuss the ending in detail, including the possibility that the students would like to have had it end some other way. Discuss those alternative possibilities.

- As a whole class, discuss how the classic has shaped the students' thinking and affected their ideas. What characters and situations had the most impact, and why? How have students' concepts and feelings changed and grown as a result of the novel? How do they imagine it was received in its own time? (This might be a good extension research project.)

- Extend the study beyond the book itself, moving the students into the culture of the time and place. Possibilities include:
  - a period "fair"—Victorian, Romantic, Wild West, Colonial, or international
  - a facsimile newspaper reporting events from the novel and including editorial commentary and book reviews
  - an investigation of music from the period or region
  - a photographic display of technological inventions from the era
  - biographies of authors, politicians, and artists from the period or country

- Have students choose a contemporary problem, issue, or setting and discuss how characters in the novel would respond to today's world.

- Have students consider differences between the world they live in and the world the author has created. How are women viewed in the world of the novel? How are ecological concerns treated? What is the view of nature? What is the nature of work? How is leisure time spent?

- Let students consider the novel across media. Have them create a picture book or comic book version of the story. How might the story be translated into a daytime television program? a situation comedy?

- Have students engage in an imaginary dialogue with the author or the characters of the novel. Let them choose a format that suits their relationship with the author or characters—a debate, a talk show, or an exchange of letters or e-mail.

## Selected Readings

Clark, Carol Lea. 1996. *A Student's Guide to the Internet.* Upper Saddle River, NJ: Prentice Hall.

Oliver, Eileen Iscoff. 1994. *Crossing the Mainstream: Multicultural Perspectives in Teaching Literature.* Urbana, IL: National Council of Teachers of English.

Teasley, Alan B., and Ann Wilder. 1996. *Reel Conversations: Reading Films with Young Adults.* Portsmouth, NH: Heinemann.

Whaley, Liz, and Liz Dodge. 1993. *Weaving in the Women: Transforming the High School English Curriculum.* Portsmouth, NH: Heinemann.

Workman, Brooke. 1992. *Teaching the Sixties: An In-Depth, Interactive, Interdisciplinary Approach.* Urbana, IL: National Council of Teachers of English.

# Summary and Troubleshooting

# Five Problems in Teaching Literature

Problems with students' reading endure. The most-recent brouhaha over reading came in the wake of the "failure" of whole language in California, with the hew and cry about students' inability to read resonating throughout the country. The problems discussed here are, in part, reflections of the ongoing debate about how students learn to read. We believe that the press and politicians often simplify the issues and want to find quick fixes and panaceas to the complex issues involved in helping students become willing and able readers. The problems that all interested professionals continue to be concerned about center on the following:

## Problem One: The Nonreader

No matter how carefully we plan or how valid our teaching strategies, there are always kids who struggle with texts, who cannot process print successfully. Some of these are students who started out reading just fine, but ended up being alienated or bored by school and stopped reading. Some are students who just never got hooked on reading and were never helped to discover what it means to read. Some are students who can read but don't.

Too often, in classrooms where everyone reads the same thing at the same time, these kids are just flat out-of-luck. They fall farther and farther behind and read less and less. So our first answer to what to do with the nonreader is to individualize. Take every opportunity to provide students with reading that is appropriate to them, to find materials that allow and encourage all students to read what interests them and what they are capable of reading.

We think that the policy of "the right book in the hands of the right kid at the right time" helps to solve some of the problems of the student who can't or won't read. In addition, a range of materials that provide support for students who struggle is important. Comic books, newspapers, magazines, and picture books all provide lots of context clues that make reading easier. In addition, very practical books that are directly related to

students' lives and interests can help students read. Car repair manuals, music catalogs, computer information, cookbooks, and job applications can sometimes provide the motivation and the prior knowledge that will aid students.

Finally, students who have never understood what reading is need strategies for understanding what reading is and how it works. They need to know that reading makes sense, that reading is more than decoding to sound, that their own knowledge and experience play central roles in how they make sense of what they read, and that they don't have to know every word in order to read, that they need to monitor whether or not they are understanding. Collaborative and paired reading gives students opportunities to make sense together.

# Problem Two: The ESL Student

A related, but somewhat different, problem from that of the nonreader is the growing number of students who are not native English speakers/readers. If you've read the chapter on popular culture and the classics, you know that we're committed to literature instruction that begins with the student's own culture. For ESL speakers/readers, that means acknowledging their competence in their native language. We are advocates of bilingual instruction, which offers instruction in both English and the students' native language, and are strongly opposed to the "English only" movement, which would limit bilingual education and reduce acceptance of multilingualism in society. In many cases, then, non-native English speakers may be encouraged to do free or guided reading in their native language, while focusing on English in their common class readings. As we have suggested, too, *all* readers need plenty of support, and oral and dramatic reading in English is an especially valuable tool to use with both ESL and native English speakers who have difficulty processing print.

Of course, not all ESL students will have books available in their native languages, and not all students are literate in their native languages. These students' experience with reading and writing will come to them through English. While we would encourage and allow students to use their native languages to sort through ideas, we would also encourage an immersion in English in the classroom. Again, reading material that provides context clues with pictures (such as picture books, CD-ROMs, and magazines), audiotape/booksets that allow students to listen to and see language at the same time—videos that allow students to see images and hear language at the same time, all help students develop their competence in English. Using writing with reading provides students with further opportunities to explore and experiment with the language. And working in small groups with native speakers gives shy students chances to speak and practice what they are learning about English. An important note: Overcorrection of ESL students while they are becoming fluent in English inhibits rather than encourages language growth.

# Problem Three: The Basal Reader or Adopted Anthology

We don't envy the position of textbook publishers, who are open to criticism on many fronts. Publishers have been attacked for the inanity of stories like the old *Dick and Jane* readers. There have been resolutions passed against basal readers at national educators meetings of English because of the overemphasis on snippets of literature and a narrow phonics approach. Yet publishers also receive complaints that they have forgotten phonics in favor of whole-word and whole language approaches. When basals have employed literature from outstanding children's writers, parent groups have hauled the books to school board meetings to object to their contents as being everything from perceived satanism to alleged fodder for bad dreams.

High school literature anthologies have been attacked both for their deadly dull chronological-historical approach and for their just plain fatness (or avoirdupois—they're a drag to carry around). Yet when publishers have offered thematic, multivolume, slim texts focusing on accessible literature for a wide range of readers, those series have not sold well. The upshot is that publishers tend to stay with their bread-and-butter programs and these in turn tend to be conservative and well in arrears of the best current thinking about reading and literature.

Most of you teach or will teach in systems with adopted textbook programs. Teachers—new teachers in particular—are expected to teach the text. It's well and good to talk of individualized, multicultural, multigenre reading, but the textbook must, of necessity, remain at the core.

There are several ways you can work with or around the adopted textbook:

1. It's important to emphasize that *if a text is stressing an obsolete or wrong-headed approach, it's probably not going to produce results anyway*, so you don't need to feel guilty if you limit its use. If a text overworks phonics or reduces literature to mere history (with the most difficult and obscure works first and the fun stuff at the end) or to the mechanics of technique, it will not advance students' literacy. You need not feel that you are shortchanging students by not dwelling at length on the text.

2. *Textbooks can be restructured and refocused by their users.* In the end, *you* determine how the material is to be taught. Even the worst of the elementary school basals and high school anthologies that we've encountered contain a number of good stories, poems, plays, essays, and even study questions. If you pick and choose you can use the textbook flexibly and as a convenient collection of materials.

3. *You can always supplement the textbook.* We learned as first-year teachers that *nobody* objects to "enrichment." There's very little to prevent you from going well beyond the text to use school and community libraries and resources. Frankly, we find that the biggest obstacle to moving beyond the text is *teachers'* conviction that they must cover the text, a set curriculum, or a list of common readings. If you were raised in a system that taught mostly common books, or if, like many of us, you were taught literature in a conventional fashion but came to love it nevertheless, you may find it difficult to let go of your own traditions. We have struggled with this ourselves, having written our share of college papers involving abstract analysis of the critical content of books and not having such a bad time doing so. But our own teaching of diverse students persuaded us that what worked for us and for a lot of other English majors just wasn't the ticket for the majority of students. For too many kids, the traditional approach just doesn't work. As we suggest in the previous chapter, this doesn't mean abandoning our literary heritage (even as that heritage is translated into basals and anthologies), but putting it in a fuller and, we think, richer context.

# Problem Four: The Critical Self/ The Critical Colleague

Many teachers suffer from a self-censor who constantly critiques and carps, who can never let anything go, and who can never say, "That's good enough." This critic is one's own past training and experience speaking. For example, we use a great deal of small-group work in our reading/literature classes, yet there's a part of us that continually asks, "Shouldn't you deliver a lecture on this? Shouldn't you be leading a scintillating whole-class discussion?" If that self-analysis stays within reasonable limits, and you can become reflective about your philosophy and your practice, forcing you to say, for instance, "No, I don't think a lecture is what these students need at all. They talk more and learn more in small groups than they do in class discussions anyway." Keeping a teacher journal and conducting good teacher research is one way to channel your dialogue with this alter-ego teacher.

Of perhaps greater concern are other teachers, often those at the next grade level, whose teaching philosophies differ from yours and who peer at you over half-glasses in the hallway.

These teachers, whose reality and life-and-death power sometimes grow in your imagination, look at the students you send each year and find them wanting. The students' grammar skills are weak, and they obviously haven't studied enough spelling (issues we take up in subsequent sections). In literature/reading, the complaint seems to be that the previous year's teacher (you) did a poor job of covering the syllabus, including that basal text or anthology we discussed as Problem Two.

These teachers speak louder as students move through the grades and into the secondary schools, and the most vocal of all is the college professor who indicts the entire K–12 school system: "Why, I can't even make an allusion to *Huckleberry Finn* or *Paradise Lost* without explaining it" or "My students can't seem to write a single coherent paragraph analyzing and critiquing a literary work articulately." As college professors, we frequently receive letters or requests from secondary school curriculum committees asking us to identify a dozen or so works that students entering the university should have read. Presumably the same letter goes to other professors, leading to the compilation of a book list or syllabus for high school juniors and seniors. We respect the intention of the letter writers, but we decline to send our choices. Instead, we mail a letter like the following:

> We strongly urge you not to compile a book list of "must reads" for your students or to focus this year's instruction on getting students ready for next year.
>
> Far more important is that your students be *readers*, that they know how to find and choose books they want to read, that they read actively and inquiringly, and that they feel confident in speaking up or writing out their reactions and analyses.
>
> Instead of a set curriculum or list, we encourage K–12 teachers to make their classrooms into reading centers with as many different kinds of texts as their students can read profitably. That will include some classics of children's, young adult, and adult literature, but it may include a lot of reading material that won't "stand the test of time," yet will be enjoyed by the students at this time.
>
> The student who will be most successful in college (or the next grade level) is not necessarily the one who has read traditional masterpieces cover-to-cover, but the one who has just plain read widely: fiction, nonfiction, drama and poetry; science fiction and fantasy; good children's and young adult literature; some best-sellers; some entertaining romance novels and detective fiction; and some scare-the-socks-off-you thrillers. We think students also ought to have thought analytically about films and television to see beyond their surface content, and to be able to react to and critique the popular media as well.

There's no crash course in "college reading" that will prepare your students. What's more important is that students have experienced, throughout their K–12 years, a reading/writing curriculum that helps them grow from their present level to one that's just a little bit more sophisticated. If all of us teachers focus on helping each of our students grow during their time with us, the next level—including college—will take care of itself.

For those of you under attack in your own building we can suggest a few ways of dealing with the problem. First of all, suggest that teachers who differ on what they consider correct practice get together and form a teacher research group. Questions about differences in approach can be formed into research questions and explored honestly and conscientiously. Everyone can learn from this sort of exchange.

Second, pass along information about teacher meetings that have been important to you as you developed informed practice. Invite colleagues to local and regional meetings of the National Writing Project, the National Council of Teachers of English, and the International Reading Association.

Third, pass along handouts from the meetings you attend, professional books that you've found worthwhile, and catalogs of professional publications that demonstrate the best thinking in the teaching of reading and writing. Talk about the books and university courses that have had an impact on your thinking.

If all else fails, simply try to avoid people who denigrate your work. We have talked with a number of friends and colleagues who teach in hostile environments who have found that their greatest rewards and relationships are with their students in dynamic learning situations behind closed doors.

# Problem Five: Censorship

Censorship is an absolute killer of intellectual inquiry, teacher morale, and a progressive reading/literature program. It's also something akin to guerrilla warfare and terrorism, for there simply isn't much of a defense one can offer when censorship occurs. Yet, lest we sound too self-righteous about the whole thing, let us state that we can understand the position of the censors: They are deeply concerned about their children's welfare, they believe books can harm people (just as English teachers believe books can help people), and they feel that as taxpayers they have a right to say what goes on in the schools.

Probably the best single defense against censorship is an articulate schoolbook-adoption policy. How are the books for English language arts classes selected? What is the policy on individualized reading of books from the school library? From the public library? If there are books that, for one reason or another, have been deemed as inappropriate for use in the schools, they should be identified clearly. In formulating policies of this sort, parents should be integrally involved, though in an advisory capacity, with the paid professionals—the teachers and administrators—forming the policy that is finally approved by the board of education.

Nonetheless, numerous censorship cases have arisen even after procedures have been established and followed. All it takes is one parent writing one letter to the editor saying, "I don't care what they did in committee, I object to this book." In addition, schoolbook censors are well organized nationwide, so that often, despite policies being followed, a vocal and articulate minority can turn a community into a battleground.

To our way of thinking, however, the simplest inoculation against censorship is also pedagogically sound: Individualize your reading program. Although censors are occasionally successful in getting titles removed from library shelves, they have never been able to censor what somebody else's child chooses to read on an individual basis. If your program is individualized, and if, perchance, a parent objects to a book his or her child is reading, common sense suggests that you let the child drop that book and choose another. The case ends there. As a way of heading off problems, you might even send home book lists from time to time, showing parents the range of choices open to their youngsters.

Nevertheless, if you find yourself or your school to be the target of censorship, ask for help. Such organizations as the American Civil Liberties Union, the National Coalition Against Censorship, the Coalition for Academic Freedom, the National Education Association, the National Library Association, and the American Federation of Teachers all have an interest in the right of the teacher to teach. The National Council of Teachers of English can also supply support, as can its political action group, Support for the Learning and Teaching of English (SLATE).

# t · h · r · e · e

# Ideas for Teaching Oral and Written Composition

In English language arts studies, composition was the growth industry of the 1980s and continues to thrive at the dawn of the twenty-first century. Composition still struggles for equal time with reading and literature, but it is not the clichéd stepchild that it was twenty-five years ago. In elementary and secondary schools, thousands of teachers have learned about new approaches to composition that emphasize ways of engaging students in *using* language rather than concentrating on language form. At the college level, a generation of composition specialists—people who actually like to teach writing as well as literature—have deepened the body of formal research into composition. And at both levels, a growing body of writers-teachers-researchers is exploring new approaches to improving writing instruction.

The approach we explore in this section of *The English Language Arts Handbook* is what we call *experiential*. The label is deliberately ambiguous, for it applies to both students' general experiences—what they do, think, and feel—and their experiences with language—how they use oral and written language in their everyday lives. Our philosophy can be summed up in two basic premises:

1. *Children learn to use language through the experience of using it for purposes they see as valuable and interesting.* We didn't invent that idea: John Dewey articulated it eloquently over three-quarters of

a century ago. Another way of phrasing this notion is simply that people *learn* what they *do*. If we want students to learn to write, they need to write; if we want them to use oral language better, we need to find them tasks and occasions that allow those skills to develop. However, as we suggested earlier in this book, we don't mean to imply that all language learning happens by magic. Students benefit from structured language experiences and response and feedback from other users of language, including the "expert" teacher. However, educators ignore the language the young person brings to school at their own peril, for it is this foundation of language and experience that provides the basis for growth: The student can only start where he or she *is*.

2. *Students' experiences provide the fundamental energy that drives their language.* It is the stuff of life that creates good writing, writing worth doing. Both *direct experience* (memories, successes and failures, relationships, hardships) and *vicarious experiences* (books, films, music) provide the impetus for composing, for reflecting on and shaping experience, for finding ways of understanding, and for sharing that understanding. We would like to believe that English language arts classrooms could find ways to both honor students' experiences *outside* school and provide additional important experiences *in* school that students see as worth their thinking about, exploring, and communicating.

# Chapter Eight

# The Process of Composing

The title of this chapter has, by the dawn of the twenty-first century, become a cliché in English language arts, and teachers can be heard touting their use of The Process in their classrooms, while critical colleagues can be heard sneering "Oh, he's one of those process teachers." In fact, the term has come to mean a variety of ways of teaching—everything from the flexible writing workshop where process is seen as recursive and "messy" to the classroom in which the teacher teaches prewriting on day one, drafting on day two, revising on day three, copyediting on day four, and publishing on day five. (Actually, we have even heard of a teacher who simply teaches those terms, then goes on to teach the old five-paragraph theme.)

The "writing process" movement, developed under the leadership of Wallace Douglas (1963), James Moffett (1983), Donald Murray (1968, 1982), Donald Graves (1983), and others, has been considered a revolution that caused a paradigm shift, a new way of seeing and understanding the philosophy and practice of the field. *Process writing* overthrew an earlier focus on *product*. Rather than focusing on the forms of writing, established language structures that students were asked to reproduce, process theorists argued for paying attention to how a piece of writing evolves and how practicing writers shape and develop their ideas into forms. The notion was that novice writers could be engaged in the processes, activities, and strategies that experienced writers use and that valid products would naturally follow.

We've been convinced for a long time that the process approach is valid, but we're concerned that the process paradigm has been turned into a new pedagogical formula replacing an old one. We've witnessed "process" teaching in which teachers march students through the "steps" of the process, in which grammar lessons exist alongside the writing process, in which students do sentence-combining drills apart from their own writing, and in which classical forms—description, narration, exposition, and argument—have been taught using a "process" approach.

We also understand the arguments of so-called traditionalists who point out that one can teach the formal elements of essay writing and still be concerned with helping students have something to say before they compose ("invention" in classical rhetoric has become the "prewriting" of process theorists). And we certainly agree that "form" (including form in whole pieces, form in grammatical usage, and form in spelling and mechanics) must be a necessary part of what teachers address when teaching writing. However, there is a fundamental difference in how these two camps view learning. While the process paradigm emphasizes skills-learned-by-doing, the product paradigm emphasizes skills-taught-prior-to-doing.

There must be—there are—middle grounds in all this, positions that allow a teacher to place appropriate emphasis on skills and processes to help kids compose successfully in recognizable and conventional discourse forms.

Our own middle ground is an experiential approach, which takes neither a rigid product stance nor a process stance, but rather focuses on the experience of composing text about the experiences one has in real life. In real life students need to put their writing into "grammatically correct" (or simply "appropriate") language. Our real life observations also teach us that real writers sometimes agonize over what they write, often doing multiple drafts and revisions, but sometimes bang out a polished piece and get it right the first time.

Our approach to the process of composing, then, is not a formula or pattern for implementation, but a philosophy or attitude that asks:

1. What sorts of ideas and experiences provide the impetus for young people to write?

2. How can we provide opportunities that support students' interests and goals?

3. How can we help students discover language and use form in language to accomplish what they wish?

In particular, it's important to emphasize that we don't see any need to isolate skills instruction from the actual process of composing. Traditionally, that instruction has been offered at two points: before the fact of composition (through lessons in grammar, rhetoric, style, vocabulary, spelling, etc.) and after the fact (mostly through error correction). Current research points to a flow or continuum between getting ideas into language and figuring out just how to do that. Skills mastered in the context of composing are more likely to stay with the learner than those learned in isolation.

# An Oral Language Base

You may have noticed that we've shied away from using the term *writing*, using *composing* instead. (We don't like the term *composition* very much, though; it has a sort of schoolroom sound and, for some reason, always reminds us of a big wad of fresh, wet bubble gum stuck to the bottom of a shoe.) We like *composing* because of its potential for broad use, its musical overtones, and its application to any sort of creating with language. We can compose our ideas in song, speech, art, dance, or mime. When we compose in writing, we can do so in essays, poetry, drama, or fiction. But we also compose in oral language. In fact, for most people, by far the most significant composing they do is in their *talk*.

Some suggestions we have for building effective use of oral language and creating a base for writing include:

- Become aware of your students' use of oral language. What is their language like when they are using it for their own purposes? Instead of quelling the tumult at the beginning of class, spend a few minutes listening:
  - What are students talking about?
  - What sorts of conversations are animated? Why?
  - What skills are the students demonstrating in their use of oral language? What makes sense to them that doesn't make sense to you?
- Be willing to drop what you're doing when students obviously have something powerful and important to talk about.
- Discover ways that everyone in class can get a share of air space. One teacher we know uses a "talking stone." Only the person holding it may talk, and he or she must pass it along. Another teacher gives each student a certain number of chits or tickets. Each time a person speaks, he or she must give up one ticket. When a student's supply is depleted, he or she is done speaking for that discussion. Each student is encouraged to spend at least one ticket. While we don't wish to artificially shut someone down or make someone speak, we think this method can help distribute talk in the classroom.
- Use lots of small-group and paired discussion. You may wish to have students take particular roles in small-group management, so they can see and explain how people are communicating, how leadership emerges, who acts as mediator, etc.
- Try operating one day without speaking to the whole class. Handouts and overheads might provide the class with instructions, or you may put students in charge. (An Australian methods instructor we heard about tells his students never to talk to the whole class at once. Now, that's commitment to the value of small groups.)
- Set some time aside for student-selected discussion topics. Put a suggestion box on your desk for students to propose topics.

- Have students explore "talk" on the Internet. Many observers of the Internet suggest that e-mail and real-time chat rooms are much closer to oral language than they are to written language. Have students conduct those comparisons.

- Make oral language projects options when assigning activities for individual or group work. Or, have students make an oral presentation to accompany their written or artistic projects. (Speaking in front of groups remains one of the biggest fears of the U.S. public, one that creates real limitations for people. We think giving students many opportunities to speak before others will alleviate this problem.)

- Pay attention to gender and cultural participation patterns. Think of ways of helping less-aggressive girls and boys or students from cultures that don't promote speaking up. Create safe situations (such as taped reports or reports to a group that give them a chance to use oral language.

- Allow exploratory talk. Encourage students to use oral language to work out their ideas. This might be particularly important when students are shaping their initial responses to literature or working out an idea for a paper they want to write.

- Acquaint students with varieties of English to diminish bias against speakers of various dialects or speakers whose native language is not English (more on this in Chapter 11). Invite into your class speakers whose native language is not English. Ask Indians, Jamaicans, Cambodians, Chinese, Japanese, Mexicans, etc., to talk about their language and their experiences learning English.

- Make a place for storytelling in your classroom. We still like the old primary school show-and-tell as a model for bringing students' experiences into the life of the classroom. Stories are the stuff of life (or, in academic terms, "narrative is a primary act of mind"). Encourage your students to be storytellers, swapping anecdotes, experiences, tall tales, jokes, future fantasies, and dreams. Invite in local storytellers (your local arts or humanities council might provide funds).

- Have students write scripts. Writing dialogue in which each character sounds different and language reflects character attunes students to the ways people talk.

- Have students compare oral language done for different purposes and audiences. How is their conversation with their grandmother different from their conversation with their friends? How does their talk to their parents differ when they're asking for a favor from when they're mad about being grounded? In addition, have them compare oral language and written language. What different characteristics can they list?

# A Reading Base for Composing

We discuss reading and response in detail earlier in this book. Here, we'd like to talk briefly about what we see as the relationship between reading and writing. The research points to the notion that reading and writing are related activities, that learning to write supports students' skill development and understanding of what it means to read, and that learning to read gives students ideas and experience with language. We think that there are a number of good reasons to include reading in the writing classroom:

1. *Reading gives writing students vicarious experience and new ideas to ponder.* While we believe that students have tremendous experiential resources from which to draw for their writing, we also think that students come to know how others think and feel through reading; they gain perspective on people's ideas and opinions; and they garner factual knowledge.

2. *Reading helps students assimilate ideas about form.* In fact, we think students gain a much greater sense of how stories, essays, and poems work from wide reading than they do from completing story maps or having lessons in the construction of an argument. The structures of the written language are so diverse and complex that students are best served by having plenty of opportunities to discover them through experience.

3. *Reading provides students with lots of stylistic and linguistic options to play with.* Again, we would caution against enforcing the use of metaphors, requiring dialogue, or pushing students to create allusions. They will see all of these as they read, however, and we are amazed at how frequently such devices appear in our students' writing without our even so much as mentioning them.

The reading/writing workshop (Atwell 1987, 1997) provides students with the opportunity to move from reading to writing and back again. Students come to see themselves as authors, identify with the processes and approaches of professional writers, and explore and experiment with their own writing in ways that they've discovered through the world of books. Students should be encouraged to write in the genres they are reading.

# Knowing Yourself As a Writer

The *Paris Review* interviews with writers, begun in the 1960s, helped to develop interest in the process of writing by exploring how the professionals did it. We were fascinated to learn that Robert Frost composed only on a lapboard, that Mary McCarthy fictionalized parts of her autobiography because she felt her fictions were closer to the truth, and that Henry Miller felt a dynamism when composing on the typewriter (and had a hard time writing after his eyesight failed) (Plimpton 1962).

Aside from the general interest of such factoids, we came to see that professional writers varied widely in their habits and began to question the wisdom of having students all write at the same time on the same topic. Now, we can't arrange for all students to exercise all their idiosyncrasies in the classroom. (We heard of a kid who wanted to do his writing in his locker, by flashlight.) And we need to follow Wallace Douglas' (1963) advice to distinguish between writing *behaviors* (pen versus word processor, lapboard versus desk, night versus morning) and the more fundamental *processes of composing* (finding ideas, getting started, revising procedures). But we find it very helpful to learn about our students' writing behaviors and processes with questions like these:

---

- What's the best piece of writing you've ever done? What makes it your favorite? How did you go about it?
- When do you like to write best? What's the worst time for you to write?
- With whom do like to share your writing? Why?
- What kind of feedback do you like to get? Who's given you good response to your writing?
- What sorts of school assignments have you enjoyed? Which have been difficult?
- Would you categorize yourself as a quick starter or a procrastinator? What's your relationship to deadlines?
- Do you like to write in silence or with background noise? What sort of music do you prefer when you write?
- What sort of tools and equipment do you like to use for writing? Pen and legal pad? Word processor? Pencil? Felt-tip marker?
- Do you prefer to write in class or at home?
- What can we do to make this class a more comfortable place for you to write?

---

Along these lines, we very much like the idea of setting up a "write place" (see Figure 8-1) in the classroom where students can go to work on their writing projects.

**Figure 8–1** ∘ **A classroom writing corner**

# Idea Gathering

Although you may have a collection of writing prompts or story starters in your "write place" for students who have completely run dry and need a little pick-me-up, you will want to move them quickly past relying on such stimuli and into thinking about what *they* have to say. Frequently, when students say they don't have anything to write about, they simply lack confidence that the ideas they have are good ones, or they lack belief in the value of their own experiences.

We demonstrate that students have plenty to write about by doing some of the following:

- Directing a guided imagery activity. As we talk, we have students write about the places we take them. For example, we ask them to think about the time they received their first scar or had the first accident in which they got hurt. We ask them to visualize and write about who was there, what kind of day it was, what happened just before the accident, who responded first, how you reacted, etc. We've done this about the first birthday they had, the first crush they had, and the first pet they had. Knowing something about your students' past experience can provide you with ideas about what sort of guided imagery activity would work with them.

- Administering interest inventories. We use a number of these. Sometimes they ask that students answer questions: What do you like to think about? What do you like to read? What's the most magical moment you've ever experienced? If you weren't here, where would you like to be? What do you hope you will be doing ten years from now? Twenty years? Have you ever lost anyone important—through death or moving away or having a falling out? Sometimes our interest inventories are just categories under which students can make lists: friends, hobbies, goals, sad memories, glad memories, pets, family, foes, favorite films, heroes, leisure time activities, etc.

- Having students keep process portfolios of their works in progress. On the very first day of class we distribute plain manila folders and ask students to begin a their list of things they can write about on the inside cover of the folder. At the beginning, some students only have one or two things they think they want to write about (of course, some can fill up a whole column), but once they are writing regularly and sharing their writing their lists begin to grow.

- Sharing our own lists of ideas we want to write about. Bring in things you are writing to share with your students. We think the best writing teachers are teachers who write. They can inspire students, commiserate with students, and share their struggles about where to go next with their writing.

- Bringing in things we are reading. As we mentioned in the previous section, we believe that reading can be a real inspiration and source of ideas for writers. Share a morning newspaper article, something you read about students in one of your professional journals, or a section of the novel you are reading.

- Brainstorming on the board for ideas for writing following a common class activity—reading a story, seeing a film, going on a field trip, hearing a speaker, or watching a TV documentary.

- Having students keep a writer's notebook. Though you might want to call it a journal, we like *writer's notebook* because of the implication that students are maintaining it to collect and explore ideas for their writing lives. Remind them to be on the lookout for tidbits that they can use in their writing—overheard conversations; flashes of beauty when the sun or the moon creates certain effects or when the trees sparkle in a certain kind of light; a funny story someone tells; something they see on television that they want to keep thinking about; a pattern they notice in their parents' conversation style—everything is fair game for the writer. We once had a student who kept a writer's box. She jotted down notes on whatever was handy—a napkin, the back of a piece of homework, the telephone notepad—and put them in her box. Every once and a while she'd pore through it to look for ideas and new directions.

# Writing to Somebody with a Face

Our experience has been that students write with more energy, commitment, and interest when they are writing for *real* purposes to reach *real* audiences, whether large or small, close or distant. Working on this premise, some graduate student friends of ours at the University of British Columbia developed a course called "Writing to Somebody with a Face," aimed at having all writing read by someone other than the teacher. Their course involved having students write all manner of letters, memos, notes, and essays.

Some places and people to write to:

- Other students, of any age or geographical location. Set up a letter exchange within the class, between classes, or between schools. Check your school or local library for the addresses of pen pal associations.

- Electronic correspondents. Chatrooms, e-mail, and newsgroups all provide ways for students to instantaneously access others across the nation and around the world. (We know teachers at schools that do not provide access for students or give them their own e-mail addresses who allow students to read and post messages through their own e-mail accounts.) In addition, most of the correspondents we list here are accessible electronically, and students can be helped to improve their online skills by writing e-mail.
- Political figures. Most politicians will write back, even if only a form letter. Have students write to congressional leaders, town council members, the mayor, the U.S. president, and world leaders.
- Business leaders. With school-to-career programs blossoming around the country (for good or for ill), the relationship between the business community and schools is strengthening. Students can ask questions about careers and internship possibilities, the reading need in and requirements of a job, and ways a business benefits the community.
- Service organizations. Service learning is becoming a more significant aspect of education, as community/school ties are developing. Students can write to ask what organizations' needs are and how they may be of help to homeless groups, food banks, elderly and children's services, animal protection agencies, and environmental organizations.
- Media organizations. Students should be encouraged to be active in presenting their views of the value and effectiveness of programming in television and radio news and entertainment.
- Authors. As students come to see themselves more and more as practicing writers, they can communicate with authors whose work they have read and enjoyed. Some authors have web pages that allow e-mail access and are willing to answer questions from students.
- Newspaper editors. Some newspapers publish virtually every letter they get, and others are much more exclusive. Help students develop the habit of using writing to make their views known. One valuable contribution students can make is to inform the public about their experiences in school, since a good deal of information about schools comes from external, rather than internal, sources.
- Celebrities. Students who have heroes among athletes, musicians, and actors might like to send fan letters, but they should be warned that they might not get a personal response.
- Family, friends, and relatives. Although the art of letter-writing is said to be dead, we all still appreciate getting notes and letters. Use special occasions to remind students of this possibility. (Students who use e-

mail might compare an e-mail message with a handwritten note to see the differences in the way language is used in the two media.)

# The Writing Workshop

Dozens of books have been written about ways to conduct the writing workshop—for students from first grade through college—over the past twenty to thirty years. Although each teacher has his or her own processes and procedures for a productive workshop class, most share a number of common principles. Workshops emphasize:

1. Student engagement. In order for students to work productively in small groups and pairs, they need to be invested in their work; they need to believe it is valuable.

2. Student choice. Student investment presupposes some choice. When they have the opportunity to choose their topics, to decide what they need to work on, and to have control over how much time they spend, students will commit to their work.

3. Student ownership. Although students will get a good deal of response and feedback from one another and from the teacher during writing workshop, they need to be responsible for making decisions about what they revise, what they publish, and what they put away.

4. Student independence. All of these principles revolve around the notion of students becoming thoughtful, self-reliant, and responsible. The writing workshop helps students learn those behaviors by practicing them.

Obviously these principles can't be put into effect overnight. Students who have become accustomed to being told what to do and how to do it won't come into your workshop classroom ready to work independently and with their peers. Here are some suggestions for ways to begin:

- Develop strategies to break down the common writing period in which everybody writes the same thing at the same time. The writing workshop model encourages students to pursue their work at their own pace. In its simplest form, the workshop consists of set days of the week when students know they will be working on their writing. In a more complex form, students are in reading *and* writing workshops five days a week, following their own pace in all their literacy work.

- Establish a "works in progress" file. Students can keep one or several papers in a file for future revision. Most writers find that letting papers cool in the file for a period of time allows them to approach their work with fresh insights. As time passes (and as you offer various avenues for publication), students polish up works for presentation to an audience.

- Promote critical/editorial talk. Not nasty, red-penciling talk, but productive engagement among peers who help one another solve problems at all phases of the writing process. You may wish to conduct some whole-class workshops to provide a model for talking about writing. Put your own writing on the overhead, show where you're having problems, ask for suggestions, and demonstrate how you might use the suggestions to revise your draft. Revise in front of them, so they can see what that means.

- Discuss organization as something that develops out of your grappling with your topic and as a method of discovering ways to approach material. Show how webs and clusters (see Figure 8–2) can help you discover both aspects of your topic and the relationships among the various ideas you can use. Offer brainstorming as another technique, and, perhaps, the informal outline. (We have problems with the formal outline because we couldn't always come up with a "b" under No. 1 or all the other parallel structures required.) Get a hypertext program for your computer and show students how to use it. (Some students and teachers like to plan using a paint program that lets them add embellishments. Figure 8–2 was prepared on such a program.)

- Help and encourage students to compose on the word processor, which can make their work as writers so much easier. They can begin with words and thoughts in any order, then move them around, expand them, and delete them as their thinking takes shape.

- Use contract grading. We praise this method earlier in this book and find it especially advantageous in a writing workshop. Here students are basically told that the more (quality material) they write, the better their grade will be. Because you don't grade individual works, you are freed to work with students during the process.

- Use process and showcase portfolios, so you can look at both the progress your students are making and at the pieces they consider their best. When making final evaluations, ask students to present their best work in a showcase portfolio with an introduction evaluating and reflecting on their own work.

- Have works-in-progress readings, where your young writers select the best, most engaging, and most tantalizing paragraph or page in

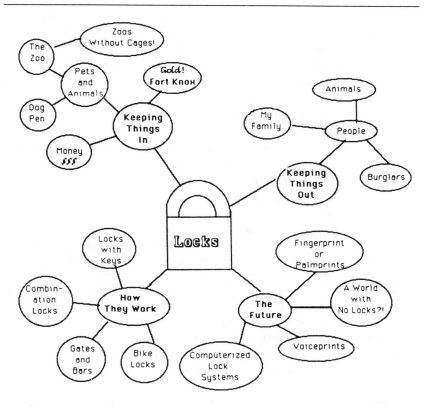

**Figure 8–2 ○ One way to cluster ideas**

their draft writing and read it to the group, thus generating interest in the final product.

- Distinguish among some of the following terms and concepts in writing:

  - A *freewriting* draft. Writers explore their ideas, perhaps in multiple directions, pursuing ideas where they take them.

  - A *first* or *rough* or *hack* draft. Writers use this draft just to get ideas down and to say what they have to say, knowing they can go back to it later.

  - *Cut-and-paste* (something we used to do literally with scissors and tape, now adopted by some computer programs as a metaphor for moving text around on the page).

- *Revising*. Here writers go back to their work to reconsider their initial ideas and approaches, then make changes in the *substance* of the work—adding things, moving them around, integrating new information, and working on effective openings and closings.
- We like to make a distinction between revising and *editing*, which (in our writing workshops) refers to fine-tuning of style, vocabulary, and effectiveness.
- We make a strong contrast between this and *copyediting* or *proofreading*, which (again, in our parlance) focuses exclusively on matters of surface correctness: usage (or grammar), spelling, punctuation, and capitalization.

- Develop an organizer chart or file so that you can keep track of where students are on given writing projects. Some teachers we know have students create a file card for each piece they begin writing, then update and refile it in a box on the teacher's desk as the piece progresses. Others have figured out how to do this on a wall chart or poster, again with the students taking responsibility for the record-keeping. One elementary school teacher has her students write their names on snap-on clothes pins; as their work progresses, the pins are moved along the edge of a writing process chart. The teacher can see at a glance what everyone is up to.

- Recognize the recursiveness of the writing process. Not everyone moves in a nice orderly, linear path from rough draft to publishable piece. Sometimes the "hot topic" (Graves 1983) springs full-blown from the student's pen and needs little revision and editing. Sometimes students will start a project, move to another one, and go back to the first. Students revise as they draft and even fix errors as they go along. And lots of things never get published (or need to).

- Put concerns about correctness in context. We discuss this vital issue in Chapter 10, "The Red Pencil Blues."

# Publish, Publish, Publish

Make the writing public. Don't let kids toss finished papers into their backpacks; don't let those compositions sink to the bottom of the gum-wrapper compost heap in students' desks. Some possibilities include:

- Organize a writing fair where students present their best work, nicely copied and bound, illustrated or "graphicked" as much as possible. Invite parents, the principal, and other classrooms to readings at the fair.

- Create magazines (or "Zines," as kids have dubbed them) on topics under study in the classroom. Have students write interviews, feature articles, advertisements, letters, and reviews. Distribute copies to students in the class and beyond. We heard about a high school in Harlem, New York, that has a webpage for student writing and publishes its students' webzine.

- Designate an author's chair, where kids who have finished work sit and read to the class.

- Write for national contests and publication. Check your library for books for young writers that list places of publication. Also check *Writer's Market Place* or *Literary Market Place* for possibilities. Art and writing contests for kids can also be found on websites. We've heard about The Refrigerator (www.seeusa.com/refrigerator.html) and The Freezer (www.seeusa.com/freezer.html), but things change quickly on the Internet, so look around.

- Establish a schoolwide or districtwide Young Author's Day. Formats for these events vary from kids coming together to read their own work to visits from professional authors who talk with the students about their work. One cautionary note: Young authors need to be celebrated daily in the individual classroom, not just once a year in a flashy public extravaganza.

- Instigate arts and crafts projects to accompany and show off writing. Our book *Gifts of Writing* (1980) suggests a number of ways in which kids can create attractive books of their own, including cloth-bound books, minibooks (postage-stamp-sized), big books (done on poster board), bigger books (done on the painted sides of refrigerator and other large cartons), scrolls, accordion books, folding books, and others. Our motto in that book is "Make your writing look as good as it reads." The title suggests another element of our philosophy: that students should come to think of writing as something to give, with pleasure and pride, to other people.

- Put short chunks of writing on the chalkboard—it's a bit like building a sand castle, but a good way to give short-term publication to a bit of writing.

- Put things on the bulletin board. (A British teacher once told us her supervisor would chastise her if she didn't change her bulletin board regularly. The only way she could do that, of course, was by putting up lots and lots of student writing. Jolly good show, we say.)

- Instigate hallway publishing. Designate the wall outside your classroom as the place where student writing projects are published. Interestingly, we've heard of very little vandalism or theft of such projects. Students are likely to respect the hard work of their peers.
- Publish and distribute broadsides, leaflets, and brochures. These minipublications are cheap to produce and you can flood the school with kid-written, -edited, and -produced work.
- Keep an annual scrapbook in your classroom featuring what students regard as their best or most typical writing, accompanied by an autobiographical note and a photograph. Treasure these, and we're not just being sentimental.
- Ask your librarian to establish a "kid-produced" shelf in the library where students' books can circulate like the professional publications.
- Place kid-produced work in your reading corner where students can read one another's work during free-reading time.

We discuss the role of word processors in editing and revising papers in Chapter 10, reviewing how they can help students get their papers into the best possible shape. Computers are enormously helpful at the publishing end, too. Students can:

- Use desktop publishing programs to lay out final copy for magazines, books, and newspapers.
- Insert clip art, original drawings they create in paint programs, or artwork that has been scanned and digitized. (Color printers have gotten cheap enough to make them practical to use in the classroom to produce elegant final copies with illustrations.)
- Print multiple copies of their work.
- Submit their work to websites. Websites for kids' writing from elementary school through college are springing up quickly. Have kids explore submitting work to one of the varied sites available. In addition, some sites allow for online discussion of writing.

Finally, we suggest a way of publishing that was told to us by John Dixon in a summer institute in London. He got the idea from a British secondary school headmaster. The headmaster had a blank bound book with a green cover. Whenever he encountered some good or interesting writing, he would cry out, "I must have that forever! Copy it into the green book, please!"

We rushed right out of the institute and found a green book and have been using it quite happily in writing classes ever since. We've added one twist: At the end of a class or course, we give our students a mock final examination, an author identification quiz based on readings from the green book. Our students invariably, and perhaps not surprisingly, score 100 percent on the exam. The writing that has gone into the green book has become *memorable*—what a great tribute to the writers who have written in it!

## Selected Readings

Douglas, Wallace. 1963. *An Introduction to Some Basic Processes in Composition*. Evanston, IL: Northwestern University Curriculum Center in English.

Graves, Donald. 1983. *Writing: Teachers & Children at Work*. Portsmouth, NH: Heinemann.

Moffett, James. 1983. *Teaching the Universe of Discourse*. Portsmouth, NH: Boynton/Cook Publishers.

Murray, Donald. 1968. *A Writer Teaches Writing: A Practical Method of Teaching Composition*. Boston: Houghton Mifflin.

# Chapter Nine

# Extending the Dimensions of Literacy

We are daily confronted by a broad range of language forms: radio, television, advertisements, plays and drama, street mime, signs and placards, music lyrics, soap operas, newspaper editorials, found poetry, sports stories, offers we can't refuse, memoranda, letters, literature, and plenty of messages exhorting us to contact someone at www-dot-something-or-other. In the schools, however, we tend to zero in on a single composition form or discourse mode: exposition. Although elementary school children are free to write stories, poems, and plays, such "frivolity" decreases by the middle school/junior high school years as teachers concentrate more on preparing their charges for the expected rigor of college or the "real world." It all ends with the magnum opus of many people's high school years: The Research Paper.

Without denying the usefulness of clear, coherent expository writing, we want to point out that the function of the *word* in society is changing dramatically in this electronic age. Much exposition comes to us by way of television, film, computer terminal, and even fax. Although we don't rely on print the way we used to, print is anything but dead. We may not read extended expository essays very frequently, but we see print employed in new and imaginative ways on everything from faxed restaurant orders to a PBS series on the history of language. Composition is an act whose boundaries are expanding as rapidly as new media extend their limits.

We cannot possibly teach all students every discourse form they will encounter in the remaining sixty (or will it be one hundred?) years of their lives. But we can prepare students for this expanding world of discourse if, instead of restricting literacy to exposition, we see that our task as composition teachers is to aim for diversity. A good comp program, we think, will allow students to compose in as many forms as possible, in imaginative as well as expository forms, and in public as well as private forums. Students will write to inform as well as to entertain; they will write stories and plays, as well as tightly organized essays; they will compose in popular and media forms as well as traditional school genres. A list of just a few of the possibilities is provided in Figure 9–1.

**PERSONAL WRITING**
Journals
Diaries
Sensory writing
Writer's notebook
Feelings
Sketches
Observations
Reminiscences
Autobiography
Monologue
Free response
Calendars

**IMAGINATIVE WRITING**
Fiction
Fantasy
Adventure
Science Fiction
Riddles
Jokes
Poetry
Collaborative novel
Stories
Dialogues
Epitaphs
Songs

**INFORMATIVE/PERSUASIVE WRITING**
Essays
Editorials
Reports
Letters
Telegrams
Bulletin boards
Labels and captions
Reviews
Newspaper artcles
Magazine essays
Booklets
Directions

**POPULAR FORMS**
Ads
Commercials
Propaganda
Posters
Flyers
Popular journalism
Satire
Imitations
Song lyrics
Concert reviews

**DRAMA/ORAL ENGLISH**
Mime
Charades
Improvisation
Creative drama
Writer's showcase
Debate
Discussion
Show and Tell
Interviews
Puppetry
Game shows
Choral reading
Readers theatre
Conversations

**MEDIA COMPOSITION**
TV scripts
Radio programs
Slide-tape
Soundtape
Montage
Collage
Animated film
Commercials
Videotape
Bulletin boards
Magazine layout
Storyboard

**Figure 9–1 ○ Extending the range of composition**

To explore the possibilities for composing, try an experiment using this list. Simply pick a topic or idea—politics, preserving the planet, our town, South America, myths and legends, love—and brainstorm for possibilities: How can you (or your students) "compose" about this subject in, say, media forms or drama or cartoons? (Figure 9–2 shows some of our noodling on the topic "Exploring Our Town.") For any one of those topics, students can follow the rubric or checklist in Figure 9–3, which shows how they can develop it further.

Sometimes teachers question their own competence to teach beyond the familiar domains of expository writing: I'm not a poet, advertising whiz, or scriptwriter. I've never made a video. How am I supposed to do this? Figure 9–3 provides one answer: Engage the students in figuring out how a medium or mode of discourse works. (If you like, you can call this "rhetorical analysis.")

Have kids collect and study samples of the form—and here's where the reading/writing connection becomes obvious. As students become writers they also become more interested in how the literature they read works. If they want to write a television sitcom or a commercial to videotape, they become analytical about how those forms work. Ask them to make some generalizations: What makes a good story? A good television show? An effective poem? The purpose is not to come up with hard-and-fast rules for the genre, but to help students grow toward an intuitive understanding of how it works. In such analysis they may discover that successful stories have many elements (not just character, plot, theme, and setting). In studying TV they may discover a formula for situation comedies, but they may also see that their favorites break the formula in certain ways. As they read poems, they may discover (thank goodness) that not all poems rhyme; that not all poems describe birds or flowers; that poems, too, succeed by breaking some of their own rules, by challenging and surprising a reader. This rhetorical analysis is not strictly a secondary school or college-level activity, by the way; the very youngest children can see systematic elements in the stories they read and like.

We also find it useful with students to learn more about writers and how they work. You can imagine some aspects of the creative act by looking at the product, but it's also useful to have students learn about the writing process by reading about writers and writing. Have students read interviews with writers (many are available in professional publications) and read about how they work in such reference materials as *Contemporary Authors*. *Writer's Digest* magazine is also useful for practicing writers. In it writers talk about their own writing and provide tips for writers who are trying to break into the business. There are also online resources for learning more about writers, and many contemporary writers have their own websites that students can visit and get up-to-date information

List Composition
Topics for:              Exploring "Our Town"

PERSONAL WRITING

Visit your old elementary school and write about your memories.

Write about some of your favorite "haunts."

Tell about what makes your neighborhood unique.

IMAGINATIVE WRITING

Write a poem about your street.

Imagine Our Town in 2001. What will it be like?

Write an imaginary story about a crime or mystery set in Our Town.

INFORMATIVE/PERSUASIVE WRITING

Write a letter to the editor of the paper about a change that is needed.

Describe the resources of Our Town to a person who has just moved here.

Investigate the entertainment sources available in Our Town to a person your age.

POPULAR WRITING

Write an ad or commercial for Our Town.

Interview a public official about his or her role in Our Town.

Debate a needed improvement in Our Town.

DRAMA/ORAL ENGLISH

Dramatize the founding of the city in 18--.

Prepare a reader's-theater reading of writing about Our Town.

Bring in historical artifacts from the "early days" and discuss.

MEDIA COMPOSITION

Borrow the videotape unit to prepare a short program about the community.

Prepare a feature story - with photographs - of the downtown area.

Create a slidetape introducing a stranger to Our Town.

**Figure 9–2 ○ Identifying composition topics**

WRITE YOUR TOPIC HERE: _Our Town_

WHAT FORM (DISCOURSE MODE) WILL YOUR COMPOSITION TAKE?
_Video of old houses and buildings._

WHAT ARE YOUR AIMS AND GOALS?  WHAT DO YOU WANT TO
ACCOMPLISH OR COMMUNICATE WITH THIS COMPOSITION?
_I want to show that there are still many historical buildings in Our Town._

WHO IS YOUR AUDIENCE? _The Cable TV channel audience._

WHERE CAN YOU FIND SAMPLES OF THE FORM YOUR COMPOSITION WILL
TAKE? _Discovery channel, Public broadcasting._

WHERE WILL YOU FIND INFORMATION ON YOUR TOPIC? _Library._
_Interviews with owners of older buildings._
_Visit with local architect.     Visit to_
_Our Town Historical Society_

WHAT PROBLEMS DO YOU THINK YOU MAY HAVE IN DOING YOUR
PROJECT?  HOW CAN WE SOLVE THEM? _Mostly using the_
_equipment. I will take the beginning video class_
_at TV Channel 11 before I start the project._

**Figure 9–3 ○ Developing a composition topic**

about what the writer is doing. Some of these offer opportunities for students to ask the writer questions.

You might also find practicing writers in your own community who would be willing to come in and talk to your students about their craft. Chances are that your town has at least one writer for children; somebody who has scripted and produced a play; someone who writes about sports, business, world news, or community affairs for a local magazine or newspaper; or someone who has done oral family histories, biographies, or autobiographies. Have writers talk about where they get their ideas; what kind of research they have to do to write in their genre; what they do when they get stuck; who reads their drafts; how they go about revising; what their favorite piece of their own is; and who their favorite author is. As students practice the craft of writing and see themselves as writers, they will have their own questions to ask authors.

And, as you are beginning a new medium or type of writing with your students, don't underestimate their knowledge, perceptiveness, and problem-solving skills as writers. One way to ensure that you can help them in this problem-solving process is to *join* them: Compose with your students and participate in the conversations. "Well, how do we go about producing our own cable TV show? Whom can we ask? What can we read? Let's start working with a script and some equipment and see how it goes."

# A Potpourri of Ideas for Expanding the Dimensions of Literacy

- Get a video camera and do an "Introduction to Our Class" as your first video. Give each student thirty seconds to tell his or her name, interests, and a quick anecdote that reflects something interesting about him or her.

- As an alternative to "My Summer Vacation," have students write tall tales about their summer away from school.

- Have students create class biographies the first week or two of class. In pairs, have them interview one another, write rough-draft bios, revise for accuracy, and publish the biographies in "Introducing Us."

- Have students design their own webpages. The introductory page should include pictures, important data, and graphics to make the viewer want to read on. Using links, students can add information about their hobbies, family, and pets, and samples of their writing. Find a program or person to help get the webpages up and running. Continue adding to the sites throughout the semester. (If you're financially or technologically in a pinch, "mock" webpages can provide an excellent model for students to provide a multidimensional look at who they are.)

- Support satire. Kids live in a crazy world, and encouraging them to write satire gives them a chance to comment on it in a time-honored fashion. Let them satirize TV shows, films, cartoons and cartoon heroes, commercials, politicians and political campaigns, etc. (We find kids' impulse and ability to satirize quite intriguing from an adult standpoint. To do successful satire, you must understand the conventions of the mode or genre you're satirizing. That kids do satire so naturally shows that they're soaking up more than content from public discourse: They're learning its rules, too.)

- Start an open-ended story as a class project. Someone in the class leads off by writing the opening. In succeeding days and weeks, students add to the story. One of our cartoonist friends has taught his students to create stick cartoon figures with lots of personality. The class now creates ongoing sagas involving their stick-figure characters.

- And speaking of cartoons. . . The world of cable television has spawned a whole new generation and whole new genres of cartoons—from those made for preschoolers to those for adults that comment on social and political events. Have your students create their own "contemporary" cartoon in which characters reflect the ways of the world as your students see it.

- Have students write their cartoons, music videos, or literature dramas collaboratively. The rich language of creating, planning, problem-solving, and negotiating is worth a world of lectures on language skills.

- Have students create a sales pitch for something generally unsellable (e.g., a year-old boiled egg). They can learn a lot about the language (and ethics) of advertising this way. Just having them brainstorm pitches for unsellable products should be fun.

- Have students find and join online chatrooms to talk about issues and ideas with people whose lives and experiences are very different from their own. Teachers report changes in their students' view of the world when they start "hearing the voices" of students from Japan and Australia and Turkey.

- Borrow a set of art slides from the art department or library and have students put together a slide show using well-known paintings and taped readings of their favorite poems.

- Have students create a "checkbook" character. Acquire some blank checkbook registers and have students compose a mystery spender through his or her checkbook entries.

- Let students explore the worlds of the magical and fantastic. Have them create their own versions of E.T., the Hobbitt, and Dr. Seuss fantastical creatures and place them in a narrative.

- Get letter-writing started in your class, with students writing both imaginary letters and ones that can be mailed. Letters can go to:
  - yourself

- a close friend
- an archrival or enemy
- family
- teachers
- your boss
- a member of the clergy or a social leader
- a movie, television, or music star
- a person who lived in the past
- an imaginary being
- someone yet to be born

Topics for letters can include:

- current problems
- world issues
- something the writer's been meaning to say
- something that the writer is worried about
- what the writer wants to do in the future
- an ideal world
- speculations on the year 2050 or 3000
- a review of or a response to something in the media
- something the writer wants to vent about
- a story the writer wants to share

- Use group collaboration to have students create a television magazine program. Using video- and audiotaped interviews and research, students put together visual features on the hot topics of the day. Use your school's video network to show the program throughout the school.

- Explore cyberworld with your students to see what's available on the Internet. Scores of resources are available for aiding in this search, but all of them seem to add that the world of cyberspace is so enormous and changes so quickly that you will need to see for yourself. Have students find ways their voices can be added to the clamor. (We'll talk later about the dangers here. Suffice it to say that you may need to secure parents' or guardians' permission to allow students to search online.)

- Have students write the message exchanges of an (innocent) Internet romance. Stories abound about people who have found each other across space and time. Let students create their own version.

- Use whatever you have available in the way of computer technology to enhance students' writing. Desktop publishing, paint, and draw programs; clip art; scanners; and color printers can allow your students to create dazzling publications to distribute to wide audiences.

# Imagination, Creativity, and Writing

Like many writing teachers, we've long been uncomfortable with the traditional division of writing into *creative* writing and the *other stuff*, usually meaning nonfiction prose, which parses out as "exposition." Obviously, creativity is not limited to poetry, drama, and fiction; nor is it limited to people who prefer to compose in those forms. We like the view of creativity David Holbrook offers in *The Exploring Word* (1963) and *Children's Writing* (1967): He suggests that all students are capable of "creativity," that is, of grappling with their own experience and getting it into words.

Some of our colleagues prefer the term *imaginative* for the writing of poetry, drama, and fiction, and use the term *imaginative nonfiction* to include a wide range of contemporary nonfiction prose by writers such as Annie Dillard, Tom Wolfe, John McPhee, Rachel Carson, Stephen Jay Gould, Isaac Asimov, and Joan Didion.

We want to be on the record as favoring the synthesis of imagination and writing in any form (including schoolroom exposition and the research paper). Although we begin with the modes traditionally seen as creative—drama, poetry, and fiction—we hope to make a case throughout this chapter that all students, K–college, should engage in varieties of imaginative writing, from the poem to the research project.

## Composing Through Drama

We have emphasized the importance of an oral language base in composition. It's important to stress that composition has a dramatic base as well. In *Teaching the Universe of Discourse* (1983), James Moffett shows that all communication involves a kind of dramatic tension between *I* (the speaker, writer, actor) and *you* (the listener, reader, one acted upon). In drama people play all of those roles, alternating between the *I* and the *you*. Whether one is talking about the relatively easy task of having students read aloud or the complex one of launching a full-fledged stage production, drama deserves a fuller, richer role in the play of English/language arts.

Elementary teachers are often more comfortable with *creative dramatics* than secondary teachers are. Imaginative play is an important addition to the language arts program at any level. Scripting and theatrical presentations seem to come more easily to secondary students. At both levels, the writing of drama is a powerful exercise in the imagination and in composition skills.

Drama and play-making are especially useful in classes where there is a diversity of competency and skill with English. ESL students and students who struggle with written English have a number of advantages when working with drama.

---

- Drama is a collaborative activity. Students work together in making decisions about staging, scenery, props, and blocking.
- Drama draws on our natural sense of oral language and dialogue. The language students *use* is the stuff of plays.
- Drama involves the whole self. It requires us to tap our own emotions and put them into characters on stage.
- Drama works with visual and physical order, as well as linguistic order. It forces us to organize. Students have to figure out where to put the furniture, how to get the body off the stage, and how to include off-stage information so the audience will know what is going on.

---

Since drama involves all of these aspects, from the physical to the visual to the linguistic, it's important to involve students in lots of different kinds of dramatic activity:

---

- Help students relax and become comfortable with their bodies and with using their bodies to explore their ideas and imaginations. Younger children do this easily. Adolescents need time and patience. Try these exercises:
  - Students lie on the floor, and as you name parts of the body, ask them to become aware of each part, how it moves, and what they can do with it.
  - Bring in a bag of objects (hairbrush, sponge, brush, can opener, dustpan, eggbeater). Ask groups or pairs of students to choose an object and prepare an improvisation centered on it. Or, have students create as many ways of using the object as possible and present them to the class.
  - Pair students off and have them take turns doing mirror images of one another, imitating gesture, movement, and facial expressions.
  - Ask your students to imagine they are a block of ice, melting in the warm air; an ice-cream cone at a Fourth of July picnic; a hot dog in the microwave. Use guided imagery, talking them through their

sensations, and have students use their bodies to respond to the imagined sensations.

- o Have your students lie on the floor and close their eyes. Tell them to imagine being underwater swimmers as you describe what they see on a South Pacific dive.

- Have your students pantomime:
  - o A great machine in which they are interconnecting parts. Have one student start, then have other students add to the machine by "connecting" with a part that's already in action. Have them add sound, too.
  - o A bank robbery, with students playing robbers, tellers, security guards, and customers. All demands, reactions, and emotions must be expressed without words.
  - o Completing an ordinary task, without the props: making and buttering a piece of toast; feeding the hungry and excited dog; changing a baby's diaper; frying a couple of eggs.

- Explore radio plays with your students. Tapes of old radio dramas and comedies are widely available. After listening to some samples your students can write scripts and then tape-record (or present live) a drama of their own, complete with sound effects.

- Use puppets for improvised plays; puppets offer self-conscious students, in particular, the kind of anonymity they may need to participate fully in dramas.

- Do shadow plays with young students, again supplying just the bit of protection from audience scrutiny that some kids need to take off.

- Create a variety of television-style talk shows as a bridge between drama and oral language. Students improvise their conversation, but must remain in character.

- Make connections with literature, finding the dramatic elements of a piece of literature and bring it on stage. Have your students:
  - o Read, read, read aloud so they become comfortable with interpreting literature in their own voices.
  - o Turn works of literature into readers' theater. Have students script sections of fiction that are mostly dialogue. The essential narration—the part of the story not told through dialogue—is assigned to a narrator.
  - o Dramatize a poem, song, or story, translating the narration into speaking parts for all the characters.
  - o Conduct imaginary interviews with characters from a story, poem, play, or novel.

- Create dramatic monologues based on the life of an author or on one of the characters from a novel.
- Place characters from a historical novel in a contemporary scene.

(Keep the video camera around for many of these events.)

## Composing Through Poetry

Poetry is the most difficult of the imaginative forms to teach, we feel, because students often develop early misconceptions about it. As children, they delight in the singsong qualities of verse, and before long, they think that all poems must rhyme, a notion that's reinforced in many language arts classes, where rhyme and meter are presented as the most important characteristics of a poem. As students get older, they often encounter modern poetry that seems obscure and difficult, or ancient poetry that also seems obscure and difficult. If they write poetry, it's often in a fixed form, which subordinates ideas to structure. And for some reason, our profession has developed a tradition of teaching poetry *units*, which walls off poetry and ignores its natural connections with human thought and other discourse.

Here are some ideas for "teaching" poetry (or better, simply using poetry as a natural form of expression). First, some don'ts:

- Don't isolate poetry in separate literature or writing units. Offer poems as reading along with other literature; present poetry as a writing option alongside fiction, drama, and nonfiction.
- Don't overstress poetic traits and the characteristics of meter, rhythm, and metaphor. To do so is akin to saying that the most important thing about an essay is its paragraph structure.
- Don't describe poetry and poets as different from the rest of the literary universe. Don't claim that poetry is "more powerful" than prose or that poets have "deeper sensibilities" than other people.

Now, some do's:

- Immerse students in good poetry. In thematic units; in studying about a particular time or place; or in looking at an era in American, British, or world literature, include lots of poetry. Include a variety of poems, not just ones that represent one or two prominent poets.
- Allow students to learn how the genre of poetry works by reading lots of different kinds of poems. Rather than pre-teaching what a poem is, have students describe and define poetry based on their experience.

- One aspect of poetry is its sensory and imagistic language. Encourage students to locate this kind of language in ordinary experience—in the language of advertising, in the language of other forms of literature, and in their own writing.
- Have students look, too, for clever and original language use, for new ways of seeing and saying things. Advertising often catches people's attention with its catchy language. Kids might also hear their younger brothers and sisters express their observations in original language.
- Have students keep a scrapbook or a place in their journals for "poetic language."
- Encourage students to think of poems as ways of expressing their ideas, their perceptions, and their experiences in vivid, sensory, physical language.
- Have students who like to write poetry collect and bind their work in the fashionable "thin volume."
- Have students make a book of illustrated poems in which the words and the pictures work together to create meaning.
- Create a "poetry kaleidoscope," a bulletin board that is a constantly changing display of poems by both kids and the writers you and they admire.
- Highlight kids' favorite poems by having one or two students start every class by reading (or better yet, reciting from memory) their best new poetry find. Make sure there are lots of books of poetry in the classroom from which students can choose.
- Get a poet to come to your school, probably with the aid of a grant from the state arts council. Help students see that poets are ordinary (but not-so-ordinary) people who write about the same sorts of things that students reflect on in their own writer's notebooks.
- Have kids experiment with their own writing by turning ideas for essays into poetry, or turning a short story idea into a poem.
- Provide students with lots of sensory experiences (through music, visually beautiful films and documentaries, art slides, field trips, etc.). Talk about those sensory experiences and the language that can express them.
- Have students use literary characters and events as the source for their own poetry.
- Have students write poetry about their passions—football, skiing, dancing, playing the clarinet, horseback riding, singing, camping—in poems.

- Create a literary magazine, and publish lots of your kids' poetry. Have your kids submit poetry to the school magazine or newspaper.
- Invite interested students to explore fixed forms of poetry, like the sonnet, carefully and cautiously. Although we question the wisdom of having all students write in obligatory forms, we also recognize that there are kids in any class who enjoy seeking out and experimenting with forms, from haiku to the heroic couplet (with the limerick happily in between).

## Composing Through Fiction

Of the so-called creative forms, getting students to write fiction is probably the easiest. We all have storytelling impulses within us, and youngsters come to the elementary grades ready to create wonderful fictions (and ready to have those same impulses channeled into drama as well). John Rouse (1978) has reminded us, too, that so-called nonfiction is "fiction" of sorts, that any "true" story is something we abstract from experience and interpret for a reader.

To sustain and develop your students' powers as fiction makers:

- Let them write stories just about any time. Having writing workshop or free-writing days when they can write anything they want encourages students to be making stories in their heads before they walk in the door.
- Encourage oral storytelling and encourage students to write down the stories they tell.
- Bring a storyteller into the class. Have students discuss what makes a good story. Encourage them to think about those elements of story when they write.
- Bring fiction writers to class (again with the aid of your state's arts council or a writers-in-the-schools program) to read and discuss their stories, where they get their ideas, and how they write.
- Have students discuss their writing online with other writers of fiction, both professional writers and other student writers. Have them publish their pieces online.
- Talk about fictionalizing experience as a means of telling a story. Have students tell a story based on their own experience, but encourage them to make things up to make the story more believable, interesting, or complex (or to protect the innocent).

- Integrate research and fiction. Encourage students to do research to make their stories more believable—to learn more about the city of the setting, the animal behavior, the historical period, the manners and dress of a country.

- Allow students to relate their research in fictional form. Tom Romano (1995) invites his students to write multigenre research papers based on studies of people. Encourage students to use poetry, letters, newspaper articles, and songs to tell their research stories.

- Bring in the film version of a piece of fiction students have read. Ask them to compare the filmed and written versions. What can they accomplish in writing that can't be done on film?

- Have students learn about the elements of fiction by reading and writing fiction. Discuss with them such issues as character, setting, plot, and theme as they work on their stories. Ask them to articulate their discoveries. What makes an intriguing plot? What makes an interesting character? How do you create a setting that seems real?

- Have students develop notions for plot by asking the question "What if?" What if the power grid across the U.S. broke down for a week? What if a teenage girl's presumed dead father appeared on her doorstep? What if an asteroid were going to plow into the earth in twenty-one days? What if two children got separated from their parents in downtown Chicago?

- Encourage students to visit the webpages of their favorite writers to learn more about the writers and what they are working on. This sort of immediate accessibility to writers gives students a greater sense of being a part of the writerly world.

- Encourage students to publish their work online and to participate in conversations with other writers across the country and across the world.

---

# Brass-Tacks Writing

Sure, it's important to extend the imagination, to let students write creative forms as well as exposition. But what about the need for students to write for the job, for college, and for the real world? Enter "brass-tacks writing."

We debated that phrase for some time before selecting it for use in this book. Some would call what we're discussing here "practical discourse," the writing of business, academia, and society at large. However, that ignores the reality that fiction, poetry, and drama are also practical modes. Others prefer the term "exposition," but as we will show, writing in this domain involves much more than writing essays, exams, or research papers. Brass-tacks writing includes memoranda, letters, editorials, applications, proposals, and a host of other forms.

Brass-tacks (or "nuts-and-bolts") writing is the sort the public generally regards as basic, the kind that will help kids succeed in school and society, the stuff that Johnny and Jane allegedly can't produce.

We think composition programs can meet the demands of brass-tacks writing in new and interesting ways. Kids need not shut off their imaginations when they write essays or business letters. What they have learned by writing drama and stories can serve them well when they write examinations and term papers. Organizing a poem can also help a student learn to organize a persuasive essay.

## Workaday Writing

One of the easiest ways to help students focus on the use of writing for practical purposes is to have them empty a wastebasket. That's right: Dump it out on the floor and sift through the trash, looking for writing that has been *used* by virtue of its having been thrown away. Our own wastebasket—dumped at this writing on the study floor—is representative; it contains:

> Brochures from a bank, credit card company, and public utility informing us of bargains and proper procedures (all came tucked in with monthly bills).
>
> Canceled checks and a scratch sheet for an unbalanced checkbook.
>
> A Three Musketeers bar wrapper listing caloric contents, fat grams and percentages, and ingredients (some of which are unpronounceable).
>
> A used grocery-shopping list.
>
> A note from one of our teenage sons telling us what documents he needs for his driving test.
>
> A hard copy of an e-mail message describing Internet projects for the schools.
>
> A Christmas catalog from Kmart.
>
> A letter from a friend.

Workaday writing is more than writing that gets tossed in the wastebasket. We also have notebooks full of workaday writing (including several we filled in preparing this book) and files and folders and boxes in varying states of disarray where we keep materials. Generally, workaday writing is *writing that gets a practical job done,* and the point of the wastebasket exercise is to show just how much of such writing there is in the world.

Another interesting trait of workaday writing in schools is that teachers seldom grade it. This is writing that students do for their own purposes: to remember things, to organize ideas, to collect information. As a teacher, you can increase the amount of writing students do while showing them the value of brass-tacks writing and not burdening yourself with themes to grade. Just raise their practice levels and consciousness of functional writing. Have students write:

---

- Class notes of all sorts: notes on their reading, notes on lectures or presentations, notes on projects or experiments. Teach kids how to take reliable and dependable notes, and from time-to-time project a student's notes on a transparency to help the others see how it is done.

- Learning logs. These are a step beyond garden-variety notes. Here students not only write down facts and concepts, but reflect on ideas as well. "Do boys' and girls' interpretations of 'Story of an Hour' differ?" "What alternative versions are there to the view that Columbus discovered America?" "Which artists' versions of Ophelia are closer to your own image of her?" Learning logs can also be collections of students' *mis*understandings (and give the teacher a chance to "instruct" at the point at which it might be useful).

- Freewrites responding to class material. Ask the students to anticipate concepts or write about their prior knowledge before you teach; have them write midstream or summary commentaries in response to ongoing class activities. Give lots of opportunities for kids to use writing to *think* about stuff.

- Suggestions and questions. Have a box on your desk where students can anonymously leave suggestions for classwork, questions about aspects of their schoolwork they're having problems with, or notes about general issues they would like to pursue with you in private.

- Notes to each other. One of our friends has designated parts of class time in which students can pass each other notes about their own business. If, during individual or group work, the class becomes too noisy, ask kids to conduct business in writing rather than talking (responses to one another's papers; ideas for group projects).

- Progress reports. If you feel like you're losing a handle on who's doing what, or if you want to have students keep you informed periodically about what they are doing, have them write briefly about where they are in their project, and how things are working out, how they're doing at keeping on schedule.

- Abstracts, summaries, précis. Students can use these forms to condense some reading into notecard-sized form for remembering later, for keeping a record of their accomplishments in reading, and for managing research.
- Self- and class-evaluations of their own performance, of a class unit, of a semester course to evaluate their learning and your own teaching.
- Notes across curricula. Have students write to other teachers to show the connections between what they are doing in your class and what they are doing in history, drama, art, or psychology.

## Brass-Tacks Writing Projects

One enormous advantage of brass-tacks writing is that it has real potential for connecting students to the rest of the world, of connecting school learning with the issues, problems, and events in their communities. Two recent emphases—school-to-work (or careers) and service learning—provide opportunities for students to engage in activities that have significance outside school. While we wouldn't want students to see their educations as being of value strictly in terms of work skills, we believe that students can see value in writing in the community. Moreover, they can have a positive impact on the world through community-based writing.

School-to-work programs give students the opportunity to go into the workplace and see what sort of work goes on in various professions. In addition, students may have the opportunity to "shadow" workers whose jobs they are especially interested in knowing more about. In many of these programs, the English language arts teacher is of little consequence. However, we think that helping students see and study the language of the workplace is extremely valuable to their understanding of both the material expectations of the job and the subtler psychological and human dimensions of the workplace.

Have students:

- Study the written materials. What sorts of manuals or guidelines are used in the workplace to describe people's jobs and responsibilities and set work specifications. How are responsibilities spelled out in writing? Characterize the writing: Is it easy to read? Overly complex? Friendly? Formal?
- Watch what people read and write during the day. How much work is done using word processors? Are forms or form letters used? What

use do employees make of e-mail? What sorts of memos are sent and received? What is written by hand?

- Explore oral language. What is the role of oral language in this workplace? What's done by telephone? What's done face-to-face? How is oral language used to get work done, to solve problems, to answer questions, and to socialize? How much talk is there up and down the hierarchy? How much talk is there among peers?

- Observe problem-solving. What do workers do when they need a question answered? Look in a book? Call someone? Ask other people in the workplace?

Service learning involves children of all ages in volunteer work in their communities. Sometimes these projects are small and simple, like planting a tree on the school's grounds or in a park, but sometimes they are much larger. Students have been responsible for planning and maintaining the plants in a local park; they have volunteered at preschools and retirement communities, reading to those who can't read themselves; and they have been involved in environmental and helping-the-homeless projects. Not only does this sort of activity serve the community and provide a model for citizenship, it also has the potential for providing students with opportunities to use language to serve the community. School and community writing projects include:

- Letters to the editor and to public officials describing a need students see in the community—a skateboard park for teenagers, a shelter for homeless people, a service for abused women. Reading the local paper will help students be aware of the community's needs and provide models for effective letter writing.

- Proposals to public or school officials outlining specific plans of action for school or community needs: how to save a community wetland, how to provide safe after-school programs for elementary school children.

- Investigations of problems: recycling, bicycle paths and bicycle safety, environmental impact, neighborhood cleanup and beautification.

- Press releases for school or community events.

- Newspaper or feature articles describing a worthwhile new project to get financial and volunteer support.

- Plans or proposals for service learning that students would like to engage in, goals for what they want to accomplish and how they want to go about meeting them.

- Evaluations of volunteer learning projects, including self-evaluations of what students accomplished on the job and what they learned, and evaluations of the project itself.

- School improvement plans to be shared with teachers and administrators—how to improve the lunch program, how to improve student relations, how to make the school safe.

- Articles for the newspaper that provide the good news about kids—stories of their contributions and successes.

- Internet searches to learn about what other schools and communities are doing to solve problems similar to the ones that your community is facing.

- Participation in newsgroups and listservs that are community minded.

- Audio- and videotapes, cable TV presentations, and live plays that dramatize community needs or show kids' accomplishments in their communities.

---

You don't have to engage your students in service learning projects to heighten their concern for the world around them. Bringing in videos about world and community problems, daily local and national newspapers, discussions of what they hear and see on radio and television will help your students see ways in which they can use writing and talking as means for working to solve problems. We can't anticipate what sorts of writing students will need in their careers five, ten, or fifteen years from now, but we can help develop in them a sense that (1) they can and should have an impact on the community and world in which they live, and (2) language is one very important medium for making an impact.

## The Academic Writing Scene

The projects and activities we have suggested on the past several pages prepare students for college as well as real life. Brass-tacks writing usually emphasizes the traditional academic skills of marshaling evidence and presenting it effectively to an audience. Our own experience teaching first-year college students suggests that rather than mastering a limited range of forms like "the five-paragraph theme" (or the most recent foolproof formula for putting together an essay) or "the research paper," students need to develop fluency in a wide range of brass-tacks writing forms. If they achieve that broad competence, they can quickly and successfully adapt to the specific demands of Professor Smith's history term paper or Dr. Jones' logbooks in computer science.

Moreover, we think that the notion of the research paper has been too narrowly confined in terms of how it is researched, how it is written, and who benefits. Everyone benefits from researching, from finding out answers to burning—or just interesting—questions. And the process of researching can be both enjoyable and enlightening. As the world becomes smaller and the sources of evidence more diverse and available, students are well-served by exploring ways in which research can fruitfully be launched. We have the following suggestions:

- Introduce your students to a range of resources—the reference library, the children's library, the media library, archives, museums, people, and the Internet.

- Demonstrate the strengths of different resources. The children's library has books with simplified information; the media library lets you see as well as read; people can give you a personalized picture and answer your specific questions; and the Internet provides multiple perspectives.

- Teach students to use the Internet. This involves not only the mechanics of operating searches that will yield the information most closely tied to the students' topic but also ways to sort the junk from the good stuff, people's wacky opinions from substantiated evidence. Help them find online newspapers, magazines, and websites that are time-honored and reliable.

- Engage students in discussions about what to do when they have conflicting evidence about their topics. Discuss ways students can explore "alternative" and "standard" sources to discover facts and well-argued positions.

- Use interactive Internet sources—e-mail, chatrooms, and newsgroups—to ask questions and discover experts who can answer their specific questions (keeping in mind the caveat about wackos).

- Provide alternative ways students can report their findings. We mentioned the multigenre research paper in which students use poetry, fiction, letters to the editor, letters by and about the subjects of study, advertisements, songs, and dialogue to illuminate their subjects. Allow students, too, to create scrapbooks, documentary video- or audiotapes, and stories or plays to show what they've discovered in their research.

Teachers may feel intensified responsibility for their students who are going on to college. While we're sure that students who've had rich literacy experiences in school will fare well in college, you may want to introduce some specific strategies to your students addressed directly to the college experience:

- Have your students survey last year's seniors who have gone on to college about the demands placed on college students. This is a good brass-tacks writing project for seniors finding out answers to their big questions. Have students ask for copies of college students' papers, complete with professors' comments. Or, invite last year's students to visit your class during their spring break and share their experiences with your current students.

- Have students locate the webpages of the colleges they are interested in. Most of these will have ways to contact the director of the writing program. Encourage students to contact that person with questions about the college's first-year writing program. Some colleges will have names of students who can be contacted by prospective applicants who have questions.

- Teach students to use a concise handbook of usage, spelling, and writing form. Help them get to know their chosen handbook backward and forward so they can solve their own manuscript problems some distant 2:00 A.M. in the dorm.

- Help students learn to analyze assignments. Here again, real samples will help. What does a professor mean when he or she says "explore," "analyze," "synthesize," "argue," or "persuade"?

- Have your students get to know their own writing processes and study habits. Self-knowledge of strengths and weaknesses, of successful and unsuccessful strategies, can go a long way toward helping students get themselves organized during the early, chaotic, bewildering days of college.

- Encourage students to think of the audience for their academic writing. Usually this is the professor or graduate student teaching assistant of a class. We wish that most academic writing was done "for real," but in fact it is often designed to reach a limited audience indeed: the person who will grade the paper. Knowing that can help students understand what to put in their writing.

- Above all, help students K–12 become inquiring, researching, thinking, *composing* human beings. More than knowing the mechanics of the research paper and the five-paragraph theme, college-bound students need to be spirited thinkers and writers. If teachers will help them *compose* in the fullest sense of that word, exploring the extraordinary dimensions of imagination and discourse, students will handle their academic writing with competence.

# Selected Readings

Boiarsky, Carolyn. 1997. *The Art of Workplace English*. Portsmouth, NH: Boyn-
    ton/Cook Publishers.

Crotchett, Kevin R. 1997. *A Teacher's Project Guide to the Internet*. Portsmouth,
    NH: Heinemann.

Romano, Tom. 1995. *Writing with Passion: Life Stories, Multiple Genres*.
    Portsmouth, NH: Boynton/Cook Publishers.

Tchudi, Stephen, ed. 1993. *The Astonishing Curriculum: Integrating Science and
    Humanities Through Language*. Urbana, IL: National Council of Teachers of
    English.

Tchudi, Stephen, and Stephen Lafer. 1996. *The Interdisciplinary Teacher's Hand-
    book*. Portsmouth, NH: Boynton/Cook Publishers.

# Chapter Ten

# The Red Pencil Blues

The scene: A language arts classroom, could be upper elementary, could be secondary. The cast: Typical students and teacher.

**Teacher:** (*entering from the hallway door, brandishing a sheaf of papers*) Class, I have finished grading your papers.

**Class:** (*sotto voce*) Mutter, mutter, mutter.

**Teacher:** (*distributing papers to the class*) On the whole, these were much better than the last ones. In fact, I'm encouraged that you're really working hard to improve your writing.

(*As the students receive their papers, they flip to the back page, searching for the grade.*)

**Joe:** (*whispering to Stan*) Whadid she give you, Stan?

**Stan:** C-plus. (*He stuffs the paper into his book bag.*)

**Joe:** Wadid she say about it?

**Stan:** (*shrugs*) Who cares? I never understand what she wants. Last time I thought I did great, and she gave me a D. Time before that I turned in a thing I did in fifteen minutes and she gave me an A.

**Teacher:** (*continuing to distribute papers*) I think we're making real progress in here, don't you?

**Students:** (*in chorus*) Yes, Teacher.

The details of time, place, and situation may vary, but almost every teacher has played the lead in a scene like this. Having spent the better part of an evening or weekend writing thoughtful comments on papers, we return them to students and watch as the kids flip to the back, see what damage has been inflicted by the grade, and ignore the instructive comments.

We wind up singin' the red pencil blues.

Of course, no trendy English language arts teacher uses a red pencil anymore. Research and teacher lore have taught us that "bleeding" on kids' papers, accentuating errors in crimson, has negative effects on their writing.

We have also rejected what might be called the red pencil mentality, which says that the teacher's principal role is that of error corrector and Super Grammarian. These days, English language arts teachers try to make their comments supportive and generally positive, and they try to focus the negative comments, perhaps choosing one particular item for discussion each paper.

Yet marking, grading, and editing themes still causes more than its share of problems for teachers, and remains what we still refer to as the theme-correcting *burden*. In our experience, the number-one reason teachers give for not assigning more writing is the fact that they have to comment on it, and they're just not certain it's worth all the time and energy.

Fortunately, current practices in teaching composition offer some fresh, even inviting, alternatives. In particular, the interest in composing as *process* has encouraged teachers to move away from their traditional role as evaluator of finished products toward that of writing guide or coach. We're now more interested in helping students learn how to revise and edit their own papers than in showing them what they did right or wrong after the fact. Even concern for correctness, usage, and mechanics can be incorporated at appropriate stages of instruction.

To engage your students in a process approach to writing:

1. *Treat students' writing as a process in meaning making rather than as an exercise in learning to write.* That is, the primary purpose of composing is to create something that other people will read successfully. Although as teachers we want students to learn to write better, we must carefully avoid turning students' papers into a proving ground or testing facility for writing skills (and we must have confidence that students *do* learn to write by writing).

2. *Engage students constructively in taking responsibility for their own work.* In the long run, the students themselves will be the ones who must make changes in their writing and accept the praise and criticism their work receives.

3. *Use peers as readers and audiences.* Both readers and writers learn about writing as give-and-get response. As they gain experience in this role, their feedback will become more and more helpful and writers will benefit from a genuine sense of readership in the classroom.

4. *Teach from a workshop perspective, offering help when it's needed in the process of composition.* Having students revise, edit, and correct in class is a perfectly valid use of "company time," and a better use of your time than taking home stacks of papers to grade. Answering students' questions when they need those answers goes a lot further toward solving writing problems than marking papers after the fact.

5. *Skeptically assess the effects of your comments on student papers, and grant students the right to ignore your comments or act on them as they see fit.* We English teachers may well have overrated the value of our comments on papers. What do students learn as the result of our comments? How do individual papers change? How does students' writing change over the long run? Classroom observation and the experience of writers suggest that even the best-intended, psychopedagogically framed remarks are often misunderstood, mis-used, or ignored. The bottom line is that writers gradually figure out things about language as they work. (And hours and hours of our marking time could be better spent.)

These five principles do not, by any means, lead to a quick cure for the red pencil blues. Putting them into action is difficult. What do we do with kids who "just don't care" about their writing? Or the student whose chronic spelling problems make his papers absolutely unreadable? Or the student editors who give one another bad advice? Or the student who con-sistently ignores our advice and consistently writes drivel?

Too, we know a number of teachers who have tried to organize their classes into workshops where students take responsibility for their own writing, but who abandoned the idea, saying that it just didn't work. Stu-dents wouldn't stay on task or talk about writing in their writing groups, and they didn't like other students reading their writing.

Employing a new pedagogy, we know, is no easy task and will not lead to easy successes. But it seems to us superior to singin' those old red pencil blues.

So, how can you go about setting up a writing workshop that will be helpful to students? How can you teach the process of revision? How can students be helpful to one another as editors? How can correctness and copyediting become natural parts of the workshop? Where does grading factor into all of this? We offer some answers to those questions in the remainder of this chapter.

# The Writing Environment

Right out of the chute it may be necessary for you to change some habits. Often students come to you with stereotyped images of the teacher as theme grader, with no inkling that there are other ways to go about writ-ing than to submit a paper and wait to find out what was done wrong. (However, we should also state, from our perspective in the university, that increasingly the students who come into our classes seem to have been in a writing workshop and have had at least some previous experience in this mode of instruction. Praise be to their elementary and secondary teachers of "writing as process.")

Still, at any level, launching a writing workshop requires preparation and explanation. Here are some strategies that we've found helpful:

---

- Begin by explaining the idea of a writer's *responsibility* to the reader. This is not the nagging sort of responsibility we invoke to get children to clean up their rooms, but recognition that composing is a personal act with personal rewards and consequences. You are the one whose name goes on the paper; you are the one who needs to be the bottom line, the "buck-stops-here" writer/editor.

- Place strong emphasis on *choice*—choice of writing topic, choice in how to use time, choice in what and how to revise, and choice in selecting groups. We want students to make good decisions, and we want them to take responsibility. Of course, there will be times when you may want everyone doing the same thing, but in order to be invested in their work, students have to have the commitment and passion that follow from making their own choices.

- Provide lots of time in class for students to work alone, to write, revise, self-edit, and copyedit their writing. There are several good reasons for using class time in this way. First, given today's busy schedules, kids will often not have time to work at home. Second, and more fundamental, this sort of focused time allows you opportunities to hold conferences with students (more about this later). Third, and perhaps most important, is that it demonstrates the importance of taking the time and the responsibility for making a paper as good as you can before taking it to your peers or a teacher conference.

- Strive for an atmosphere of *serious play*. Some may see this as an oxymoron; we see it as essential to productive classrooms. No doubt, writing is work. It requires concentration, energy, and patience. But, ironically, working on writing that we are committed to is energizing, satisfying, and, well, *fun*. Students should be able to work alone and with one another in quiet groups, they should be able to confer with another student or with you, and they should be able to move around the room freely to refer to classroom resources. They should be able to laugh when writing is funny and exclaim when they are delighted or surprised.

- Help students individually and collectively develop criteria for assessing the papers they're writing. What will make a good personal narrative, letter to the editor, or personal research paper? It's often helpful to develop or have students develop rubrics or checklists of things to look for in their writing: detail, focus, aim, and appropriate beginnings and endings.

- Distinguish between the "phases" of revising, editing, and correcting papers. We generally discuss revision as a matter of working with content, editing as focusing on matters of language and style, and correctness as dealing with matters of mechanics and usage. It's most important that students not blur these distinctions; in particular, many of your students will come in thinking that "revising" simply means "proofreading" or even "copy it over, in ink." At the same time, it's important not to march through these phases in lockstep manner. Writers may, in fact, do some correcting as they are composing; they may do some revising as they are working with style and a new thought occurs to them; and they may be doing their final copyediting and change some words to make the work "sound better." Writing is *recursive*; writers move back and forth among various tasks as they work.

- Have students develop their own portfolios and record-keeping systems. We've suggested process and showcase portfolios—the first for keeping drafts and the second for keeping the best of a student's completed work. The process portfolio may hold information about the number of papers completed, ideas for new papers, a personal editing guide and spelling list (for the writer's particular bugaboos), and notes on process. In addition to a student's best papers, the showcase portfolio may provide the student's introductions and self-evaluations of final bests.

# Peer Response Groups

The heart of a process/workshop pedagogy is a small group of students who, with teacher guidance and support, offer one another reactions to their papers and editorial advice. Peer groups can meet often during the writing process: as students are thinking about what to write about; as they are discussing what to include and where to get information; as they are drafting and putting together their ideas; as they are polishing and correcting; and at the end for sharing.

Some ideas for peer response groups:

- Let students form their own peer groups. Some teachers we know argue against this, preferring to structure groups so that they contain a mix of better and poorer writers, and so that friends don't always work with friends. Despite the problems that self-selected groups sometimes present, we think they form a much tighter writing community than teacher-structured groups.

- Suggest that students name their writing groups: The Magic Pens, The Awesome Editors, Will's (Shakespeare) Light and Power Company.
- Assure students that they know how to help one another in class. (They will be skeptical.) Two useful exercises:
  - Have students describe the best and worst film they have ever seen. They will have strong and definite opinions (and will probably disagree). As they provide evidence in support of their opinions, point out the critical standards they are employing.
  - Invite students to write or improvise a parody of a current television show. In doing so, they will automatically employ critical and evaluative standards and (if you want to use some terminology) knowledge of *rhetoric*.
- To get some diversity and cross-ability response, occasionally invite students to discuss special topics—using dialogue, solving spelling problems, beginnings and endings—and allow them to share their attempts in these areas.
- Encourage students to be *helpful* editors. Each student in your class has certain skills and talents as a language user that he or she can employ. Make it clear that although not everybody (including you) knows everything about writing, in your classroom community you know quite enough to help one another out in important ways.

## Strategies for Writing Groups

- Don't let students apologize in advance for their papers. The natural instinct is to say, "Well, this didn't turn out the way I wanted" or "I don't like this very much." Outlaw such self-deprecating and self-defeating introductions.
- Give students a variety of ways to present papers. Some kids would like to read a draft aloud to their classmates. Others would prefer a "paper pass," where everybody's draft is read and commented on in silence.
- Model helpful response. Demonstrate response as a natural process in which you talk about what strikes you in writing, what caught your eye, what interested you, what got you thinking, and what confused you. Response isn't usually giving advice, but explaining what the writing *does* to and for you. The writer decides what to do about that. Ways to model:

- Project a paper on the overhead (a paper written by one of last year's students, with the name removed) and hold a discussion about how the class could make helpful remarks.
- Pass out one of your own drafts, take a deep breath, and ask the students to help you out. (In so doing, you'll also model how to respond to reactions—*not* defensively.)
- Put some students in a "fishbowl"—a small group in the center of the room—to conduct a discussion among themselves. Afterward you and other students can discuss how this went.
- Work with small groups occasionally to help them when they're stuck or to provide additional ways of responding. But be careful not to take over groups that are working to establish their own procedures.

- Structure some peer-group sessions so that students have some ideas about what to look for in papers. Have different focus sessions on such matters as:
  - Beginnings. What makes a good beginning? How well does this one work?
  - Word pictures. Describe for the writer the visual images this creates in your mind.
  - Socko, boffo language. Tell the writer about all the knockout phrases in his or her writing.
  - Structure. Does this piece flow well from beginning to end? Could we follow it easily?

  One of our favorite sources for such peer-group activities is Peter Elbow's *Writing with Power* (1981). It contains scores of ideas for peer-group responses.

- Help students continue to see options in their pieces by continuing to write as they are receiving response. Have peer groups suggest ways in which new ideas can be integrated into the piece. Have them unsettle drafts in the following ways:
  - Add dialogue to a piece that is all narrative.
  - Add descriptions of characters or places that aren't described.
  - Develop a person (nonfiction) or a character (fiction) or an idea that's barely introduced.
  - Develop a counterargument to each of the major assertions presented.
  - Tell what happened before or after the events of the story or narrative.

- o Change the point of view of the piece.
- o Add examples for each of the ideas presented.
- More ideas for focus in peer groups:
  - o Have the writer give the history of this paper, including why he or she chose to write it and the kinds of problems that have been encountered in the process.
  - o Encourage the groups to begin with praise—not hollow praise but focused reactions that say "I liked X because of Y."
  - o Ask students to read one another's papers aloud. Having somebody else read your paper not only relieves anxiety but helps a writer hear his or her work in a new way and with someone else's voice.
  - o Have writers explain to the group what they are having problems with and what they would like the group to focus on.
  - o Alternatively, have writers keep completely silent as others are talking about their paper so that they don't influence what readers focus on.
- Do writing about writing in peer groups. If groups members are not talking, if they're not doing substantial discussions of the work at hand, have them write out comments to give to the writer.
- Have students write a running commentary as another student reads a draft paper aloud. The idea is for respondents to jot down their instantaneous reactions to the piece, useful information for any writer to have.
- If your students are very reluctant to share comments orally, allow them to write letters to the author about the work. Such letters should not be anonymous, but they should be prepared carefully and thoughtfully. Putting criticism in a letter often makes it easier for student editors to comment.
- Have peer groups present one another's writing when they have completed pieces. Student A can read student B's work aloud. Student C can introduce them both, explaining what the group liked about their papers. Or students A, B, C, and D can combine forces and do a dramatic presentation of E's work. (Roll the video camera.)

## Students with Limited English Proficiency

We believe that all of the above activities are appropriate for students whose native language is not English. Students who are learning English should be encouraged to immerse themselves in writing in the same way native speakers do. They should be asked to write about what they are interested in, and their writing should be regarded with the same serious-ness and be given the same careful attention as the writing of proficient English speakers. In a developmental model, we emphasize responding to students where they are.

The biggest problem we have encountered with students who are non-native English speakers is their insecurity. They are frequently afraid to speak or write because they have been made to feel their language is inad-equate or incompetent. These students need special encouragement, sup-port, and praise for their efforts to communicate. Moreover, they should work with the same process as other students in the class, with meaning as the central concern of composing, followed by attention to structure, style, and correctness. Premature attention to surface issues in language strangles both thought and fluency. Have faith in growth over time.

### The Teacher's Role in Response Groups

For the most part you want to keep yourself out of the assessment, or at least operate behind the scenes. It's possible for the teacher to sit in on groups, even make comments from time to time, but you must be cautious so that you don't take over the group or disrupt its natural flow. We "float" during response groups, watching for unproductive groups. We have no reservations about intervening if a group isn't getting the job done, and we occasionally offer comments as we tune in to the work of a group. If we've done our job right, however, the groups come to run on their own.

# Conferences

Holding conferences with students about their writing operates in a mid-dle ground between peer-response groups and teacher-written comments. The conference is a particularly efficient use of teacher time, because you can spiel out more words per second than you can write. More important, you can find out what students need and zero in on their problems. In a few colleges, conference teaching has seemed to work so well that pro-fessors have actually abandoned common class meetings and spend all their time working face-to-face with students in their offices. We have strong reservations about that approach, however , because in it we feel both the loss of the classroom community and an increased student depen-dence on the teacher. Some elementary and secondary school teachers, dissatisfied with peer groups, nonetheless run workshop classes where students work alone on papers while the teacher circulates conducting brief conferences. Many combinations are possible.

Our rules of thumb for conferences:

- Keep them brief. It's tempting to develop your ideas at great length. Learn how to make your conferences directed, usually to one point that either you or the students has raised.
- Let the students talk. Let them describe the problems they're having, even though their perceptions may differ from your own.
- Respect students' privacy. The downside of classroom conferences is that other kids can hear what you're saying. Be cautious.
- Let students suggest solutions to their own problems. Don't always be the answer person.
- When you do suggest solutions, present them as alternatives, allowing students to see several ways of proceeding.
- Don't let conferences become centered on proofreading. This is not an effective use of your time. Focus your energies on matters of content, style, and language.
- Don't be so businesslike in your conferences that you forget to ask kids, "How's it going, generally?" Take a few seconds to discuss the weather, the ball game, the new shoes.

## The Teacher as Editor

We think it's important for teachers to supply as much help as possible during, rather than after, the fact of composition. We find that the more time we put in on classroom discussions and conferences, the less time we need to spend writing comments on papers. However, there comes a time for just about any teacher when written comments become important. Some principles and strategies to keep in mind:

- Make your first response to the paper that of a reader, not a grammarian. React to the content. Make laugh marks in the margin if it's funny. Do versions of the smiley face. Tell the student what has moved you.
- Think of your response as a letter to the student rather than as a set of instructions rectifying a problem composition.
- Give reasons for your positive responses. We think that positive comments are just as (or more) useful to students as advice, but students need to understand *why* something worked for you, not just that you thought it "good."
- Work hard to understand what students have written. We see that as a major responsibility of the teacher. We absolutely disagree with

teachers who refuse to read "sloppy" papers or who red-line a paper if it contains too many errors or is difficult to decipher.

- Don't feign ignorance or confusion when students have simply written clumsily or outside the boundaries of standard English. Do explain the ways in which writers can make it easier for readers to grasp what they have in mind.

- Make suggestions in terms of the paper's content rather than using abstract terminology. Tell students concretely what seems to be the problem or what needs to be done. Not: "You've made an incomplete comparison," but "You never finished telling me why Ford trucks are better than Chevies."

- Make suggestions that help students solve their own problems. Encourage them to revisit their data or experience, thereby adding more depth and detail.

- Encourage students to develop their own standards. Provide support through your comments so that students can develop their own concept of "good writing" and confidence in their own decisions as writers.

- Don't cover too much. Resist the temptation to make this the one composition that will solve all the student's writing problems forever.

- Explore alternative ways of writing back to students.
  - Put your comments on sticky notes so that you don't have to write on the paper itself.
  - Reserve your comments for the end of the paper, leaving the pages clean (and resisting the temptation to mark errors).
  - Sit at the word processor to respond to students' papers, writing brief notes and letters commenting on the whole.
  - Test out the interactive network at the computer lab to see if it makes sense to put comments *into* word-processed papers via a software program.
  - Have students turn in a blank cassette with each paper and make all of your comments orally.

- Don't read too many student papers at once. That's obvious, of course, and sometimes reading a stack is unavoidable. Try staggering due dates, both among and within classes. Orchestrate your oral conferences and your written responses so that you are not compelled to read every last composition in the barrel tonight or this weekend.

- Develop a system in which students tell you what kind of response they want. Some of our colleagues have students put a sticky note on their papers, saying "read and respond," "read and edit," "read and appreciate," or "read and ignore." The only problem that they have found is that frequently they would like to comment on papers that say "read and ignore," if only to congratulate a student on a job well done.

- Above all, see your role as that of helper, not enemy. Your job (as we see it) is to help students succeed with the papers they've written. If these compositions are successful with their chosen audiences, no doubt the learning we all want to see will take place.

# The Question of Correctness

When the teacher takes editor's pen or pencil in hand, the issue of what to do about surface correctness emerges instantly. What do you do? Should the teacher correct every spelling error? Every error in mechanics? Every case of nonstandard usage? Should you put proofreading symbols in the margin—*sp., punc.*—and have students find the problems and solutions themselves? The dilemma is complicated by the fact that parents seem to be very critical of teachers who *don't* identify every error, and if parents had their way, red pencils might be standard issue for every teacher.

We take up the issue of correctness in more detail in the next chapter. For the present, however, it's important to remark that we think surface correctness must be subordinated to matters of content and style when a teacher responds to writing. The growing body of evidence suggests that correctness does make a difference to students when they're publishing their writing, so keeping the audience at the forefront helps. In particular, having students write in a workshop setting where they can get help regularly makes it easier for the teacher to teach correctness with a fighting chance that the concepts will take hold in students' minds.

Moreover, we suggest taking an analytical (rather than critical) stance toward errors. This means asking some questions about errors. What errors does the student make? (Be careful about generalizing from a few students' writing to all students' writing.) Are the errors in this paper typical or a simple "mistake"? Do a student's errors indicate carelessness (in which case the audience and purpose of the piece may not be clear or important to the student), lack of time, or a stage in the student's developmental awareness? Are errors the result of "interference" from the student's first language? Do the errors represent a pattern? We think that understanding why students make errors helps teachers think about how best to deal with them.

The strategy that has worked best for us in elementary school, secondary school, and college classes is to stress the distinction between content and surface correctness, that the one precedes the other. We also give students the responsibility for handling correctness. Students can successfully use handbooks and dictionaries to find solutions to many of their problems. A simple oral reading by a student will also turn up many errors that are simply ones of omission or accident. Peer groups can also do much of the polishing work on any paper that students write.

In some cases, however, we find it necessary to include work on correctness in our written comments. This is particularly true when students are not native speakers and writers of the language, and it's sometimes the case with students who simply have chronic usage and mechanics problems or even—though we dislike the word—disabilities. Then we will often focus on a particular problem and, for one paper or several, show the student how to manage it successfully for his or her own purposes. We also make it a point to tell the students precisely why we're working this way, and we regularly find ways in our written comments or conferences to praise the student for the content of the piece.

And, believe it or not, we have also had students ask us for more help with correctness matters. Sometimes this comes from an inappropriate fear that "my grammar is bad; my English teacher said so." At other times, it comes from a realization on the part of the student that he or she has a problem and, quite simply, wants to solve it. In such cases we're quite willing to work with students. (Often we have told classes, "If you want specific help with usage or spelling or punctuation, say so at the top of the paper.") In these instances, our first job is to figure out whether or not the student truly has a problem. If it's real, then constructive teaching is possible through written comments or conferences, and, what's more, is likely to be successful.

## Grading Compositions

Having remarked above that the reader/teacher ought to be on the side of the student, rather than being the enemy, we now turn to the inimical process of grading. If you're not careful, your best-intentioned work with student writers, your carefully and humanely written comments, will be wasted in the eyeblink it takes to see a grade.

In our ideal world, student writing and other composing would always be "graded" pass/fail, successful/in progress, credit/no credit. And we comment in several chapters that contract grading is about as close as we've been able to come to that ideal. Another good alternative is portfolio grading, where students receive a mark for showing growth over time or for having completed particular kinds of assigned writing. In addition, we like using showcase portfolios and letting students choose the best of their work to be evaluated, and develop or help create the criteria that will be used to evaluate their writing. If you find it necessary to put individual letter grades on student papers, we recommend the following:

- State your grading criteria at the beginning of the assignment. In fact, type them up and run off copies for the students to study.
- Engage students in setting standards for grades. What makes a "good" story or an "excellent" piece of research writing? As students develop these criteria, they will also come to understand how the criteria apply to their own work.
- Break your grade into components: clarity, organization, structure, style, correctness. Weight these factors to show students precisely what you value (presumably matters of content over those of correctness).
- Include the writing process as part of the grade. Give credit for preliminary proposals, first drafts, second drafts, and polished copy, thus rewarding students who undertake the process seriously and productively (and we'll warrant that those who have will produce higher-quality writing).
- Have your students write self-assessments as they turn in their writing. (We don't recommend having students *grade* their own papers.) As students reflect on what they've written, they're more likely to understand the grade you've assigned to their work.
- Explain your grades. Never slap a B or C on a paper without explanation or with a short phrases like "too short" or "not enough detail." Make certain that students understand what your grade means and how they can do better the next time.

# Selected Readings

Tchudi, Stephen, ed. 1997. *Alternatives to Grading Writing.* Urbana, IL: National Council of Teachers of English.
Weaver, Constance. 1996. *Teaching Grammar in Context.* Portsmouth, NH: Heinemann.
Yancey, Kathleen Blake, and Irwin Weiser, eds. 1997. *Situating Portfolios: Four Perspectives.* Urbana, IL: National Council of Teachers of English.

# Summary and Troubleshooting

# The PTO Discusses Writing

The scene: The assembly room of most any school. The occasion: The English language arts teachers have developed a new composition program and have spent the evening describing it for interested parents at a Parent Teacher Organization meeting. The teachers have discussed writing-as-process, oral language foundations for writing, editorial groups, and the development of editing skills through publishing. The time has come for questions from the parents.

**Principal:** . . . and so we thank the language arts teachers for this informative presentation. I know they stand ready to answer your questions.

**Parent 1:** Well, this all sounds very interesting, but I really am puzzled as to why our children write so badly in the first place. I mean, when we went to school, it was pretty much expected that we would write and write well. What happened to destroy that?

**Teacher 1:** You raise an important set of issues there. With all due respect, I'd have to urge us to be careful about reminiscing about our own past education. Granted, many of us in this room may have grown up writing, but the "writing problem" has been around for a long, long time. Even in "our" day, in meetings just like this one, parents worried about the bad writing of their children.

**Teacher 2:** But certainly the role of language in people's lives has changed, hasn't it? We use the telephone more than ever; we get much more of our news and entertainment through television and the electronic media. The students I see don't have the same motivation to write that we may have had in the pre-electronic dark ages.

**Parent 2:** Then why is there so much focus on *writing?* Didn't somebody once say, "Print is dead"? Or at least dying?

**Parent 3:** Not in college it isn't. My older kids have had a terrible time writing in college, so I want to know why the school hasn't done its job in the past, why it has waited until now to do something.

**Teacher 3:** It's an interesting contrast, isn't it? On the one hand, the demands for writing (at least in college) are as greater or greater than ever. On the other hand, we have the feeling that electronic media have altered the need for us to write at all.

**Teacher 4:** And we've tried to account for that in our writing program—or, perhaps, I should more accurately call it a *composition* program. As you've seen, we plan to have students write—or compose—in many different forms and genres, to write poems as well as essays, scripts and stories as well as exposition.

**Parent 4:** That's precisely what bothers me. All this emphasis on *creativity* and *expression*. I mean, come on, now. We're not raising kids to be poets or playwrights; we're raising them to go to school and then to get out and get good jobs. I think the program is focusing too much on frills.

**Teacher 4:** But if I could jump back to the previous point. The one about preparation for college or the workplace. The research in writing has helped us see that just concentrating narrowly on writing like the essay or the business memorandum doesn't really produce highly literate students. They may know the forms, but that doesn't mean that they'll be able to conquer new writing tasks successfully.

**Teacher 3:** Ironically, the very fact that we concentrated so much on essay writing in the past may be, in part, why students have so much trouble in college.

**Parent 4:** But *poetry?*

**Teacher 5:** We're not trying to make poets out of your children. But we do recognize that writing a poem or a script or a short story or any of the so-called creative forms involves students in organizing ideas and using language in ways that are fundamentally helpful even in practical writing. We don't want kids to write rhyming memos filled with metaphors and similes, but it's true that writing poetry with force and imagery does encourage one to write compactly, precisely, and without wasted words. Aren't those also the traits of a good memo?

**Parent 5:** I'm concerned about your standards, in whatever they write. Like, the other day, my daughter came home with a composition from language arts and there were four misspellings and some grammatical errors. Nobody had bothered to correct these. Don't teachers know the difference anymore? Don't they care?

**Teacher 6:** Of course we care, and, believe it or not, most of us can still spell and use good grammar. In your daughter's case, what she brought home was a draft of her work. The errors hadn't been corrected because she hadn't reached the proofreading stage. We get to that when students are preparing final copy.

**Parent 5:** It makes no sense to me. An error is an error. In my day, when we made a mistake, there was no coddling; we were told when we were wrong.

**Teacher 6:** So how do you feel about writing today? Do you like to write?

**Parent 5:** Me? Oh good grief, no. I'm not a good writer. Never was. I could never get it right for my teachers, so I certainly don't do much of it now.

**Teacher 6:** Well, that's part of the point then, isn't it? Your experience is actually quite common. People who have been overly corrected or overly criticized are often so afraid of making mistakes, they just quit writing. In our program, we put errors into an appropriate context, and we do, honestly, teach students to correct them when they are finishing up their work. But to dwell on errors too soon, too much, doesn't correct those errors. All it does is make people self-conscious about their writing.

**Parent 6:** So where's the proof? I mean, you've given us a lot of talk about this program—a lot of claims that if you don't correct errors and don't just teach essays that students will learn to write. But where's the proof? I mean, do you have some test results we can see?

**Teacher 1:** Well, there will be test scores coming out. The students have just taken their state assessment, and we are just as concerned as you parents about how well your children do. We have confidence that our students' experience has allowed them to meet the minimums required by tests and given them valuable knowledge and skills not measured by standardized tests.

**Teacher 2:** But where's the proof, you ask? We have portfolios for each of your children in which we assess their progress, and with their permission, we will share these with parents. In addition, they have prepared showcase portfolios, which contain their best work to date, with their own assessments of progress.

**Teacher 3:** Students have also created individual bound books, which are propped along the back wall. Please enjoy those during your refreshments later. And remember, please, that these were created by all our students, not just the "gifted" or the college bound.

**Teacher 4:** And we also have copies of a small magazine our students have produced, and the kids have done all of it, from writing and editing and proofreading down to doing the page layout on our desktop publishing program.

**Parent 7:** I'm interested in my child's access to computers. We don't have a computer at home, and from what I understand, they will be pretty important for my child's future, no matter what she plans to do. Will she get lots of chances to learn how to use one?

**Teacher 5:** We're working on getting greater computer access in our classrooms and media center in order to give all kids a chance to do their composing on a word processor, to learn how to do spell checks and grammar checks during the writing process, and to do polished publications and final copies printed on the computer.

**Teacher 4:** And we're teaching them to be careful with those editing and spelling programs. I had one student who rewrote "Goldilocks and the Three Bears," only she spelled bears B–A–R–E–S throughout the paper. But yes, we realize students need word processing skills, and they learn them very quickly as they compose on the computer.

**Parent 6:** What about Internet access and using the computer for research? Shouldn't students be using all those wonderful resources that are so readily available?

**Teacher 1:** We certainly recognize the need for students to have access to the Internet, and we should be connected soon. You're right that there are many rich and wonderful resources—magazines, newspapers, catalogs, and people around the world—and we certainly want students to make use of both the interactive and the traditional resources on the web. More important, however, is teaching students to use those sources well. There's a lot of junk out there and we want students to learn to make distinctions between the good and the useless.

**Parent 5:** How do we know that our kids aren't going to sites that are inappropriate for them? I don't want my child reading pornography.

**Teacher 2:** We'll send permission slips home for you to sign before we let your child do Internet searches, and we'll ask kids to sign agreements to use the Internet for appropriate school purposes. And just like with other library research, we'll be talking with kids about what they're finding and how they plan to use it. We think that kids basically have good sense about this and are eager to use the Internet well.

**Teacher 3:** We'd love to have you come to our classes, work with kids on their research. . .

**Teacher 5:** In fact, we can use parental support in so many ways. We're having a Young Authors' Conference next month, where youngsters of different backgrounds from all over the district will get together to read and share their writing with each other and with adults. We could use some parent volunteers for that program, too, parents to meet with small groups of authors and to help them share.

**Teacher 4:** And we could also use help in our publishing programs, and in assisting students in proofreading their own work, so you could see how the system works. . .

**Principal:** Enough. Let's not scare them off, eh? But clearly, parents, these teachers respect your questions and value your ideas. We hope you'll stick around for more talk and that you'll remain interested in our program far into the future.

# f·o·u·r

# Ideas for Teaching Language

**language** (lan'-gwij) [Middle English, Old French, from *langue,* tongue, language] An arbitrary system of signs and symbols by which people communicate and interact.

The dictionary definition just begins to hint at the possibilities and problems of "langwij." It shows, rightly, that our language is deeply rooted in speech and that we use an "arbitrary" and conventionalized set of symbols to communicate. That is, it seems to be part of human nature for people to select collections of sounds, to assign meaning to them, and to string them together at high speed in order to transmit messages. This process seems to us little short of a miracle, part of the larger miracle of humanity in general.

But the dictionary—limited as it is to conveying mostly the denotative or "content" part of words—cannot begin to encompass the true miracle of language: its magic and mind-boggling properties and capabilities, its poetry and its science. Words refuse to hold still for scrutiny, much less dictionary making; sentences coil and recoil upon themselves in infinite variety; discourse stretches farther than the eye can see or the ear can hear.

Nor does the dictionary say anything about the teaching of language. It might have added:

**language**. "the use of which drives English language arts teachers and their students crazy."

Or: "that which upsets everybody but few people are willing to do anything about."

More positively, and moving beyond the limits of the dictionary, we'll offer the following:

**language**. "The unifying element of the language arts."

Or, more positively still:

**language**. "Source of endless possibilities for exploration and inquiry."

We think the potential of language to serve as both the *content* and the *medium* of English language arts is extraordinary. In classes for the youngest to the oldest students, we can explore how language systems work; how they shape and are shaped by people; how they serve as media for the declaration of learning, expression of emotions, elucidation of facts and concepts, and articulation of truths and lies; and how they form the very fiber of curses, spells, incantations, prayers, pranks, wishes and dreams, plans and designs, and, above all, *literatures* in every land and culture.

That's why people hold language in such reverence and even awe:

"In the beginning was the word." (Genesis)

"Perhaps of all the creations of man, language is the most astonishing." (Lytton Strachey)

"People's speech is the skin of its culture." (Max Lerner)

"If you will scoff at language study how, save in terms of language, will you scoff?" (Mario Pei)

One of the continuing challenges to the English language arts teacher is that language is used so widely, yet understood so poorly by its users. Everybody, it seems, is an expert on language, and everybody and their brothers and sisters is an expert on language teaching, on what school teachers should be doing, about the alleged decline of language, and about the good old days of grammar and spelling. (And everybody and their siblings have equal stores of bad stories about language: about communications failures, about saying the wrong thing at the wrong time, and, unfortunately, about an English teacher who made them feel ashamed of the way they talk.)

Our aim in this section of *The English Language Arts Handbook* is no less than to demystify language study and explore its fullest dimensions, for you as a teacher and, indirectly through you, for generations of students.

We'll begin by examining what is traditionally the most limited aspect of language in the schools: grammar and its associated concerns of dialects and correctness. Without ignoring these standard curriculum components (the components many parents and administrators misperceive as being the heart of our discipline), we'll go on to show the kinds of language explorations that teachers can engage in to help kids feel at home in the linguistic milieu they've been a part of from the day they were born. We'll show how language study is not only a way of unifying English language arts studies, but of bringing coherence to the whole school curriculum.

And we'll offer the theory and the challenge that every class, every day, provides opportunities to help students become smart, critical, well-informed users of language, whether it's their mother tongue or a second or third language. Hog-tied by standards, shipwrecked in seas of bureaucracy, or bedeviled by conflicting mandates, you, the teacher of

English language arts, can turn every utterance into an opportunity for study, not in the gradgrindian sense of conventional linguistic scholarship (though who knows, many of your students may find language interesting enough that they want to follow it as a career), but in the sense of joyful inquisition and linguistic gamesmanship.

Proof? Say the following ten times rapidly without laughing: "The pickled Pied Piper pontificated pugilistically." If you succeed, conduct a tongue-twister duel with your local champion.

# Chapter Eleven

# Grammar, Dialects, and Correctness

Grammar as a doomsday device!

We first encountered the term "doomsday device" in Stanley Kubrick's classic film *Dr. Strangelove*, released in 1964 at the height of the cold war. A doomsday device, as Peter Sellers/Dr. Strangelove explains, is a nuclear-equipped intercontinental ballistic missile programmed to go off whenever radiation levels reach a certain point. Thus, if a population has been totally wiped out in a nuclear attack, the doomsday device will launch a counterattack, even if no one on the planet is left alive!

Not long ago, we recalled the doomsday device when we saw a seemingly innocent photograph in the newspaper: A girl in her early teens was filling in blanks on a worksheet, and if you turned the paper at an angle, you could read its title: "Relative Clause Pronouns." An accompanying article explained that an area middle school teacher was going against the current fashion and actually teaching students grammar. "Without it," she explained, "they are lost." Just how they were "lost" was not explained in the newspaper, and we were perplexed, since research into formal grammar instruction throughout much of the twentieth century has failed to reveal any significant relationship between knowledge of grammar and the ability to use language in speech and writing.

The student in the phonograph—that innocent and probably dutiful young person—seems to us to be a twenty-first century doomsday device. If the research is correct (and we'll discuss more about why we think it is), that student will not necessarily benefit from filling out blanks and identifying relative clause pronouns, but we confidently predict that at some point in the future, maybe twenty years down the road when she has a teenager of her own, she'll go off and launch a counterattack, berating her child's English language arts teacher for failing to teach grammar. You've heard the refrain, we're sure: "Why, in my day, we knew grammar and talked right. Young people nowadays just don't have any respect for good grammar!" We also believe that her explosion will have no more effect than a nuclear missile fired into a land from which human life has already been exterminated.

Over the years, grammar has probably generated more discussion, debate, acrimony, and maybe even fistfights than any other component of the English language arts curriculum. There are teachers who say they are "for" grammar, and those who are "against" it (never mind that both use "grammar" every time they open their mouths to speak). There are traditionalists who call for a return to sentence diagramming, cultural pluralists who want a broadening of the definitions of correctness, and eclectics who say, "I'll do whatever seems to work as long as test scores go up (and nothing seems to achieve that purpose reliably)."

The brouhaha over grammar has had a debilitating effect on English studies, for instead of discussing how to get kids to read more, write more, think more, and talk more articulately, we've spent entirely too much time debating whether or not students ought to be studying transitive and intransitive verbs, gerunds and gerundives, and the reality of a dative case in English. (Grammatical query: Do language arts teachers *lay* or *lie* better?)

Seldom have combatants in the great grammar debate bothered to begin by following a simple rule from general semantics and common sense: Define your terms. As lexicographers know, words used in diverse situations take on multiple meanings. What angry parents mean when they ask "Why don't you teach our child grammar?" is not what teachers mean when they say "I don't teach formal grammar," which is not what linguists mean when they say "Grammar provides the rules that everyone must follow in speech." In case you've never looked it up, here's what Webster's tells us about the origins of *grammar*. First the derivation:

> Old French *gramaire*, from Latin *grammatica*, from Greek *grammatikē*, from feminine of *grammatikos*, skilled in grammar, from *gramma*, letter, from the root of *graphein*, to write.

It's interesting to note the very close connection between grammar and the written word. Linguists recognize that there are important differences between the grammars of spoken and written English. However, schoolteachers will be quick to tell you that errors in written English cause particularly violent responses from the public.

Now the definitions of *grammar:*

1. The science of treating of classes of words, their inflections, and their syntactical relations and functions.
2. A treatise on grammar.
3. Manner of speaking or writing, with reference to grammatical rules.

(*Merriam-Webster's Collegiate Dictionary, Tenth Edition*. Copyright © 1998 by Merriam-Webster, Incorporated)

A key distinction must be noted between the first and third meanings:

The first meaning is that of a linguist or an informed language arts teacher: Grammar is a study of the system of English, how words fit together in our language. (We'll call that grammar[1].) The third meaning, grammar[3], has to do with language in actual use in society: In the eye of the public, grammar[3] is extraordinarily broad in scope, ranging from whether to say "may I" or "can I" to good penmanship to double negatives. In fact, grammar[3] probably ought to be called "language in use," because it has many elements (such as penmanship and politeness) that have little to do with grammar.

Grammar[2] is a textbook, technically a "treatise" on grammar. But as often as not, you'll find that a grammar[2] book contains a wide range of information about the language, some of it having to do with the way sentences are put together, but much of it actually peripheral, including telephone manners, how to address a letter, and how to look up topics in the library.

For generations, teachers have presented grammar[1] (the system of English) through grammar[2] (handbooks of usage and style) in the hopes of changing what students do with grammar[3] (speaking, writing papers, using good English). Has it worked? Generations of schoolchildren know intuitively that the answer is no. And, as we noted in our discussion of the doomsday grammarkinder, nearly a century of research in this topic has failed to show a connection. In study after study, researchers have presented grammar[1] and later measured students' use of language, looking for improvements (sometimes in what we might call grammar[4], standardized tests and worksheets decontextualized from language in use—i.e., grammar as doomsday device). And in study after study, they've come up with no significant differences.

We must be cautious in interpreting such studies, however. Clearly some people (children and adults) are capable of translating the abstractions of grammar[1] into operations they can execute in their speaking and writing. For example, we know people who can distinguish between feeling *bad* and *badly* by observing that one word is an adjective that can be applied to objects while the other, as an adverb, describes or modifies an action. Thus *bad* describes one's physical state, while *badly,* used to describe feeling, would describe tactile skill. Others of us either have to look it up every time or memorize a rule or slogan: "To feel badly means you've got no sense of touch."

The research into applications of grammar[1] necessarily has to be conducted with large numbers of students, so perhaps it's not surprising that the results are a wash. For every kid who understands the abstractions and applies them, there's at least one other kid who feels bad about the whole thing and cannot make those connections. We've long believed that if you could separate those students who have a propensity for learning through abstract principles and teach them grammar[1], you could probably show some effects on their language use. But most teachers teach heterogeneous learners (even in so-called homogeneous classes), so a pure grammar[1] approach is likely to fail.

We don't want to argue that grammar[1] should never be taught or should be taught only to those who have a propensity for learning from it. But we do want to make clear our research-supported conviction that the wholesale teaching of grammar[1] (or its poor cousin, the textbook, grammar[3]) to all kids with the expectation that they will all become model speakers/writers of standard English was an inappropriate language-teaching goal from the outset.

If the research evidence does not justify teaching large amounts of grammar[1] in an effort to make children write and speak better, what should we do, especially given the clamor of parents, administrators, and school leaders for more grammar? Grammar[1], Grammar[2], and Grammar[3] all have a place in the school program. Teachers would be wrong (not to mention naïve) to say that they don't care about correctness or that grammar doesn't matter. The problem, again, is in blurring distinctions and teaching one form of grammar thinking that it will produce changes in language use. We'll take up each of the grammars in this chapter.

# Teaching Grammar[1]: The Systems of Language

Both linguists and teachers have discovered that exploring the way English (or any language) operates can be engaging and rewarding for students *if* it is separated from the felt need to change people's language behavior. That is, grammar is interesting to examine in its own right. Try some of the following with your students:

- Say "good morning" to them, and no matter what they reply, ask them how they knew what you meant. How did they know you meant "hello" or "let's get started," rather than "mornings are inherently good" or "this particular morning is good"? Use the discussion that follows to help students see that they are competent in a very sophisticated language system. (Also teach them that wonderful Australian greeting and farewell, "G'day.")

- Bring in copies of Lewis Carroll's "Jabberwocky," with its nonsense words:

'Twas *brillig,* and the *slithy toves*
Did *gyre* and *gimbal* in the *wabe:*
All *mimsy* were the *borogoves,*
And the *mome wrath outgrabe.*

The italicized words were coined by Carroll to create images, and students enjoy talking about words like *slithy, toves,* and *brillig* to see why and how those words carry meaning, even when they aren't in the dictionary. Further, in an elementary parts-of-speech lesson, students can understand that *outgrabe* is some sort of action, while *toves* are things and *slithy* is an attribute or characteristic of a *tove.* In the process of discussing this knowledge that the students already possess, you can refer to terms like *noun, verb,* and *adjective,* which they've probably met before if they're in fifth grade or above.

- Teach parts of speech independently of rules of usage. That is, don't muddy the waters of teaching *nouns* and *verbs* by immediately introducing rules for the agreement of *subject* and *predicate.* We've found that one can teach recognition of basic parts of speech quite rapidly from the middle elementary years on up using some of the following approaches.

  - Instead of using textbook lessons, teach parts of speech using readily available materials: newspapers, a textbook chapter, school memoranda. Start with the stuff of life: the nouns and the verbs, the objects and the actions. Introduce *is* as an equal sign, the *verb of being. Adjectives* and *adverbs* follow, along with the concept of modification. Don't fuss overmuch with connectors: *determiners, prepositions,* and *interjections.* Over time, work these gap-bridgers into the discussion. (For a more detailed discussion of this approach, see Chapter 6 in Lee Thomas and Stephen Tchudi's *The English Language: An Owner's Manual* [1999]).

  - Have a debate over which is more important, nouns or verbs (a debate that will likely end in a draw).

  - Analyze parts of speech in newspaper headlines, noting how the lack of connectors sometimes leads to ambiguities.

- Teach simple sentence diagrams. (This may seem like heresy to some antigrammar teachers, but if separated from usage rules, sentence diagramming is easy to master and does give students a visual sense of grammar[1].)

- Teach parts of speech through the structural grammarian's device of substitution frames. That is, instead of (or along with) traditional definitions, show students that particular slots in sentences are filled with similar words:

The (*noun*) walked.
The cowpoke (*verbed*).
She came (*preposition*) the party.
"(*Interjection*)!" he shouted.

You and your students can experiment to develop a series of substitution frames that reliably identify parts of speech in (*adjective*) situations. Along the way you can reinforce students' realization that they have already gotten a great deal of grammar under control just by mastering the language.

- Experiment with plurals of nonsense syllables: one *wonkaloony*, two *wonkaloon*_____. What's the rule in English for turning unfamiliar words into plurals? Also discuss some of the irregular plurals in English (one *deer*, a herd of _____). (As an offshoot, also explore some of the interesting group names we have in English for collections of critters: a *pride* of lions, a *flock* of sheep, a *gaggle* of geese. Have students create some imaginative group terms of their own, e.g., a _____ of football players—perhaps a "punting"? A _____ of cheerleaders— possibly also a "gaggle"?) How is it that students can automatically supply the correct plural for a nonexistent word?

- Changing parts of speech. Students can also intuitively change actual or nonsense words into other parts of speech. Thus, if a person *outgrabes* (verb) regularly, he or she is an *outgrab*—(the noun form). How do you turn *belch* (as in "What a magnificent belch") from a noun to a verb? (In this case, the form is the same in the present tense, as in "I belch you." But why is that previous example both English and non-English? How does one use "belch" as a verb?)

- Study Esperanto. This artificial language, created by Polish opthamologist L. L. Zamenhof in 1887, has been studied and learned for over a century and has an estimated seven million speakers worldwide. The grammar of Esperanto is simple and regular and, taught to students, helps them understand English grammar as well (for the same reason that students of Latin often find their understanding of English grammar deepened). For the first of a free series of postcard lessons, write the Esperanto League of North America, P.O. Box 1125, El Cerrito, California, 94530.

- Compare foreign languages. If your students are studying some Spanish or French or maybe Latin, or, praise be, if they come to you as native speakers of Chinese or Japanese or Yiddish or Italian, have them describe the grammar (or system) of that language for students to study. How do different languages communicate meaning? Does word order matter (it certainly does in English)? Are words in the language inflected with endings (or beginnings) that signal meaning?

- Teach your grammar[2] textbook, *selectively*. If your school has an adopted grammar series or if the curriculum requires coverage, you can do so without destroying students' love of language.
  - Separate the grammar[1] information from correctness.
  - Don't assign all forty-seven fill-in-the-blank usage exercises for each lesson.
  - Supplement sterile textbook examples with newspaper clippings.
  - Help students keep straight on the distinctions between the three grammars, even if the book doesn't.
  - Invent your own "fun and games exercises" for students. Have a Noun Day when every kid brings in a favorite object/noun, then creates adjectives to describe it and adverbs to describe how he or she feels about it. Play charades with verbs. Invite kids to write a paragraph using only verbs of being (is, will be, was, were), then have them write a paragraph using only active verbs (punch, kick, claw, grammarize).

# How Much Grammar[1]?

When should grammar[1] be taught? How often? To whom? With what expectations?

We'll start with a negative: We wish diligently to avoid the traditional school pattern of teaching grammar (parts of speech, sentence functions, usage rules) over and over and over. If you look at many adopted text series, you'll see that this is precisely what happens; it's the same material year after year, a tacit acknowledgment that grammar didn't "take" the first or second or third time. Moreover, despite periodic allegations from the public or the press that nobody teaches grammar anymore, a simple poll of students (and their parents) will quickly establish the facts: Everybody *has* had grammar, probably more than once, probably several times, and, for the most part, without salutary effect.

More positively, we find that in every language arts class there are opportunities to discuss language-as-system every day:

- A kid tells a joke. Did we get it? Jokes are essentially linguistic tricks involving turns of phrase, and this is for all jokes, not just puns. Collect jokes; analyze jokes; let your students figure out what in language makes something funny. ("Why," asks a cartoon character, "doesn't the dictionary spell *phonetically* phonetically?")

- Somebody uses a simile or a metaphor: "The referee was blind as a bat." "He was blasted." Pause for a moment to note how this language works by substituting a surprising word, a mind-expanding word, for one we would ordinarily see in a syntax slot.
- Students are puzzling over a poem—a sonnet by Shakespeare, a limerick by Lear, a goofy verse by Shel Silverstein. Opportunities arise for us to help kids see how syntax works, how we go about unlocking language puzzles in literature. Wordsworth writes:

The City now, doth, like a garment, wear
The beauty of the morning; silent, bare,
Ships, towers, domes, theaters, and temples lie
Open unto the fields, and to the sky.

Take time to savor the images, the pictures, then have students look at the way the poet uses grammar[1] to effect: How does the metaphor work? What is the effect of the lists? Did anyone notice that the poem rhymes? How did Wordsworth have to shift his syntax to get those lines to come out rhyming?

- Collect the language of billboards and bumper stickers, morals and maxims, clichés and truisms. How does each of these create a grammatical one-liner? What is effective about their use of grammar to pack a lot of punch into an eyeblink's worth of language?

# Grammar[2]: Books About Language

A major publisher reissued its basic high school handbook with the claim "It's passed the test of time with millions and millions of students." That's the sort of sentence we'd like to turn over to a group of students for linguistic analysis. Like many advertising claims, it implies much and explains very little. Which "millions" of students spoke up in favor of their dear old schoolhouse grammar book? How much time has passed (and how slowly did it creep)? What tests were passed (and who gave them)? The fact is that school grammars (grammars[2]) have largely failed the test of time for millions of students according to such simple criteria as (a) whether or not the students learned to use language with a reasonable degree of correctness, (b) whether they came to understand the nature of language itself, and (c) whether they are at ease with themselves as speakers/writers.

As we've suggested, the typical school grammar is an odd mix of description and prescription about language, a mismatch of instruction and drill, a curious combination of half-truths about contemporary usage. In recent years, texts have been superficially modernized, often with reference to "the writing process" and by shifting instruction into boxes euphemistically labeled "editorial workshop" or "mini-lesson." So we see the school grammars[2] as having remained largely unchanged, except for cosmetic and semantic alterations from time to time.

Nevertheless, there are some good books describing language that can be helpful to teachers and students, especially if we keep in mind why we are presenting material to students and what we hope to accomplish.

---

- Adult books on grammar. Instead of spending (literally) tens of thousands of dollars buying (literally) tons of grammar books, school districts should invest in smaller numbers of *adult* grammars. No, these are not X-rated. They're accessible "linguistic treatises" that help teachers (and perhaps a few advanced senior high students) learn more about the language. In particular, if you feel a little shaky about your knowledge of grammar (and, in our experience, just about everybody does), you might look at a book that describes grammar from a linguistic, rather than prescriptive, point of view. We've listed our personal choices of good adult grammar books at the close of this chapter.

- Usage handbooks. Here we favor short, well-indexed reference books rather than thick compendia. Our personal favorite at the moment is Diana Hacker's *Pocket Manual of Style*. This thin spiral-bound book, with the table of contents and index inside the front and back covers for convenience, includes brief, well-illustrated discussions of clarity, formal grammar, usage items, punctuation, and mechanics, all arranged in a user-friendly fashion. There are a number of similar short usage books on the market; check your local trade bookstore to find your favorite.

- Dictionaries. Here again we stray a bit from the definition of grammar[2] as a treatise on syntax, but obviously dictionaries are an important source of linguistic information for students, and most dictionaries carry enough information on grammar and usage that they qualify under this category. We think it's important that dictionaries be seen as helpful tools, not as punishment. Thus we don't have much faith in dictionary drills ("Look up these ten peculiar and little-known words"), and we don't believe in forcing dictionary use ("Don't ask me what it means; look it up!"). We do think kids should have dictionaries handy and feel comfortable using them. One of our favorite activities is to have students "adopt" a word—a curious one like *skulk* or *winnow* or *flaunt* or *flout* or *founder*—then look it up in the dictionary to become an expert on its origins and meanings. We then hold a get-acquainted session where people wear their words as name tags. (Ah, I see you are flaunting the fact you are a flautist!)

- Spelling guides. A big problem with dictionaries is that one needs to know how to spell a word to be able to find out how to spell it. (Not unlike looking up "phonetically.") A handy alternative is a list of commonly misspelled word; these are often available commercially, sometimes on a single laminated sheet that fits in a notebook. Even better, we think, is for kids to create their own "spelling demon" lists of their personal troublesome words, which are often much shorter than the commercial lists. We like lists because students can scan them quickly and find the word they need without flipping through many pages. Of course, for simplicity, explore:

- The spelling checker. As more and more schools and kids have access to word processors, it makes sense for teachers to encourage the use of this tool. Although some people have argued that the spelling checker is the work of the devil (like the hand-held calculator that has allegedly eliminated knowledge of the timestables among kids), we fully endorse the use of the computerized spelling list, and think it may well have pedagogical value. As a spelling checker scrolls through a student's paper, it not only identifies irregular spellings, but offers alternatives. To make use of the alternatives, the student has to think through what he or she wrote and what the standard spelling might be. In the case of words that are not in the program's lexicon, the student can make a conscious decision to add the word to the list. Rather than destroying spelling skills, we think the spelling checker can be a useful ally in developing them. Of course, the spelling checker is not perfect; in particular, it is blind to homonyms and cannot tell *their* from *there, too* from *two*. Even here, then, the checker encourages growth in spelling by forcing students to take responsibility for their decisions.

- The thesaurus. The utilization of thesauri thrusts numerous scholars into portly misfortune because they utilize phraseology possessive of inappropriate implications. (We wrote that last sentence by substituting thesaurus synonyms in the sentence "The use of the thesaurus gets a lot of students into big trouble because they use words with wrong connotations.") Occasionally a thesaurus (either a paper version or the one built into a word processor) is useful for finding just the right word or for locating a word that is on the tip of your tongue. (You can find that word by looking up its synonym.) Show students a thesaurus; explain how it works and caution against misuse; and keep it on the reference shelf.

- Secretary's manuals. These little volumes, available inexpensively in paperback, are a gold mine of information. A good secretary's manual contains all the usage advice of a schoolroom grammar but places it in a less pedantic, more useful form. A typical secretary's manual contains spelling lists, some basic rules of usage, disputed usage items, business letter format, information on library use, and tips on manuscript preparation. Dollar for dollar, they are the most practical grammar[2] around.

- Computer grammar checkers. We're interested in computer grammar[2] programs for their immediate use in helping with proofreading, but also for their indirect effect: They teach a little grammar, spelling, mechanics, and usage on the side. For example, our word processor includes a "word alert" program (for usage items), "phrase alert" (for clichés and some grammatical constructions like passive voice), and a "punctuation check." When it flags something in our writing, it offers a brief, practical lesson: Don't put a comma after "than." Do you mean "to," "too," or "two"? Students who receive such online help with their writing can pick up a great deal of grammatical information on their own. The problem with such systems, we find, is that the knowledge they offer is more sophisticated than many novice writers can assimilate. That is, you have to know grammar and usage to use the information. (In turn, if you know grammar, you probably don't need the computerized grammar checker.) On the whole, however, we think most of these programs are modestly helpful, and a quicker source of information than a book version of a grammar[2].

# Grammar[3]: Dialects and Correctness

As just about everybody knows, English usage is not constant. It varies from one part of the country to another and within regions. The hill country accents of Tennessee are not those of West Virginia; Texans don't talk quite like Oklahomans; you can easily separate a true Down-Easter from a Bostonian, even though they both speak a New England dialect. Usage varies in vocabulary, syntax, intonation, and pronunciation, and it differs according to ethnic origins, social settings, educational contexts, and content. And of course, dialects are also a reflection of one's native and second language. Moreover, the conventions of usage change over time.

The point is that usage—grammar[3]—is not always determined by hard-

and-fast rules or even by written-down rules; it is, as Robert Pooley noted in 1945 in his classic book, *Understanding English Usage,* a product of custom and tradition. It's also a byproduct of face-to-face contact, for whenever dialect communities encounter one another, they tend to exchange language along with information, commodities, or punches. The basic structure and vocabulary of English grew from such encounters between Celts, Anglo Saxons, Danes, Romans, Normans, and the church. Today it continues to change with new cultural forces and encounters. Language is, to use the terminology of current scholarship, a matter of *social construction;* to use a language, you have to buy into the culture of its users, *even as you contribute to that culture and change its language.*

For many years, English language arts teachers taught a status dialect, standard English (SE), essentially the form of the language presented in usage handbooks and the language spoken by six o'clock newscasters on national television. It is a "prestige" or standard dialect more as a result of the power of its speakers (the white majorities in England, New Zealand, Australia, Canada, and the United States) than of any innate superiority or elegance. As linguists point out, *all* dialects "work"; each form of speaking or writing is essentially as successful as any other.

Thus teachers are no longer in a position to say that the "best" or proper form of the language is standard English. (Actually we should say standard Englishes; for despite some national or international common characteristics, the SE in London is clearly different from that in New York or Auckland or Sydney or Toronto.)

Yet we also know that SE (in its various forms) *matters.* Kids who don't use standard spellings will have their job applications rejected; those who employ nonstandard usage in placement tests will wind up in remedial writing courses (even though they may be quite articulate). Folks who write in standard English have a better chance of having their letters to the editor published; those who speak SE will be listened to more carefully in public settings than those who don't (if the latter can even work up the needed moxie to speak publicly in the first place). There are several alternative approaches to SE available to the teacher. Advocates of the various positions are:

1. *Enforcer.* The enforcer is the traditional schoolteacher who will accept only standard English in the classroom, who feels it is the duty of the school to get all students talking and writing this real-yet-ephemeral dialect. Among the enforcers we also list the members of the "English only" movement, who are, with all-too-considerable success, having English declared an official language, and trying to force people who do not have English as a first language to convert to our "mother" tongue.

2. *Bidialectalist.* Every person is "bidialectal" to some extent in that we all switch vocal registers and change speech codes at various times for various audiences. (In fact, as an interesting classroom exercise, have your students do their impressions of various dialects; you and they may be surprised at how much bidialectal knowledge they already have.) The bidialectal approach argues that people can retain their natural dialect (the dialect of "home") while learning to use SE for public occasions. Without attempting to demean the home dialect; indeed, while accepting and even rejoicing in its resources, the bidialectal advocate tries to nudge students in the direction of SE so they have options and are not prevented from achieving success. Unfortunately, true bidialectalism is very rare, and unless there are powerful socioeconomic forces pushing a dialect speaker to SE, bidialectal approaches often seem indistinguishable from the enforcer position. Moreover, there are serious language policy issues involved in bidialectalism. For one, bidialectalism is a "one-way street"; that is, for the most part only children from lower socioeconomic or minority cultures are asked to make the change, while children of the ethnic and economic majorities are not expected to alter the way they speak. Since, as we've seen, standard English is not a preordained or particularly excellent form of the language, the bidialectal approach can be seen as discriminatory, despite its apparently solid foundations in language.

3. *Expansionist.* This third kind of teacher argues against enforcing a single standard and, in a sense, bypasses the problems of the bidialectal model by arguing that we owe it to *all* kids to increase their understanding and use of language. An expansionist argues that the way to help people improve their competence as writers and speakers is not to force them to change, but to expand their opportunities to use language in real situations. In this camp, too, are the proponents of "English plus" (offered as an alternative to "English only"), who say that all kids ought to become acquainted with more languages than just their native tongue.

We of course recognize that standard English "matters," that there are penalties for the inability to use it in certain situations. We also state unequivocally that *correctness* matters, that the schools have a responsibility to prepare students who can write for a variety of audiences, including putting the finishing touches on surface structure.

In our teaching, then, we first of all try to individualize our instruction. Who are these students? Who is *this* student? What has been their previous experience with language? What is their range of dialects? Is "correctness" a possible barrier to their success?

Second, we adjust our response to students' work based on that assessment. For the non-native speaker of English, new to the country, new to our school, we focus almost exclusively on fluency, on helping students get down basic ideas in whatever language they can manage. Following the language experience approach, we encourage students to write about their own lives, to write from their experience prior to coming to our classroom. We introduce the elements of English usage and correctness gradually, usually in the context of the students' own writing and speech, always with the audience in mind: What changes are necessary to help this student be successful with language at this point in time?

For the native speaker who may have a nonstandard dialect, for practical purposes, we take the same fundamental approach. First we figure out where the kid is situated on the spectrum of language use; second, we try to expand the range of experiences, encouraging students to draw on their own ideas and experiences before moving on; third, we adjust our response and the reading and writing workshop to help nudge the students along, so that, once again they experience success with their chosen audiences.

Now we turn to the hypothetical accomplished student, one who, for whatever reasons, is in full control of standard English. Would it surprise you to learn that we take the same fundamental approach? First, figure out where the kid is in language skill; second, help him or her enlarge the range of reading and writing experiences; third, provide help and support appropriate for that student's needs.

Such an approach may sound extraordinarily complex, impossible to manage in a classroom of thirty or thirty-five students. However, such individualization *does* come with practice and effort; more important, it is vastly more efficient than the traditional approach to grammar. The time not spent giving endless grammar lessons and worksheets on relative clause pronouns is converted to class writing and speaking time, time for individual conferences, and time for the quick or occasional writing hint to a student. Expansionist: a little at time.

And above all, we think it is crucial that the expansionist position be firmly rooted in students understanding how language works. We include attention to dialects and correctness. We think it's very important for students to have a context for correctness; to come to understand what dialects are, in general; to know what their own dialects are; to understand the implications of owning and using various dialects; and to have a sense of the social and political impact of dialects on dialect speakers (and everybody is a dialect speaker). By understanding the nature of these issues, students are empowered for the expansionist classroom.

Some activities for the expansionist classroom:

- Have students analyze their own language. Encourage them to keep a journal noting how they adjust their language for various settings: when they talk to the principal, when they call a friend on the phone, when they call an information source on the phone, when they speak to their parents or minister or teacher.

- Have them note how their oral language differs from the written standard. *Everybody* says (or "sez") "gonna" and "gotta." What other oral forms do they use, forms like "wanna," "doncha," "comin'," and "goin'." So if these are standard speech forms, why aren't they appropriate in standard English writing?

- Have students role-play language use in various settings: a college professor lecturing a class; a business executive discussing quality control; three ten-year-olds setting up a club; a public-address announcer at a football or basketball game; a disk jockey on any of the following stations: oldies, mellowies, country and western, seventies rock 'n' roll, hard rock. Have the students discuss the language range and usage employed.

- Do imitations. First caution students that these will be done in the spirit of inquiry, not to make fun of anybody. Then ask them to present imitations of dialects, along with impressions of famous people. Although the imitations may not be linguistically flawless, they provide excellent data for discussion of dialects. How does a person imitate Texan, Appalachian, or New England dialects? What are the speech characteristics of Clint Eastwood, Hugh Grant, Rosie O'Donnell, the president, and Kermit the Frog?

- Let a boy and a girl do improvisations of the same role: a business executive worried about the stock market, an angry parent, a person applying for a job, a person trying to find directions in an unfamiliar setting. How do they approach the task differently? How much of this can be attributed to the individual's personal style (John is generally quiet; Mary is socially energetic), how much to male/female role and language differences?

- Create slang dictionaries. The more diverse your class, the better this project will turn out. Have students collect slang or colloquial expressions that separate kids from adults and kids from one another.

- Explore dialects through television. In particular, have students watch the news for a week, with a tape recorder nearby to catch interviews with speakers of noticeable dialects. Use this raw material for further discussion of how dialects work.

- Conduct a unit in which students explore their own language roots. Although they may not be able to track their own family all the way back to non-English-speaking members, they certainly can learn of the linguistic trails left by their cultural or ethnic group. What languages did your American ancestors speak? What countries did they come from? What part of the United States did they settle in first? What English words come to us from the language of your ancestry? How did those words become part of American English?

- Discuss linguistic prejudice. Very likely your students will have some deep-seated biases, overtly or covertly. What impressions do they have of speakers of a Southern dialect, a Boston or Yankee dialect, Brooklynese, English, Irish, German, Indian, or Jamaican? Help them see ways of separating people from their dialects; that is, judging them as individuals, not as users of a dialect about which we have stereotypes.

- Study the origins of punctuation rules (the *Oxford English Dictionary* is an especially useful resource here). Do students know why a period was once called a "full stop"? Why the comma was a "half stop"? Given the origins of these marks as signals for pauses, help students think about their own recurring punctuation problems.

- Spend some time reviewing the history of English spelling. Help students understand how English spelling became regularized and why, because of its diverse linguistic origins, English spelling is so maddeningly inconsistent in the first place. Some students might like to read up on the various efforts that have been made over time to simplify English spelling and purge it of its oddities. Why have such efforts failed despite their logic?

- Have students create a personal list of spelling demons and try to figure out why particular words give them problems.

- Have students explore community attitudes toward language varieties. Let them develop a list of common variations or perceived errors in language and ask people to describe their reactions.

- Much has been written and said about the alleged unemployability of speaker of nonstandard dialects. Have students in your class survey employers to discover what expectations and demands employers have for workers in various jobs.

- Learn about the "English only" movement and its efforts to establish English as a national language. Also contact the National Council of Teachers of English for information on its policies concerning students' rights to their own language.

- Above all, from this study of grammar[3], help each student in your class develop an understanding of his or her language. In a journal or notebook, students might write about:

- o Their own dialect. Everybody has one. What's yours?
- o Where their dialects stand on the sociopolitical scale. Do they have a prestige dialect, or one that is regarded as nonstandard for business or college?
- o How their dialect represents them, their heritage, their culture.
- o What (if anything) they feel they need to do to change their dialect. (Tread carefully here: Do not force students with nonstandard dialects to pledge erasure—a voluntary-under-duress "enforcer" position.) We'd be most happy if, at the end of this unit, students said, "I am pleased with the way I talk, and I know what to do for people in power to be pleased (or, at least, nonjudgmental) about my speech."
- o What are their recurring problems with written English—not just dialects, mechanics, or spelling, but problems getting ideas down on the page?
- o Their own opinion on movements like English only or efforts to force the use of standard English on all students.

A final warning: Although we've begun this section of the *Handbook* with a discussion of grammar, it's crucial that grammar itself be put in a larger context. It's only a small bit of the world of language and an even smaller bit in the world of learning and inquiry, topics we take up in the next two chapters.

# Selected Readings

Burgess, Anthony. 1992. *A Mouthful of Air: Language, Languages—Especially English.* New York: Morrow.

Greenbaum, Sidney. 1996. *The Oxford English Grammar.* Oxford and New York: Oxford University Press.

Kaplan, Jeffrey. 1995. *English Grammar: Principles and Facts.* 2d ed. Englewood Cliffs, NJ: Prentice-Hall.

Gordon, Karen Elizabeth. 1993. *The Deluxe Transitive Vampire: The Ultimate Handbook of Grammar for the Innocent, the Eager, and the Doomed.* New York: Pantheon.

Thomas, Lee, and Stephen Tchudi. 1999. *The English Language: An Owner's Manual.* Boston: Allyn and Bacon.

# Chapter Twelve

# A Curriculum for George Orwell

Over a half-century ago George Orwell, in his now-classic essay "Politics and the English Language" (1946), argued that "the English language is in a bad way." He was especially concerned about language abuses, which he felt were leading to a blurring of thought, particularly in politics. Muddled language, he argued, reflected muddled and outright deceptive thinking, and citizens needed to be on the alert for it. In his then-futuristic novel *1984,* Orwell continued his exploration of language and thinking through the genre of fiction, showing a society whose language was controlled by an institutional "Big Brother." Orwell's worst fear for the future was that citizens would be trained in "doublethink": the ability to hold and discuss two contradictory ideas simultaneously.

Although Orwell's gloomy prophesies for 1984 did not come true, most observers of the language agree that the abuses he described are rampant, accentuated by our global communications network. Even today a committee of the National Council of Teachers of English presents a Doublespeak Award to the politician or bureaucrat who utters the worst batflegab during a year (and there are plenty of candidates). The committee also bestows the more prized Orwell Award for clear and precise use of the language.

George Orwell accurately described a vicious cycle: The English language "becomes ugly and inaccurate because our thoughts are foolish, but the slovenliness of our language makes it easier for us to have foolish thoughts." He was not ready to give up hope, however, for he believed that "the process is reversible."

In the previous chapter we discuss the nuts and bolts of grammar, dialects, and usage, but we also need a chapter dedicated to George Orwell to place those concerns about language mechanics in a broader context, that of language in society. As important as matters of correctness may be, it seems to us far more important that children (and adults) come to have a sensitivity to language, a knowledge and awareness of how it functions. When we see students struggling with writing, unable to write the fabled "cogent, coherent essay," and when we see them reluctantly stand up in class to mumble a vaguely formed opinion, then we see a problem far greater than grammar and correctness.

To some extent, we believe that the problems identified by Orwell are a negative by-product of content and experience: That is, language users sometimes waffle and grope and flounder and euphemize because they aren't experienced in the world and haven't had much of an opportunity to put ideas into language. The problem of language and experience is the topic of the first two sections of this book and can be partially cured through good composition and literature programs, where kids have lots of opportunities to read, talk, and write about ideas that range from personal experience to world issues.

But there's an element of language awareness and experience that's important as well. As S. I. Hayakawa pointed out in his classic, *Language and Thought in Action* (1990), a great many adults don't have the foggiest notion what language is all about. They confuse words—mere symbols—with the objects they stand for. They use name-calling as a substitute for rational discourse. They can't follow the semantic implications of discussions. They are vulnerable to the simplest linguistic tricks of propagandists and advertising agencies.

And as we enter the twenty-first century, the perils of language inexperience have never been greater. Although Big Brother does not literally exist, one could argue that television programming has taken over many of his functions, dictating cultural beliefs; shaping the news to appeal to listeners; and blurring the distinctions between hard news and dramatized facsimiles, between honest discourse and the blather of talk shows. Moreover, advertising—of both ideas and products—has never been more widespread and more effective. Big Brother may not exist for real, but advertising could probably create him.

Our "curriculum for George Orwell," then, is essentially a program to increase language consciousness and awareness. We think it's important for young people to develop a sophisticated understanding of the complexities of language. There are hundreds of exciting activities one can use in the English language arts classroom to help students understand the nature and functions of language. Not only are these activities engaging in their own right, they have both indirect and direct payoffs in helping students read, write, speak, and even think more clearly, articulately, and powerfully.

# Language Fun and Games

### Mrs. Jaypher

*A poem to be read "sententiously with grave importance":*
Mrs. Jaypher found a wafer
Which she stuck upon a note;
This she gave the cook.

Then she went and bought a boat
Which she paddled down the stream
Shouting: "Ice produces cream,
Beer when churned produces butter?
Henceforth all the words I utter
Distant ages thus shall note"
                    —Edward Lear (1812–1888)


**To Make an Amblongus Pie**

Take 4 pounds (say 4½ pounds) of fresh Amblongusses, and put them in a small pipkin. Cover them with water and boil them for eight hours incessantly, after which add 2 pints of new milk, and proceed to boil 4 hours more. When you have ascertained that the Amblongusses are quite soft, take them out and place them in a wide pan, taking care to shake them well previously. Grate some nutmeg over the surface, and cover them carefully with powdered gingerbread, curry-powder, and a sufficient quantity of Cayenne pepper. Remove the pan into the next room, and place it on the floor. Bring it back again and let it simmer for three quarters of an hour. Shake the pan violently till all the Amblongusses have become of a pale purple colour.

                                                        Edward Lear


Edward Lear knew just about as well as anybody that language is fun and games. It's important for teachers not to forget the important role that language play has in our mastery of English. Both adults and children enjoy the humorous use of language—puns, riddles, jokes, rhymes, puzzles, and satire. Children naturally create humor through language, and they respond to it with ease, without the intervention of teachers or instructors.

Language play goes well beyond humor, for most successful users have a sense of "the play of language," a feeling for words and language that allows them to explore and exploit the richness of English to make their meaning clear. We suggest that you play language games with your students regularly—keep copies of one or two games in your briefcase at all times; play a game when things grow dull or tense; use games as worthy time-fillers at the beginnings and ending of class. This is not mere fun and games; you'll be building a reservoir of linguistic understanding in your students. The following sampler of games will give you some of the possibilities.

---

- Jumbles. Many newspapers carry anagramatic jumble or search puzzles, challenging the reader to unscramble words or to find words in a maze of letters. These games are engaging for students but also deepen their understanding of the language, including the mysterious patterns of English spelling, which make *Iyknoplamatic* a possible

English word while *Izqotywxchych* is not. After students have played some of these games, invite them to create their own (thus revealing that they have intuited and generalized from the rules).

- My Gramma's Game. My gramma likes apples, not oranges; books, not magazines; floors, not ceilings; pillows, not beds. When the clues are written out, you can see that gramma's preference is for words with double letters. Let your students create their own "gramma likes" games with words that begin with vowels, have three syllables, contain a silent letter.

- Odd Person Out. Who doesn't belong in the following list? (1) J. Randolph Adams, (2) P. Nelson Kennedy, (3) C. Quacken Bush, (4) D. Edward Blake, (5) L. Clark Grant. (Number 4 does not contain the name of a president.) Or (1) Grace H. Iverson, (2) Rachel S. Turner, (3) Diana A. Nelson, (4) Alice B. Croft, (5) Janice K. Long. (All except number 3 have first, middle, and last names in alphabetical order.)

- Panagrams. A panagram contains every letter of the alphabet: "The quick brown fox jumped over the lazy dog." That panagram requires thirty-five characters to get in twenty-six letters, and language gamesters have delighted in trying to write shorter ones, such as "Pack my box with five dozen liquor jugs" (thirty-two); "Blowzy frights vex and jump quick" (twenty-eight, but hardly recognizable as English); and "Waltz, nymph, for quick jigs vex Bud" (twenty-eight, but requiring a proper name to squeeze in all the letters).

- Single-Letter Words. Try this quiz with your students: What letter of the alphabet is a bug? (B); a beverage? (T); a vegetable? (P); something to look with? (I); a cry of surprise? (O); to be in debt? (O); the person one speaks to? (U). These do not exhaust the possibilities; your students can find more. Extension:

    A B C D goldfish?
    M N O goldfish.
    S A R.
    C M?

Hint: Translate "A B" as "baby."

- Teakettle. Have your students develop lists of homonyms: sea/see, bark/barque. Then have them make up sentences in which the homonym is replaced by the word teakettle: "I will row my teakettle (barque) and pick up the teakettling (barking) dog."

- Spelling and Vocabulary Games. While the purpose of using language games is expressly *not* to overwhelm students with instructions about language, we must point out that a great many language games also teach. *Scrabble* reinforces vocabulary and spelling and pushes students into exploring new words. The old parlor game GHOST does the same: Participants sit in a circle and add letters to a one-letter base; the person who cannot think of a letter that would lead to but not actually complete a word is the loser and receives a penalty letter from the word G-H-O-S-T.

- Punctuation Games. In *Fun with Words* (1972), Maxwell Nurnberg poses some of the following punctuation puzzlers:

    o Punctuate the following, once as a request for information, once as an insult:

    Whats the latest dope

    Answers: "What's the latest dope?"; "What's the latest, dope?"

    o Punctuate the following so that it invites one to take a plunge:

Answer:

- Exploring the Alphabet.

    o Study the origins of the English (Roman) alphabet. How did it emerge from drawings and hieroglyphics?

    o Study weirdnesses in English spelling. Create your own list of spelling demons, the words people always seem to get wrong, and figure out why these particular character combinations cause problems. We nominate *necessary* and *traveler* to get you started. Students might also discuss spelling rules such as "i before e, except after c" and determine why that rule "works."

○ Have the class propose some simplified spellings. Tell them that for years, the *Chicago Tribune* tried to get *through* spelled as *thru,* but called it quits when the idea didn't catch on. Why do we cling to our odd spelling system?

○ Bring in a guest speaker of Chinese or Japanese and have that person explain how these are word/symbol languages rather than alphabetic. Ask them to explain how a Chinese typewriter works or to discuss the debate in Japan over the use of the Roman alphabet to represent traditional Japanese words.

• Language and pictures.

○ Many teachers have their students write concrete poetry, in which the poem is shaped to represent the topic (a flower poem is shaped like a flower, for example). For an excellent resource, look for Milton Klonsky's *Speaking Pictures: A Gallery of Pictorial Poetry from the Sixteenth Century to the Present.* It reveals a number of sophisticated art/word combinations.

○ We've often used an idea proposed by Lavonne Mueller of DeKalb, Illinois, who took concrete poetry a step further and had students create a three-dimensional "word museum" for the school library (*The English Journal,* May 1974). The students studied examples of visual language—pictographs, hieroglyphs, etc.—then created three-dimensional word renderings. *Wax* was created from chunks of candle wax, left in the sun to melt. *Boxed-in* came as a series of Chinese boxes. Fun and games? Certainly. But Mueller reports that in the process, students' understanding of the relationship between symbol and object—word and thing—grew enormously.

○ In our adaptation of the word museum project, students research the history of a word, generally through the *Oxford English Dictionary,* but a desk dictionary will do. They also interview people about the meaning of the word in contemporary society. Finally, they create a poster, including graphic representations, that shows the history, evolution, and current meaning of the word. For our museum exhibit, we create museum guides with some questions and suggestions:

What's the oldest word in the museum?

The newest?

List some words that came to us from Latin or French.

List some words that entered English through Anglo-Saxon.

List some words of Scandinavian origin.

What's the most interesting or unusual word in the museum?

Which museum posters displayed their word history in the most interesting ways?

# Language and/in Society

Beyond the sensitivity to language that can be gained by playing with words and letters, students need to explore how language functions in the world around them.

We've had good success having students keep a journal or notebook of *gleanings* (a concept and term we got from Leslie Pratt at Delta College in Michigan). Students comb newspapers and magazines for uses of language that strike them as interesting, clever, deceptive, important, or imaginative. These are kept in a display notebook. (For language from radio, TV, or speech, the students write brief transcripts.) As a term or semester goes along, students become increasingly sensitive to new forms of the word in the world. We shift the focus of the gleanings from time to time, so that students look one week for samples of advertising language, another for humor, a third for political language.

## The Language of Advertising

Some have said that advertising language is the poetry of our time. Poets can't support themselves writing poetry, but an imaginative advertising writer can play with the language and make goodly bucks. Further, because so much money rests on advertising, writers tend to be very precise and careful in their research. In an advertising unit, you can have your students explore:

- Radio and television ads. With an audio or video recorder, they can capture good ads and analyze their content. What makes an ad effective? Who is the audience? What have the students purchased recently as a result of media ads? A guest speaker from the ad industry might give your students some inside stories. Also have your students create their own ads on tape.

- Billboards. Talk about them. What makes them eye-catching? How do they use words, color, and white space? Study the language carefully for cleverness and poetry. Look at the integration of art and language. Perhaps your students can create billboards (or at least posters) putting some of their knowledge into action to promote a school event or cause.

- Classified ads. Here is a gold mine of fascinating language, some of it effective, some of it not. Study the real estate ads. What does "needs work" mean in a house description? "Handyman special"? "Priced to sell"? "Price reduced"? Examine the language used to sell used cars. What's being revealed and hidden by the language? What's going on in the personals? Under "pets"?

- Jingles. What advertising songs or jingles do the students have lodged in their brains? Have they ever gotten stuck singing or reciting one over and over? How many slogans and jingles can they list on the board? How does this use of language help to sell goods and services?

- Magazine ads. Look especially for clever uses of language: "Ever wonder what your panties say behind your back?" (panty hose). "The quickest way to a man's heart is through his feet." (slippers). "Who could make light of themselves better?" (low-tar cigarettes).

- Truth in advertising. Have your students read the fine print and check out the claims of advertisers. What does it mean to say that Chevy is "the heartbeat of America"? What's going on in those Ford/Chevy/Dodge truck comparisons? What do advertisers promise? What don't they promise? Students can do especially fruitful analyses of advertising disclaimers like "Batteries not included" and "Don't do this with your own automobile."

- Waffle words. Many ads use words that seem to make a claim but do not. "No toothpaste gets teeth whiter than Bright-O" implies superiority but actually states that this product is *no better* than any other. Words like *new, improved, whiter,* and *better* leave out comparisons that would make realistic assessment possible. By collecting waffle words, students can become more sensitive to the abuse of language, not only in advertising, but in other kinds of language use as well.

## Languages of the Mass Media

This topic is a book unto itself, especially given the role of television in young people's lives. Any contemporary medium—newspaper, film, radio, the web, magazines, television—can provide material for many weeks of study and could be a topic for analysis from September to June. Media are changing so rapidly that instead of proposing specific activities for specific media, e.g., television or the Internet, we offer some general questions that you and your students can ask about *any* mass medium:

- Who pays the bills? What is the relationship between the interests of the bill payers and those of the audience?

- What does this medium do especially well (e.g., report current events, comment on long-range trends, entertain, inform)? What does it do less well?

- What are the best uses of this medium today? Have your students create their own awards for the medium you are investigating, designing categories for awards then finding winners.

- What point of view does a particular medium present? Can you detect bias in the perspective being offered by, say, a particular radio station or newspaper?

- How does people's behavior change as a result of exposure to this medium?

- How could the quality of the medium be improved?

- What are the dangers of mind control implicit in the medium?

---

An activity we've used with great success is to have students write a consumer guide to a particular medium—talk radio, music radio, public radio, network television, pay television, e-mail, the web—using the questions above as a guideline. It's particularly satisfying to have students prepare the consumer guide in the form of the medium itself, e.g., a talk show on the dangers of talk radio; a short video dramatizing a couch potato flipping through the channels; a website on website design or the advantages and disadvantages of the Internet.

## Language and Mind Control

A key feature of any curriculum for George Orwell is to discuss what we can boldly call "mind control" or more accurately and less dramatically label as "the relationship between idea and language." Aristotle recognized some two thousand years ago that words are representations of objects and ideas; John Locke noted over four hundred years ago that the mind creates its own structures and meanings for words; in the last century, linguists, semanticists, and postmodernists have documented that the things we call "truths" and "realities" are, in fact, consensual among people, not absolute structures in the universe. We filter our perceptions through language, and we use language as a rhetorical device to shape the ideas and opinions of others. Perhaps no other concept in English language arts is more important for students to grasp than the idea that language is not neutral, that we shape it to our ends and that it shapes us to its and other people's ends.

Orwell taught us about doublespeak, the political language that obfuscates and confuses, that misrepresents and befuddles. For kids in middle school on up, we recommend that teachers read Orwell's "Politics and the

English Language" aloud to their students. You'll find that even though this essay was written in 1946, students can quickly come up with contemporary examples. Some antidoublespeak activities for your classroom:

---

- Let kids write doublespeak, the most abominable, two-faced, misleading prose they can manage. This activity is not meant to justify the use of doublespeak, but to help students understand it through actual use. Encourage students to see what happens when they use long words where short ones would do (consult the thesaurus for possibilities) and when they avoid calling things by their customary terminology, preferring to employ or utilize euphemistic synonymetrics. Orwell even spells out the rules for writing and the characteristics of doublespeak.

- In election years collect statements from politicians. Have students analyze precisely what is being promised, what seems to be promised, what is mere puffery. (Save those clippings for use in nonelection years.) Turn off the sound on political television commercials and read the candidate's lips and visual imagery. What's being said through body language and graphics that is not being said in words?

- At other times, have students collect the language surrounding a hotly debated political issue—local, regional, national, or international. To what extent do speakers employ loaded words, euphemisms, or complications? How do they use and abuse facts? How do they evoke an audience response? Have students write essays arguing opposite sides of an issue. Afterward, have them describe what happened in their minds as they argued a cause in which they didn't necessarily believe. If their experience is the usual one, they may have found themselves employing language in the heat of battle that they would customarily find inappropriate or even deceitful.

- Collect newspaper articles and political columns. Analyze their use of rhetoric and persuasive language. What news and oversimplifications do the students detect? Have them write their replies in the form of letters to the editor.

- Encourage your students to identify a cause or problem around the school or your community that requires action. Have them develop proposals, editorials, and letters urging people in power to adopt their ideas. Along the way have them look carefully at their own efforts to shape people's minds. Have them analyze replies from the people in power, as well.

- Conduct a unit on "big ideas." What are the major ideas that have shaped society in the past five or ten years? Have students read some of the materials that helped promote those ideas. Good topics for examination would be the women's movement; ethics in government; environmental consciousness; and the latest war, "skirmish," or "military incursion."

- Study trends, fads, and ideas popular among young people the students' own age. Where do these ideas come from? Who persuades young people that these are good things to do? What sorts of mass marketing or mass persuasion techniques are employed? What are the major ways in which people with ideas reach school-age youngsters?

- Conduct a unit on "Issues for a Better Tomorrow." Have students think carefully about what they see as the most important problems for their generation to solve. Who is going to do the solving? What role do your students see for themselves in controlling their destiny? What role will their language play in acting out that scenario?

## The Meaning of Meaning

It's important for students of all ages to engage in the analysis of language in daily use—collecting examples of doublespeak, assessing the media, analyzing ads, and so forth. But to place our curriculum for George Orwell on a solid foundation, we need to go further, by helping students gain an understanding of the nature of language and how it is shaped by human thought. Some classroom activities:

- Let students play with the difficult task of defining language. What is language? Where does it come from? How does language mean? How do words mean? What does meaning mean? Have students choose any common word, possibly a word from their own slang or lingo, and define it as fully as possible. How did this word acquire its consensual meaning?

- Have kids speculate about how the world would change if communication changed. What if there were no face-to-face conversation and we had to communicate by writing? Or what if there were no writing, only talk? Only TV and no telephone? No telephone, only the old-fashioned telegraph? The new-fashioned e-mail? What if we communicated only by gestures, not words? Or if we communicated directly, omniscient mind–to–omniscient mind? You can do this activity in several ways, including having students write science fiction, role-play, or even try to solve actual problems using one medium of communication rather than another.

- Ask your students to keep a one- or several-day log of their encounters with language. What language forms (speech, writing, media) do they encounter most frequently? What ideas and information enter through the various sources? What means of "languaging" do students choose to use most frequently?

- Assign the task of expressing a strong opinion without using words. Students may use images (drawn or photographed), gestures, or music to get across the idea. In what ways, if any, does composing in a nonverbal medium enhance our ability to communicate? How does wordless communication slow us down?

- Explain how lexicographers gather citations of words in actual use in order to create their definitions. Have students choose a common word—*walk, run, sleep, car*—and collect citations for a week or more. Pool all these examples and then create a definition based solely on these particular examples. How, if at all, does their definition differ from that of the dictionary?

- As part of a journal writing assignment, have students explore one of their strong biases or prejudices. Where did this come from? What words do they associate with it?

- Have students collect words that are used to demean racial and ethnic minorities: *nigger, wop, spic, dago, kike.* How do these words distort perceptions? Have the students track down the origins of these terms in a good dictionary.

- As a class project, have students create a new mystery word, say, calling a hamburger a "snurfbum." Then have your class use the word, without telling others what it means. What is the response of outsiders? How long is it before other people pick up on the mystery word and start to use it themselves?

## Language and Public Policy

Our colleague at the University of Nevada, Lee Thomas, has alerted us to the fact that a "curriculum for George Orwell" has important implications for the distribution of power in society, and this is an area where our guru, Orwell, fell a bit short. Language is not only a medium of rhetorical persuasion, it is also a repository of power. Titles and ranks are words of power, as are the secret languages of magicians, shamans, and politicians. The twentieth-century language philosopher Mikhail Bakhtin has shown us something of the hierarchies of language, including the fact that we must consider not only who is speaking and what he or she says, but who is allowed to speak in the first place. Michel Foucault has used analogous reasoning to discover an "archaeology" of knowledge steeped in language, that what comes to be known as truth is also deeply embedded in language structures and opportunities to argue for truth, that knowledge itself is rhetorical in form. These are sophisticated concepts, some of them best dealt with in graduate seminars, but students themselves can explore the concepts through such activities as these:

- Who has access to the miracle of the Internet? Do some people have more access than others? Who owns computers? Where are the computers in your school located and who determines who will use them?

- How is an Internet website an exercise in power? Which websites are accessible only if you have a credit card? What do hypertext links allow you to do? In what ways do they limit your access to knowledge?

- Libraries are designed to make information available to lots of people. In what ways do libraries have the opposite effect, that of intimidating people or limiting their access to knowledge? What are the advantages and disadvantages of libraries and the Internet as information sources?

- Call up a bank and ask a question, say, about whether or not students can get free checking accounts. How easy or difficult is it to find information? Try the same experiment dialing the 800 number for an airline. How long does it take to reach an actual person? What are the implications for language and power?

- Okay, the touchy one. Invite students to study language and power around the school. Who can talk? When? What are the limits of expression placed on the school newspaper? Where are the controls to the intercom system? What do bells or buzzers signal? Maybe you don't want to take up these issues with your students, but if you don't, what does this say about your powers and freedoms and language as an educator? Just asking!

## Selected Readings

Maasik, Sonia, and Jack Solomon. 1997. *Signs of Life in the USA*. Boston: Bedford Books.
Orwell, George. 1946. "Politics and the English Language." In *Shooting an Elephant and Other Essays*. New York: Harcourt Brace. (Available in a film version quite suitable for students.)
Postman, Neil. 1992. *Technopoly: The Surrender of Culture to Technology*. New York: Alfred A. Knopf.
Simons, Herbert. 1990. *The Rhetorical Turn: Language and Inquiry*. Chicago: University of Chicago Press.

# Chapter Thirteen

# Language and Learning Across the Curriculum

L et's clarify our progression in this section of the *Handbook* dealing with language. We've tossed a stone in the pond and are watching the ripples grow wider and wider.

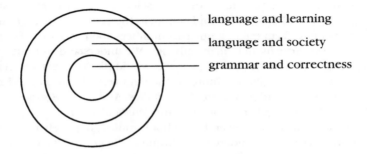

language and learning

language and society

grammar and correctness

In Chapter 11 we took up the specifics of teaching grammar and correctness, topics that loom large in the minds of the public as well as teachers. But in Chapter 12 we enlarged our view of "language" to include a range of linguistic adventures, arguing that teachers must give students a full understanding of language and its functions in their lives. Here we want to expand the perspective once again to show that "language" is not only a unifying concept for the teaching of English, but offers a way to view the whole school curriculum coherently.

In some respects, it might be useful for you to consider the implications of reading (or at least teaching) these chapters in reverse order. That is, current models of English language arts instruction imply very clearly that the best way to learn language is to plunge into it, using it successfully for a variety of purposes. That's how babies master language; that's how schoolchildren learn language; that's how each of us continues to expand his or her language use throughout life.

One answer to the question "What about grammar?" is: "My students are using language productively every day of their lives. What else do you want?" Such a reply is, of course, sassy and politically inept; don't try this in your school district. But the principle remains: A good language curriculum can begin with engagement and inquiry through words (the topic of this chapter); progress to metacognition and awareness of language as a medium (Chapter 12); and, for the sake of school, student, and society, polish up the fine points of dialect and usage as a tertiary, but by no means trivial, concern.

English, we argue, can bring coherence to the curriculum.

Of course, we must acknowledge that each discipline has the potential to offer such coherence.

Ask a scientist or science teacher what's the most important subject in the curriculum and you'll quite likely hear "Science, because it deals with the central processes of coming to know and understand the world around us. What could be more fundamental than that?" Ask a history person and you'll hear "History, because without it, people have no sense of the past, present, or future." A humanities or social science teacher might make the case for people and their values and culture as the center of the curriculum, while a mathematician might argue that numbers and processes of computation underlie virtually all human activities. We understand and value such curricular claims and visions; in fact, we would like to see more mathematics across the curriculum, more science in every classroom, and more attention to history and people in other studies. And let's not forget music, art, health, the practical arts, and any other curricular study.

The fact remains, however, that school studies are largely fragmented along disciplinary lines, kindergarten through college, and we believe that *language* has the greatest potential for providing unity and synthesis. Language is arguably the most important as well as the most common of the disciplinary common denominators. Language already is in every classroom in the world, whether that classroom is presently concerned with numbers, dates, or science and technology. We note that in recent years the idea of competence in various fields has been linked to English language arts, so that one hears of the need for increased scientific literacy, mathematical literacy, historical literacy, and so on. To explore competence in the various fields, subject-area teachers draw on language, asking students to speak or write about what they know.

But enough of the disciplinary provinciality, ours and theirs. About two decades ago, a "language across the curriculum" movement emerged as a cry for help from English language arts teachers, who realized that students needed to do more reading and writing (as opposed to more study of grammar). Students couldn't get enough practice in their elementary language arts block or their secondary English period, so English teachers pleaded, "Do more writing in the disciplines, so students will get the practice they need. Do more reading across the curriculum so students will see there is more to books than the stories and plays they read in language arts." To this cry, many teachers replied, "No thanks. I've got to cover material of my own." But in the 1970s a few people made deliberate efforts to increase the amount of language use in their math, science, social studies, health, geography, and physical education lessons, and they discovered an astonishing thing: When students read and write imaginatively in other disciplines, their learning in those disciplines increases dramatically. Language across the curriculum improves *learning* across the curriculum.

As a result, we in English language arts have broadened our claim. Instead of simply asking for support, we make a bold assertion: Pay attention to language, teach it in your classes, and your students will learn more. Further, we have come to discover the value of including the other disciplines in our own classes. It turns out that allowing students to read and write about science, math, history, health, and physical education in the English language arts class also increases students' appreciation of *our* field. From this symbiotic relationship, then, has grown what we call the "interdisciplinarity" of English. "Whole language" really means "whole learning." "Writing from experience" can include the experience of a science experiment or of devouring a history book. "Personal" reading can include a computer handbook as well as an adolescent novel.

English language arts teachers have thus become leaders in a movement that seems to be taking place in all disciplines: a push toward breaking down the barriers, toward merging disciplinary concerns and issues, and toward integrating and reintegrating the curriculum.

However, as we write, the future of interdisciplinary language arts and language across the curriculum is up in the air. On the one hand, we see great progress in many elementary classrooms toward whole language/whole learning approaches; we also see a strong push toward interdisciplinary studies at the middle school level; and we see pockets of interdisciplinary, language-centered teaching in high schools and colleges. On the other hand, the dominance of disciplinary learning is very powerful and the public, journalistic, and legislative devotion to "standards" is definitely pushing the schools back in time and back in curriculum design. We see too many elementary schools where kids still drag home deadly dull social studies texts with stupefying study questions; we see middle schools that still yearn to be "junior" high schools, focusing on disciplinary learning rather than the needs and interests of adolescents; and for every team of secondary/college teachers crossing disciplinary boundaries, we see many more individual faculty hanging on to discipline-centered teaching, with language reduced to a mere tool for testing rather than employed as a mode of learning.

The English language arts teacher who likes the idea of language and learning across the curriculum must be prepared to teach flexibly. To begin with, we should continue to focus on ways of making our own classes interdisciplinary: by including readings across the disciplines in the language arts library, by letting students explore topics in many fields and interest areas, by helping young people learn to write successfully about their knowing and learning in *any* field. At the same time, we need to seek opportunities to cross disciplinary lines: to merge social studies, geography, and language arts units in the elementary grades; to form connections and collaborations with colleagues at the higher grades.

Our teaching ideas in this chapter are designed to be used in both directions—moving out from English while increasing its boundaries—and at many different levels. They provide a sampler of possibilities that we hope you will find useful in extending your own teaching across the curriculum.

# Science

Like using language, science is a matter of observing, synthesizing, and describing the world. Teachers of both science and the language arts can help students make connections by discovering the role that language plays in learning and communicating about the natural world. Students can:

- Keep science logs, recording their observations about the natural world, commenting on them, and synthesizing their understanding. Opportunities for observation and writing happen every day in every classroom. What are those specks of dust floating in the sunlight? Why is bubble gum so difficult to get off your shoe or out of your hair? How do pencils work?

- Measure the arrival of a season and record its onset in a class notebook or scrapbook with measurements, observations, and even artifacts such as a fallen leaf or a spring flower.

- Prepare scripts for a series of scientific demonstrations for the class on, say, gravity or buoyancy.

- Collect newspaper articles showing modern science at work. Use these to create display posters explaining the scientific principles and processes involved.

- Watch *Bill Nye the Science Guy* or similar science demonstration shows on television and discuss or reproduce some of the experiments.

- Watch science documentary programs on the Discovery Channel or public or educational television channels and use these as the starting points for individual study or research.

- Participate in a "Science Soapbox," featuring mini-debates (oral or written) on the moral and human implications of issues like nuclear power, environmental protection, or genetic engineering.
- Design inventions to make people's lives better, publishing a *Book of Needed Inventions* as a final project.
- Develop better written components for school science-fair projects, writing explanations, not just labels.
- Investigate and write an explanation of why something doesn't work right: a kitchen blender, hot-water heater, automobile engine, or bathtub.
- Interview a magician, learn some of the secrets behind magic's illusions, and present your findings about how magicians seem to defy the laws of science.
- Research and write science fact-sheets for younger students, or start a "Science Facts" column in the school newspaper or newsletter.
- Read and write about the history of current technology, say, from pencil to word processor; from door latch to voice identification lock; from paper mail to e-mail.
- Research and write about careers in science; study colleges that have strong science programs.
- Write imaginary letters to the legendary figures of science: Curie, Pasteur, Galileo; write scripts about great moments in their careers; or role-play their visits to your class.

# Mathematics

In math, as in language, people translate their perceptions of the world into symbols. In some ways we envy the world of math, where symbols hold constant meanings, where $2 + 2 = 4$ is a more precise statement than Noun + Verb = Sentence. Nevertheless, math students must use real words and our wonderfully idiosyncratic language in order to understand and communicate concepts. Your students can:

- Write explanations of difficult math concepts so others can understand them. (Surprise—your students can write more user-friendly explanations than the authors of the adopted math text.)
- Interview local businesspeople about how mathematics works in their area: the auto shop, the bakery, the insurance company. Have students write a book of *Real World Math* recording these algorithms.

- Write a recipe book, including necessary measurements and calculations.

- Prepare a booklet of *Fun and Games with Math,* including puzzles, problems, perplexities, and conundrums, or write a column with that title for the school newspaper or parent-teacher newsletter.

- Design their own story problems, which will be much more imaginative than the dull ones in their textbook, and write up the answers.

- Read about the internal workings of calculators and computers and write an explanation.

- Research personal computers and prepare a consumer buying guide.

- Investigate the role of mathematics in a career they might pursue, whether it's fire fighting or playing in a band.

- Invent a better monetary system or school simulation (e.g., a school "script" based on class performance that can be used to purchase perks).

- Research and update school sports records or keep a sports statistics book.

- Perform a talk show with the giants of mathematics: Euclid, Pythagoras, Newton, Leibnitz.

- Write limericks about those worthies: "A math man named Euclid was grumpy, for his geometric figures were lumpy . . ." "A man name Pythagoras was puzzagorassed; his triangle was much too zigzagorassed. . . ."

# Social Studies

This area (which includes history, economics, government, and civics) offers perhaps the most natural connection with English language arts studies, for it's rich in writing and reading topics of interest to students of any age or level. Many of the early attempts to link the disciplines in the 1930s, 1940s, and 1950s centered on "core" language arts/social studies programs. Your students can:

- Read, read, read: fiction, poetry, drama, and nonfiction on issues in government, society, and human affairs. (What work of literature isn't, in some way, a social science treatise?) Using literature can engage students in first-hand understanding of ideas and issues in ways far more complex and rich than your schoolyard-variety social studies book.

- Write, write, write: fiction; poetry; drama; and nonfiction on the problems and circumstances of human affairs, including historical writing, futuristic writing, sociodrama, political intrigue, and biography.

- Keep logs and journals instead of conventional notebooks, recording their responses and reactions to historical ideas and events rather than simply keeping notes and writing down dates.

- Launch letter-writing campaigns to elected officials expressing well-researched opinions on current events and problems. (Be sure to proofread.)

- Investigate the judicial system and write an explanation for younger learners.

- Study the history and present and future prospects for their community, neighborhood, or school.

- Start a cable news network for the school or community public-access system, presenting a capsule of school, local, or world news.

- Read and write to participate in simulation games dealing with the colonialization of America, the supply of natural resources, international economics, world population, or other issues. Or, study an issue or problem and create a board or simulation game that represents it.

- Research their family tree, which could involve correspondence with relatives, interviews, and analysis of family documents.

- Research, discuss, and write about any current local issue, and forward the results to the appropriate governmental officials.

# Art and Music

Human beings are symbol makers, and that includes symbols other than words. The fine arts clearly open avenues for expression of some of the same human ideas, experiences, and emotions that are covered by English language arts. Students in these areas can:

- Keep response journals about the art they view and the music they hear, writing their reactions before moving on to analysis and history. (Perhaps students can find ways to respond other than writing; e.g., drawing about art or composing music that reflects what they hear.)

- Research and write about modes and techniques of expression in art—painting, sculpture, folk art, and craft. What does each medium permit in the way of self- and artistic expression? What are the limits of each? Students might conclude by writing illustrated how-to books for newcomers to an art form.

- Write a guide to old or obsolete musical instruments. What ever happened to the glass harmonica or the shawm?

- Explore electronic art and its capabilities: the synthesizer, computer art. Students might even compose music on the computer, then show their creations to the class. Exploit computer multimedia capabilities that allow students to link images, music, and words in creative ways. Create a website that is a demonstration of the possibilities.

- Write a descriptive essay exploring representations of visual experiences in another medium—for example, word paintings or sound paintings. What can be portrayed in words that cannot be shown using graphic art or music? What can be included in a painting or musical composition that cannot be talked about?

- Read biographies of major artists and composers.

- Create an arts billboard for the school or local closed-circuit television system or website, with announcements of coming attractions and reviews of events past.

- Find pieces of art and music to accompany their favorite pieces of literature; compile multimedia anthologies of literature and art; create scripts to enact the great ideas of music and art; and draw and paint to illustrate their own writing.

## Foreign Languages

The connection between foreign languages and English study runs deeper than merely mastering the grammar of one language or another. Foreign language study deepens the understanding and appreciation of language in general and helps students understand linguistic and cultural differences. Students can:

- Keep journals in the foreign language they are studying—a record of day-to-day experiences. Such a journal should not be graded for grammatical correctness; rather it serves as a way of increasing fluency, *n'est ce pas?*

- Create a foreign language joke or riddle book.

- Study words in English derived from the foreign language and prepare a poster display.

- Translate some of their own (short) writing into the target language. (Such a practice encourages students to learn, in the target language, the words, phrases, and structures they most commonly use in their native tongue.)
- Correspond with a pen pal using the foreign language.
- Study the debate over bilingual instruction and the "English only" movement. Where do the students stand on these issues?
- Read foreign language newspapers and prepare summaries (in the language) for posting on the board.
- Write in English (or the target language) about the customs, life, and culture in the home country of the language.
- Do improvisations in the language, very simple at first, moving toward full fluency.
- Prepare language lessons for younger children; tutor young learners; and read aloud to them and translate.

# Health and Physical Recreation

Yes, jocks and jockettes, there is a connection between language and sports. You can ask students to:

- Write rule books for popular sports.
- Develop how-to books for newcomers to a sport.
- Conduct surveys of coaches or team members about the projected success of Little League, Pony League, Pop Warner, or high school teams.
- Report on athletic contests for the school newspaper—not just the usual score-plus-exciting-moments gruel, but carefully crafted essays analyzing the game and its outcome.
- Write a *Brown Bag Lunch Book* including interesting and nutritious alternatives to peanut butter and jelly.
- Study food systems management—in the school cafeteria, at home, at a local restaurant. How does food get from field to table?
- Study the human heart, both scientifically and metaphorically, in essay, poem, song, or story.
- Investigate and prepare reports on drugs, alcohol, rest, exercise, or nutrition.

- Design and illustrate a lifelong exercise and nutrition plan.
- Read sports biographies, autobiographies, fiction, and nonfiction.
- Write critical reviews of fad diets.
- Investigate and report on science and sports: sports medicine, the physics and biology of sports, sports psychology, and scientific training methods.
- Study the language of sports in the locker room and in the daily newspaper.

# Applied Arts

The so-called practical fields of schooling are ideal for interdisciplinary language arts work. Language is an underlying element in fields as diverse as home economics, driver education, industrial arts, and business. Using contemporary techniques of language arts instruction, teachers can make such courses genuinely engaging. Students can:

- Write a book of rules of the road for other students coming into driver education, or prepare posters and displays of automotive concepts.
- Read the business page and follow up on current trends reported in the newspapers.
- Visit local businesses to see the roles played by reading and writing. Visit government offices for the same purpose.
- Design and play a simulation game based on a problem in business and industry.
- Study new materials being used in industry and speculate about how new plastics and alloys may be used in the future.
- Research technological developments in industrial fields and explain how industry is changing in our time.
- Research specific careers and write introductory guides on how to prepare for the career of your choice.
- Compile a guide to good writing in the particular area or field.
- Design and create things: woodworking projects, school government, field trips, a new school newspaper or literary magazine, a statue or memorial for the foyer.
- Write how-to books on all manner of topics: cooking, sewing, using power tools, taking pictures, making maps, developing photographs.

# The Integrated Classroom

Something of a buzzword in our time, "the integrated classroom" remains one of our ideals for education. Our dream of the ideal school is a K–12 (or K–college) institution not separated by grade levels and school subjects. Students would be engaged in a variety of projects, some of them for larger clusters of kids (call these "classes"), others for smaller teams or individuals. The ideas we've proposed in the preceding pages could, in fact, serve as a kind of curriculum guide for such a school. Of course, assessment would play an important part in such an enterprise, as it does in the real-world alternative to the dream school: the integrated classroom. As students complete various tasks, it is important for them—note, *them,* not just the teacher—to keep records of the skills and knowledge they've mastered. At the end of, say, writing a how-to book on making maps, a student would list the particular reading and writing skills and concepts he or she had mastered (how to "read" a map, how to label a map, how to translate words into images and vice versa); geography skills and concepts (too numerous to list); mathematics (measurement, multiplication, scaling, proportions); science (instruments of measurement, accurate record-keeping, approximation and error); history and social studies (of a particular terrain, of segments of the terrain); physical education (hiking and mapping), economics (understanding centers of commerce), and so on. Such assessment can take place in learning logs or by using checklists derived from the assigned school curriculum (especially those mandated standards).

Here are some ideas for the self-contained or interdisciplinary classroom, or for any teacher who might find them useful. Have students:

- Listen to speakers brought to school because of their particular knowledge across the disciplines, especially community members with expertise.
- Foray into the library or Internet and browse, looking for topics they'd like to know more about.
- Write plays dramatizing important moments in history. (What did George Washington's daddy say about that felled tree?)
- Visit community institutions that can shed interdisciplinary light on many different topics: universities; museums; libraries; businesses and industries; possibly even garage sales.
- Devise scientific experiments to explore areas where their book-learning leaves them in doubt.
- Read and write prophesies and predictions.
- Read and write about a community problem and propose solutions.

- Investigate the ecology of their town, including its natural and human ecologies.
- Research a decade—the Gay Nineties, the Roaring Twenties, the Radical Sixties—noting its contributions across the disciplines: art, music, sport, literature, history, economics.
- Write a letter or e-mail each week (or month or day) to a real person: political leader, news maker, hero or heroine, rock or film star, scientist.
- Write biographies of prominent citizens.

# Planning for Interdisciplinary Teaching

In the preceding pages, we've given you a number of fairly concrete ideas about activities that can be done to promote language and learning across the curriculum. We'll close this chapter with a more generic set of ideas, a kind of checklist of considerations for the teacher when planning for interdisciplinary teaching. From these, you can home-grow an interdisciplinary unit on just about any topic under and including the sun:

- Choosing topics. Start a list or file of possible topics for study and exploration. We particularly like skimming the newspaper to see what's in the news: sports, world news, regional news, local issues, upcoming events. Surfing the web will also yield areas of interest. If it's possible, and, indeed, it's preferable, engage students in the quest for topics.
- Review connections with the school curriculum. Check the state and locally mandated "standards" for your discipline and for other disciplines. What core curriculum topics can be folded into your interdisciplinary study? (For instance, "scientific method" is a common goal of science classes. What English language arts or interdisciplinary study does *not* cover methods of inquiry?)
- Generate questions for discussion. Again, engage students in the process. What do you/they/we want to know about the sun, cloning, computer art, local government, designer drugs? Link and cluster questions. What are the big ideas you want to explore in the unit?
- Look for reading resources. Create a book cart or in-class library. Surf the Internet and bookmark a series of websites that offer resources. Do an Internet search on key words in your topic: hunger, population, democracy, rain forests.

- Look for resources in math and science. What are the numerical and scientific questions linked to your quest to learn more about the weather, entertainers, cable television, religions?
- Seek out resources in history and the social sciences. How might these fields of inquiry improve your students' understanding of Elizabethan England, ancient Greece, modern America, the future of the universe, or the origins of the universe?
- Cast about for resources in the fine arts. The web is especially useful here for graphic arts, for you can find classic art and photography, contemporary graphics, and guides to museums all over the world. Check local galleries for exhibits related to local and national history, literary themes, forgotten causes, or contemporary methods of communication. Check local libraries for recorded readings or music linked to your theme.
- Seek out multicultural connections. How do other cultures view such issues as nutrition, family, neighborhood, population, and economics? In your web searches, seek out newspapers and other information sources from diverse countries. Read today's news as presented by news sources in Moscow, New Delhi, Beijing, and Nairobi.
- Design information quests to learn that which cannot be found in other sources. Create a survey or poll. Collect and manipulate statistics. Design a science project to test hypotheses.
- Translate discoveries into projects and hands-on demonstrations. What can students write, build, fabricate, display, or videotape, on the basis of the knowledge they have obtained?
- Assess. Have students carefully record and document their learning. Check off their accomplishments on the list of state or local curriculum objectives. List your students' major learnings *beyond* the home-base field or discipline. Ask students to discuss how they have answered their own questions.
- Repeat the cycle for new questions, themes, and topics. We rest our case for the English language arts as the core discipline or field from which extraordinarily exciting curriculum-wide teaching can develop.

# Selected Readings

Courts, Patrick. 1997. *Multicultural Literacies.* New York: Peter Lang.

Kuhn, Thomas. 1964. *The Nature of Scientific Revolution.* Chicago: University of Chicago Press.

Tchudi, Stephen, and Stephen Lafer. 1996. *The Interdisciplinary Teacher's Handbook.* Portsmouth, NH: Boynton Cook Publishers.

Whitehead, Alfred North. 1929. *The Aims of Education.* New York: Macmillan.

# Summary and Troubleshooting

# Sentence Diagrams from Nightmare Abbey

From time to time we dream about professional matters, and such dreamy nights often give us pause for reflection the following day. Following the advice of dream psychologists who advocate self-analysis, we keep pencil and paper on the nightstand and write down dreams that powerfully affect us.

About the time we were finishing work on this section of the *Handbook,* we had a particularly restless night, with creatures from the dark side dashing around in the corners of our mind. In the course of one nightmare, there were revealed to us four sentence diagrams that raise important issues about the teaching of language. We present them here as we recalled them by dawn's gray light, along with our commentary and analysis.

## Diagram 1

**Nobody teaches grammar anymore.**

This diagram reflects a common misperception among parents, newspaper editorialists, and even some teachers. Of course grammar *is* taught (and learned), as every native speaker of English intuitively knows. But *grammar* in this context means more than simply learning how to understand the language (a monumental accomplishment in its own right). It is a stand-in for the broad feeling that the schools are failing, the economy is falling apart, and language is in decay. (Don't we wish that grammar study could turn around a falling stock market?)

The trick for teachers who have studied the nature of language is to persuade their various audiences that newer approaches to English language arts teach grammar in all sorts of ways: through reading, writing, listening, and speaking. Should we teach formal grammar on top of that? Our feeling is that a *little* grammar (and conceivably even a little sentence diagramming) is not fatal. But does it bring about the changes in language that it has traditionally promised? Most native users of English know the answer to that one, too.

# Diagram 2

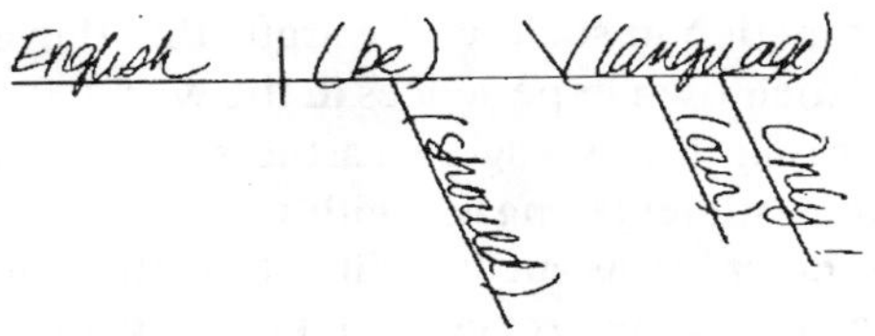

**English Only!**

The "English only" movement, designed to establish English as the legislated "official" language, is certainly a nightmarish one, having achieved enormous support in almost half the states in the union. We can be confident that laws about official language will not influence the languages that people use (unless, of course, the nightmare of a linguistic police state comes about). But "English only" is having the effect of limiting bilingual programs that give non-native English speakers a fighting chance to learn core subject matter in their own language even as they master their new, target language. Further, the movement strikes us as being xenophobic and foolishly nationalistic. Despite the denials of its advocates, there is strong evidence of racism in their motives as well. What can we do about it? For one thing, we can be politically active, supporting such groups as the National Council of Teachers of English in their efforts to fight "English only" laws. One can also join in the countermovement, "English plus," which argues that every child has the right to learn to speak more than one language successfully. Less dramatic, but far more important, perhaps, is for us to make our own classrooms truly multinational and multicultural in the literature we use and to treat non-native speakers of English as a resource rather than a pedagogical nuisance.

# Diagram 3

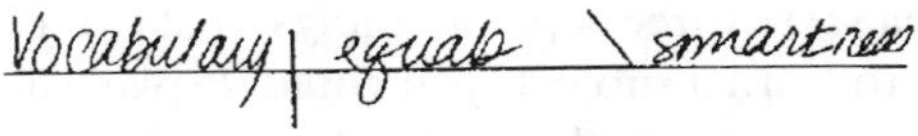

**Knowing lots of words makes one intelligent.**

The lure of vocabulary teaching is great, and one sees "vocab" units in virtually all commercial textbooks and a great many school curriculum guides. We're not against teaching vocabulary, and recognize that there probably is a modest correlation between the number of words we know and our "smartness," or knowledge base.

But in the schools teachers often turn the equation around, teaching words out of context and in isolation, thinking that if kids master the vocabulary list, their grasp of the world will be improved. How, then, do we build vocabulary? How do kids master the words and terms that are vital for them to function in society? We argue that they must acquire the language through their own experiences in the world, including the world of reading and writing. Knowledge, smartness, and education should, at best, come about as students engage with their world and their community. Vocabulary emerges as an enabling tool that allows students to employ their language in the processes of knowing and understanding.

# Diagram 4

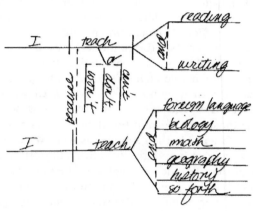

**I won't, don't, or can't teach reading and writing,
because I teach another discipline.**

The "language across the curriculum" movement has certainly been a frustrating one for teachers of English language arts, especially at the college and high school levels where departmentalization dominates.

For years, English teachers implicitly offered the view that language, content, and idea were three separate things, that (for example) you could study word lists to learn a subject, you could display language in sentence diagrams without regard to the content, and you could pass laws that make people change the way they talk.

If there's any single message to be delivered in this section of the *Handbook,* it's that language growth, development, and usage are naturalistic and inseparable from the content of human experience. Teachers of other disciplines do teach language, whether or not they say they can or will. The only question is whether they're going to do it well or badly. Or, to rephrase that, whether they're going to use language as a tool and ally or as an obstacle to learning.

The best way we know to help the unwilling or the doubting is to get them doing some writing and reading about their own subject matter, keeping journals about what goes on in their classes, and writing articles and reading essays about issues in the field that matter to them. As teachers of history, science, and mathematics read and write for real, they come to see the potential for language use in their own classes.

In this general area, we expect progress to be slow; we expect our nightmare to recur. In the meantime, we're having a wonderful time teaching language across the curriculum in our own self-contained English classes, inviting students to bring in and read and write about concerns in the worlds of science, business, politics, sports, computer science, medicine, law, education, and the like. When colleagues from other fields accuse us of poaching on their discipline, we invite them to poach on ours by becoming interdisciplinary teachers of reading and writing.

# f ∘ i ∘ v ∘ e

# The Profession of Teaching

This final section of *The English Language Arts Handbook* contains just one chapter (plus a letter). Yet it focuses on one of the most important and elusive concepts in education: professionalism. We describe some of the "peripherals" (to borrow from computer terminology) that connect with our day-to-day teaching. Like computer add-ons, may of these have the potential to contribute to our work and to our students' learning, but like computer add-ons that don't match your system, they can also lead to serious complications and malfunctions.

# Chapter Fourteen

# Colleagues, Collaborators, and Contraries

G etting along in a school or school district is not an easy task, whether you're a student teacher coming in for the first time or a grizzled veteran of twenty years or more. Like any institution, a school system is made up of people, and those people aren't cogs in a machine who always perform predictably. People have special interests, deeply held convictions, and personal needs that don't always correspond ideally with those of fellow teachers along the corridor. People were hired into the system at different times and for different purposes. The length of time teachers plan to remain with the school will vary widely and affect their day-to-day performance.

In this chapter we discuss the difficult topic of human and personal relationships for the English language arts teacher. We do this not by offering advice on how to get along with your neighbor, but by discussing the major groups (other than students) with which teachers need to work: administrators, parents, and colleagues. In each case we focus on the positive, looking at steps and strategies that you can initiate to maximize your effectiveness as a teacher within a human institution.

## Working with School Boards and Administrators

In our teaching lifetime, we've seen a dramatic shift in the relations between teachers and the people who hire them and oversee their work: the board and its administrators. As recently as thirty years ago, the relationship was one of *community*. The principal of the school served as a schoolhouse mother or father, overseeing day-to-day operations and serving as an intermediary between the teachers and the school board, which in turn seemed to be a cordial group of "family relations." That admittedly idealized relationship has changed, so that today school boards are often suspicious of teachers and their motives, and the principal is more likely to be seen as the middle manager of a business enterprise than as the pedagogical *pater-* or *materfamilias*.

The reasons for this shift are sociologically and economically complex, but three trends stand out in our minds.

1. *Teachers engaged in collective bargaining.* When we first entered teaching in the 1960s, teachers' unions were rare and were, in fact, regarded as unprofessional by many teachers and community members. Unions were something that construction workers, auto builders, and truck drivers belonged to. Yet, as many perceptive educators noted, for teachers to act as if they were members of a kindly and supportive family was not paying off: salaries and teaching conditions were bad, and "the family" wasn't doing anything to change the status quo. Unionized school districts made important gains for their teacher/union members, but along the way, the board of education became the opposition. Familial chat between teachers and board members became difficult, because each side had its list of negotiable and nonnegotiable items; each decision became a precedent for future decisions; each concession by either group became locked into a contract. Principals could no longer afford to be our pals, because they were part of management, not labor, and sat on the opposite side of the negotiating table from the teacher reps. On the whole, we think the gains earned by the unions far outweigh the losses, but it's important to note that one major loss has been the ease of communication between teachers, administrators, and the board.

2. *The American people began to doubt the effectiveness of their school system.* Actually, they began to doubt a great deal more than that, including their ability to compete on the international industrial scene, their ability to fight and win a moral war, the strength of their economic system, and the ethics of their national leaders. Much of their frustration became focused on the schools, so we have experienced a thirty-year period in which the public has increasingly felt that its schools (and its teachers) aren't getting the job done. Teachers work in an atmosphere of distrust and, increasingly, in a system where their performance is likely to be judged through legislatively mandated tests, curriculum guidelines, and minimum standards of performance.

3. *The role of the school in responding to the social and emotional needs of students began to be challenged.* With increasing racial and ethnic diversity in society, with health and human service needs increasing, with greater emphasis being placed on the needs of girls and women, the school was asked to develop programs and curricula to respond to those needs—multicultural curricula, diversity programs, health and sexuality programs, curricula responding to issues of ethics and violence. Many parents—especially those from strong religious backgrounds—began to question the role of the schools in

discussing issues of morality, sexuality, and diversity. Home schooling, the call for voucher systems, and the instituting of charter schools all had their impetus in challenges to the validity of the school curriculum to teach about values, beliefs, and human behavior.

These shifts in relationships have been especially difficult for English language arts teachers, for ours is the subjective discipline, the *human/ humane* discipline, whose aims and goals center on human behavior and human values, and whose dimensions are difficult to describe and assess. Sure, we could write a curriculum based on grammar terminology, spelling lists, literary names and dates, and correctness in writing, and such a curriculum would be accountable to and testable by local, state, and even national examinations. But we also know that such a program would not, in the long run, produce the highly literate citizens that teachers and parents want. Nor would it address the areas of human creativity, human value, and human behavior that are central to our study of literature. There is, then, a built-in communications gap between what teachers want and what the people who elect and stand to serve on the school board want.

To avoid painting too gloomy a picture, we add that positive trends have taken place over the same period of time. In general, school boards are less benign than they were in the good old days, and they think closely and carefully about what they want to have happen in their system (never mind that sometimes the thinking is driven more by the fear of lawsuits than the desire for quality learning). In addition, there seems to be greater public access to the decisions that school boards make, with opportunities for all citizens to be heard in public forums when boards are making decisions. Nonetheless, we believe that teachers need to remain active in taking positions about their own profession, their own standards, and their own expertise, so that school boards make policy and prescribe curriculum on the basis of defensible knowledge and information.

The following ideas are designed for individual teachers, but they will more likely be put in practice by groups of teachers working in concert. Ways of developing "concert" will be described later.

---

- Develop a program to inform school boards and administrators of new developments in English language arts. Routinely invite board members to participate in workshops, conferences, young author conferences, and the like. (In a survey he conducted for the National Association for Curriculum Development, Stephen learned that among the schools that had been the most successful in developing

exemplary English programs, many had routinely followed this practice [Tchudi 1990].)

- Create a newsletter for parents and administrators that describes and
illustrates the aims and new directions of the language arts program.

- Ask the board to establish literacy as a priority for the school district,
then use that declaration to work for needed support for new programs.

- Educate the board about the cost efficiency of programs and texts.
Lobby for alternatives to mandated texts and expensive prepackaged
programs. Educate the board and administrators to possibilities for
English language arts teaching that involve a range of materials and
teacher-directed curricula.

- Lobby with the board for increased materials for literacy instruction.
Ask for an in-class library and a bank of computers for every language
arts classroom in the district.

- Educate the board and administrators about the successes and failures
of current literacy programs. Write to the National Council of Teachers of English (NCTE) and obtain the names of schools and districts
that have received awards for excellent programs or curriculum
guides. Prepare point-by-point comparisons with your school district
and draw these to the attention of board members and administrators.

- Take the issue of class size for language arts teachers to the board.
Bring the NCTE's resolutions on class size to the attention of the
board, as well as other issues surrounding current teaching practice
in the language arts.

- Enlist the aid of the school administration in seeking outside funding
for English language arts programs. In these days of tight fiscal constraints, school boards are likely to help programs that show signs of
helping themselves.

- Suggest a school-within-a-school program to your school board and
administrators. In this era when charter schools are designing alternative curricula, suggest experiments within the school that emphasize interdisciplinary curricula; international and multicultural
education; multigrade and multilevel classrooms; and team teaching.

# Parents and Community Members

The board members do represent the community, and in our experience,
they generally raise the same sorts of problems and questions that community members do. Many of the projects suggested in the previous sec-

tion are intended to engage the community on the side of English language arts instruction. Beyond those, try to do some of the following:

- Sponsor articulation meetings where parents are invited to learn more about what is happening in the English language arts programs. (Alas, often only a small number of parents will come to such sessions. Be sensitive to cultural issues and to the parents who are intimidated by school. Make an extra effort to find ways to talk to these parents, who are often very concerned about the work their children are doing.)
- Hone your *English Language Arts Newsletter* to reach parents and tell them what they need to know. Among good questions for either articulation meetings or the newsletter are:
  - What do the test scores mean about my child's progress?
  - Why don't the teachers mark errors and correct my child's writing?
  - What books should my children be reading?
  - What activities or games will help my child learn English?
  - How much homework should I be seeing my child bring home? And how can I help her with it?
- Find ways to involve community service groups in the literacy program. Ask the Rotarians, the Kiwanis, the Elks, and the Moose to adopt a classroom or a school and find ways to supply it with supplementary reading materials.
- Educate yourself about how to get news in the local paper. Learn the name of the education editor and send in information on your latest projects. Learn how to write press releases that will draw attention to your program or get you free advertising on local radio and television channels.
- Start a parent volunteer program, with lots of attention to the wonderful work parents and other community members do to help students with reading and writing. Nominate your volunteers for volunteer awards.
- Hold a workshop for parents on "How to Help Your Child Be a Better Reader/Writer." Both the National Council of Teachers of English and the International Reading Association have pamphlets designed for parents on this subject. Among the ideas recommended for parents:
  - Create opportunities for open-ended conversation and discussion (the old-fashioned family dinner hour, for example).
  - Play word games with kids.

- Read aloud to children; encourage them to read aloud to one another, older to younger or vice versa.
- Tell stories to children; develop a family core of oral yarns.
- Fill the home with reading material: newspapers, magazines, books, pamphlets.
- Use e-mail instead of the phone. Have kids keep in touch with family members and friends by writing.
- Find family oriented websites, such as the Children's Television Workshop (www.ctw.org) and the Family Education Network (www.familyeducation.com), or opportunities for kids to publish online, such as KidPub (www.kidpub.org/kidpub), MidLink (longwood.cs.ucf.edu/-MidLink), or New Moon (www.newmoon.org).
- Have students explore the weather, the news, inventions, space, gender issues, and world cultures on the web.
- Help kids design study areas for reading, writing, and homework in general.
- Buy books and magazine subscriptions as gifts.
- Choose educational computer activities (graphics programs, virtual globes and maps, language and literature games, and publishing programs) as opposed to mind-numbing games when buying software.
- Help kids establish guidelines for their television viewing. Discuss television programs with your children.
- Volunteer as a parent tutor in a school or community literacy program.

# Teacherly Colleagues

Our best friends are teachers. As we said in the introduction, the ideas we present here are not all original. We've shared our problems with our teacher friends and gotten helpful suggestions; we've attended conferences and listened to the ideas of strangers who then became friends; we've given talks at conferences and gotten feedback from members of the audience; and we've been involved with professional organizations at the local, state, and national levels. Each of these associations has taught us about our own teaching, about the problems our friends share across the state and across the country (and around the world), and about new ways of responding positively to the challenges of teaching. There's no substitute, in our minds, for the learning that goes on as colleagues work together offering ideas to one another in a community of learners (whether that community is within your building, within your local professional organization, or among your alumni friends who stumbled through student teaching with you).

As we said earlier, school faculties are not uniform in their interest and commitment. Most of the old pros in teaching agree that you have to select your close colleagues carefully, that you can't work with (or reform) everybody in the building. Thus, in our own work, we've done our best to be cordial to everyone and to listen to what every colleague has to say, but to design projects and activities that encourage, even *force* us to collaborate with people who have things to teach us.

Some suggestions for developing your faculty's sense of community and professionalism:

---

- Use departmental meetings for more than business; hold them in non-crisis times to:
  - propose new ideas, programs, classes, and units
  - forge collaborative relationships among faculty members
  - develop strategies to strengthen relationships with the school board, administrators, and community members
  - develop strategies for working with faculty across disciplines
  - discuss common problems in dealing with broad issues of teaching, e.g., non-native speakers of English, discipline problems, gender issues, and civil language in the classroom
- Form a teacher research group among your colleagues to look at ways you can learn more about your students' needs and literacy growth.
- Become a teacher-researcher yourself. Whenever you start a new class or course, jot down a few basic research questions about your curriculum, your students, and your methods. Systematically collect data all term long, and when the dust has settled and grades have gone in, spend the necessary time to study and write up your findings. Type up your conclusions on a page or so and share them with your colleagues.
- Form an English faculty reading group. Use it for your recreational reading, but also to explore new adolescent literature or new multicultural or international literature.
- Form a writing group. Have colleagues "workshop" their writing the same way you advocate kids doing. Create a writers' group publication. Share it with your students.

- Try some collaborative teaching with the colleague next door. Figure out ways you can share and exchange students, get your classes together for special events, and use one another's students as audiences.

- Develop a collaborative project with a teacher in another discipline. Share ideas about Civil War literature and history with a social studies teacher. Use biographies and autobiographies of scientists in a collaborative project with the biology teacher.

- Join local, regional, and national professional organizations like the National Writing Project, the National Council of Teachers of English, and the International Reading Association. Participate in their conferences, and submit to their journals. Fight for funds to support travel to professional meetings. Make sure the union keeps this as an item in its negotiations.

- Lobby for the faculty to determine its own inservice needs. Get on planning committees for organizing the professional development activities for your faculty.

- Ask for funds to bring good consultants to your school, from good teachers in your own district to national specialists in an area that interests your faculty. (If possible, try to observe this person in action before you extend an invitation. Good writers are not necessarily good speakers or cooperative consultants.)

- Take part in summer teaching institutes. Make friends with and learn from colleagues in other districts, cities, and states. Take the ideas back to your own colleagues.

- Develop a professional library in your school. The bibliographies at the ends of each chapter and at the end of the book provide a good place for getting started. Ask for support from your administration.

- Share good books you read—both professional and recreational— with your colleagues. Ask them to share good books with you.

- Make certain the school has subscriptions to major periodicals in English education and related fields (some are listed in the "Professional Resources" section). Assign individual faculty members the responsibility of scanning one journal a month and recommending good articles to the others; we are obviously too busy to read everything we should.

- Create a mentoring system for new faculty, student teachers, and teacher aides. Share teaching ideas, resources, and information about how to find things in the school. (At the same time, spare them your personal opinions about the faculty ogres; let them form their own opinions.

- Work across grade levels. Invite colleagues from the levels above or below yours to come and talk about areas of common concern. Don't let your colleagues get into the blame game, accusing one another of not doing their part to prepare students for the next grade.

- Socialize together as a faculty. Have TGIFs, end-of-school picnics, holiday cookie exchanges, and ongoing *Scrabble* or volleyball games.

- And don't forget kids-as-colleagues. By this we do not mean that you should become buddy-buddy with the students. But they are, after all, your best resource for learning about teaching. They are the final test you must pass. With the kinds of methods we have described in this book, it's easier than it used to be to enjoy kids, to appreciate them as human beings and as writers and readers. Granted, they will drive you everywhere from up the wall to stark raving mad, but as a teacher of young people you (and we) are in a wonderful position to study, appreciate, learn from, and teach a great bunch of minds.

# Summary and Troubleshooting

# Letter to a "Young" Teacher

In 1932, Virginia Woolf published *A Letter to a Young Poet*, a book whose lead essay shared Woolf's views on contemporary poetry with a would-be poet. The letter that follows is in that tradition.

• • •

Dear "Young" Teacher,

Let's begin by saying what we mean by "young." Age has nothing to do with it.

A few years back we wrote a book called *The Young Writer's Handbook*, which we designed for "young" writers aged eight to eighty, give or take a few years at either end. That book, like *The English Language Arts Handbook*, was dedicated to people who are young in spirit, not necessarily in age or experience.

You are a young teacher because, one way or another, you find it possible to approach teaching afresh each day—or, more realistically, four days out of five. You would rather not teach this year's students by the tried-and-true (or the tried-and-wanting) methods and strategies of last year or fifty years ago. You assess students initially and finally on their personal growth, not on stereotypes or clichés.

It's not easy to remain young in our business. As a student teacher or first-year teacher arriving on the scene, you are often told "Ignore everything they taught you in college. You're in the real world now. You'll wise up when you see what this place is really like."

Add a wrinkle or two to your forehead.

You go to the principal and request funds for this or that: a new literary magazine for the writing club, more paperback books, a computer for your classroom. The reply, "We respect your enthusiasm and we think it's wonderful that you have all these innovative ideas, but we don't have the money and frankly don't see why you can't make do with the handbooks we bought you a few years ago."

Add a sprinkling of gray hairs to your scalp.

You have great ideas about developing a thematic interdisciplinary unit for your students and want to spend some extra time in the library digging out resources. Instead, you are called to a meeting to explain why your students didn't show improvement on Objective 9 of the statewide assessment.

Add more wrinkles and gray hairs, the latter surrounding a bald spot created by pulling your hair out.

Yet, young teachers are all around us. Just the other day we attended a Writing Project board meeting where teachers of all ages expressed their enthusiasm about a writing magazine they were developing for teachers, a parent/child bookmaking night to be taken into any school that requested it, and a summer writing program free to students in at-risk schools. How does it happen that beneath the increasing wrinkles, gray spots, and bald spots, some teachers remain young?

There aren't any formulas, of course, and what follows is a very short list of two suggestions. To the extent we've managed to remain young, we've operated under these two principles.

*Remain experimental.* In her *Letter to a Young Poet,* Virginia Woolf advised:

> Write then, now that you are young, nonsense by the ream. Be silly, be sentimental imitate Shelley, imitate Samuel Smiles [a nineteenth-century popular writer and journalist]; give rein to every impulse; commit every fault of style, grammar, taste, and syntax; pour out; tumble over; loose anger, love, satire, in whatever words you can catch, coerce or create, in whatever meter, prose, poetry or gibberish that comes to hand. Thus you will learn to write.

Now, you can't afford to be so flamboyant in your teaching, if only because your "products" are kids, not scraps of writing that can be tossed away if the experiment fails. But the spirit of Woolf's remarks strikes us as right: Try *anything* that seems appropriate, possible, desirable, interesting, and (we add) responsible. What is *not* known about teaching English language arts is considerable, and the most crucial discoveries will be made by classroom teachers, not necessarily by university researchers.

Elsewhere we've written about the idea of the teacher-researcher, one of the most energizing, liberating ideas to come along in education in some time. As a teacher-researcher you will, like Woolf's young poet, try many new things, but you will also collect data and evidence to determine whether or not the experiments are yielding the kinds of growth you predicted. In this way, you will successfully combine youth *and* experience.

*Be institutionally savvy.* Institutions—public or private, nonprofit or profit—are often bizarre places to work. Despite the human beings who make them go, institutions are inanimate and impersonal. You may have loved your college profs, but singing the college fight song is, in the end, like pledging allegiance to a brick wall. Institutions breed bureaucracy, regulations, and layers of ineffectiveness (including the new breed of management specialists whose job is to simplify things).

At first glance, many schools seem to rule out possibilities for the sort of experimental teaching we've described in *The English Language Arts Handbook*. But we've discovered through years of practice that there are ways individual teachers can work in, through, around, about, and ultimately over just about any school bureaucracy.

To begin with, the cliché remains true: "The classroom is your castle." This is not meant to imply that you should run your class as a private kingdom, but it does suggest that day in and day out, you're quite free to organize and structure the way you wish. Sure, there are standardized exams that have to be taken, grades that must be given, a curriculum that needs to be covered. But even within those constraints, virtually no school system limits how you approach the task of teaching; and even in the most rigid of systems, there's no effort to control the essential dynamic of teaching: the teacher/student relationship.

Beyond that, because schools are chronically underfunded and English language arts classes are further underfunded within that system, you need to become a specialist in what we call the dirt-cheap alternative. Can't get the school to fund an in-class library? The dirt-cheap alternatives include learning how to better use the resources of school or public libraries, getting kids to find books on their own, and bringing in supplies yourself. The district won't set up a computer laboratory for English students? Poems, plays, imitations of Shelley, satire, and gibberish can be composed with the dirt-cheap pencil—imagination, not hard disk capacity, is the limiting factor.

"Rules were meant to be broken," goes the saying. We offer an alternative: "Rules were meant to be understood." Concretely, this means that when the district mandates the teaching of formal grammar, you as a savvy teacher must figure out that what is wanted is not so much knowledge of parts of speech as kids who write and speak standard English. Understanding that rule, you increase attention to editing in peer-group workshops and teach parts of speech as necessary to help kids master tough usage items. (Down the hall, your colleagues are either breaking the rule by doing nothing with grammar, or following it slavishly, in neither case helping students very much.)

In short, institutions often provide far more latitude and opportunity than you might suppose, and we urge you to find ways to achieve the things you see as important, despite institutional constraints.

Virginia Woolf closed her letter this way:

> So long as you and you and you, ancient representatives of Sappho, Shakespeare, and Shelley, are aged precisely twenty-three and propose—O enviable lot!—to spend the next fifty years of your lives in writing poetry, I refuse to think that art is dead.

Far from being dead, the art of teaching language is alive and well in the hands of you young teachers, who—O enviable lot!—have the power and potential to be the most successful practitioners of our profession the world has ever known.

Our best wishes,

Susan Tchudi
Stephen Tchudi

# Resources

What follows is a list of major professional organizations and publications that we think can be of help to the teacher of English language arts. It makes no claim at comprehensiveness; however, each of these organizations and publications has proven helpful to us more than once in our careers as teachers.

## Organizations

### *The National Council of Teachers of English,*
### 1111 Kenyon Road, Urbana, IL 61801

NCTE can be somewhat baffling to a newcomer because of its Byzantine structure of sections, commissions, conferences, committees, and assemblies. Suffice it to say that one of the great virtues of NCTE is that it offers publications and study groups to suit almost any teacher's individual interest. Upon joining NCTE, the new member also becomes a member of a section—elementary, secondary, or college—and receives a subscription to a journal, *Language Arts* (primarily for elementary teachers), *The English Journal* (for secondary teachers), *In the Middle* (for middle school teachers), or *College English*. For additional fees, you can subscribe to more than one journal or to one or several of the council's other publications, such as *English Education* (principally for college English education teachers and school supervisors), *College Composition and Communication, Research in the Teaching of English,* and *Teaching English in the Two Year College*. (A particularly good buy is NCTE's comprehensive membership, which includes subscriptions to all those journals plus a copy of books published by the council during the membership year.) Probing further into NCTE, one finds assemblies, including several that might be especially interesting to readers of this book:

The Assembly on Literature for Adolescents
Assembly on Science and Humanities

Children's Literature Assembly
English as a Second Language Assembly
Junior High/Middle School Assembly
Whole Language Assembly

Most assemblies have low dues and depend very much on the vigor and enthusiasm of individual members.

## State and Regional Affiliates of NCTE

By writing NCTE, you can also make contact with your state, regional, or local affiliate. These organizations vary greatly in size but are at the very heart of English education activity nationwide. Area affiliates usually have modest dues, hold one or more annual meetings, and provide numerous committees and activity groups for the professionally minded.

## Other National Organizations

Many nations other than the United States have vigorous national organizations, in particular:

Canadian Council of Teachers of English
National Association for the Teaching of English (U.K.)
Australian Association for the Teaching of English
New Zealand Association for the Teaching of English

These organizations, along with the National Council of Teachers of English, are members of the International Federation for the Teaching of English, which promotes exchanges of information among the member nations and their national organizations. U.S. teachers who are interested in international English studies should also consider joining the International Assembly of NCTE, which has close ties with, but is not identical to, the International Federation.

## *National Writing Project,* School of Education, University of California Berkeley, CA 94720

The NWP is not something that teachers join directly; you become involved by participating in summer and year-round programs sponsored by local NWP sites, now numbering over 150 in the United States and worldwide. You can write to Berkeley or ask around to learn of activities in your region. In addition, some states have independent writing projects; these include the Michigan Writing Project, the Iowa Writing Project, the Illinois Writing Project, and the New Jersey Writing Project.

### *The International Reading Association,* 800 Barksdale Road, P.O. Box 8139, Newark, DE 13714

IRA publishes *The Reading Teacher* for preschool and elementary levels and *The Journal of Reading* for those at the secondary level. Like the National Council of Teachers of English, it also publishes a wide range of books and monographs on various aspects of its field, which in recent years has broadened to include writing and oral language as well as reading. IRA has a particularly strong network of affiliates or local reading councils that allow for direct involvement in your immediate area.

### *Institute for Democracy in Education,* 119 McCracken Hall, Ohio University, Athens, OH 45701

This group looks beyond the friendly confines of the English language arts classroom to discuss learning across the disciplines. It is particularly dedicated to student and teacher empowerment, encouraging both to be decision makers within the institution.

### *National Association for Core Curriculum,* 404 White Hall, Kent State University, Kent, OH 44242

"Core" curricula, frequently a blending of history, social studies, and English, have been around for almost half a century. This organization is concerned not only with these kinds of interdisciplinary programs, but with the concept of core or general education learnings as well.

### *National Association for Science, Technology, and Society,* Willard Building, University Park, PA 16802

NASTS is a vigorous interdisciplinary group dedicated to getting more concern for values into math and science curricula and for making connections between math, science, and the humanities. English language arts teachers interested in this area should also consider joining the Assembly on Science and Humanities of NCTE, a group that is also affiliated with NASTS, thus promoting language as a fulcrum for reducing the distance between the two cultures.

## Publications

### *Holistic Education Review,* Box 1476, Greenfield, MA 01302

An impressive professional journal with an emphasis on integrated teaching and learning.

### *The Horn Book,* 14 Beacon Street, Boston, MA 02105

This journal focuses on books for children, with articles by writers on their own work, author and illustrator process, and information on how to use the books in the classroom. The annual July issue features profiles of the Newbery and Caldecott award winners.

### *Instructor,* P.O. Box 2039, Mahopac, NY 10541

A general, hands-on, nuts-and-bolts magazine with lots of practical teaching ideas, sometimes more gimmicky than substantial. It's not enough to keep you going September to June, but it certainly helps out with good what-shall-I-do-now ideas.

### *Learning,* Box 2589, Boulder, CO 80321

Another general magazine with a focus on elementary and lower secondary school. It includes teaching ideas, research studies in plain language, trends and issues in education, teacher opinion surveys, and discussions of social issues and problems affecting the schools.

# Selected Bibliography

This bibliography represents works we think are especially important and useful to the English language arts teacher, the sort of books we'd like to see in the teacher's room library. You won't necessarily find reference to all these books in the text of the *Handbook,* but all of them have profoundly influenced the authors.

Abbs, Peter. 1982. *English Within the Arts.* London: Hodder and Stoughton.

Adams, Marilyn Jager. 1990. *Beginning to Read: Thinking and Learning About Print.* Cambridge, MA: MIT Press.

Andrasick, Kathleen. 1990. *Opening Texts: Using Writing to Teach Literature.* Portsmouth, NH: Boynton/Cook Publishers.

Applebee, Arthur. 1974. *Tradition and Reform in Teaching English.* Urbana, IL: National Council of Teachers of English.

Ashton-Warner, Sylvia. 1963. *Teacher.* New York, Simon and Schuster.

Atwell, Nancie. 1998. *In the Middle: New Understandings About Writing, Reading, and Learning.* 2d ed. Portsmouth, NH: Boynton/Cook Publishers.

Bailey, Richard, and Robin Fosheim, eds. 1983. *Literacy for Life.* New York: Modern Language Association.

Barnes, Douglas, James Brittan, and Mike Torbe. 1989. *Language, the Learner, and the School.* Portsmouth, NH: Boynton/Cook Publishers.

Barr, Mary, Pat D'Arcy, and Mary K. Healy. 1982. *What's Going On? Language! Learning Episodes in British and American Classrooms, Grades 4–13.* Portsmouth, NH: Boynton/Cook Publishers.

Baskwell, Jane, and Paulette Whitman. 1986. *A Guide to Classroom Publishing.* Toronto: Scholastic.

Bayer, Ann. 1990. *Collaborative-Apprenticeship Learning: Language and Thinking Across the Curriculum, K–12.* Mountain View, CA: Mayfield.

———. 1984. *Writing Instruction in Nineteenth-Century American Colleges.* Carbondale, IL: Southern Illinois University Press.

Berlin, James. 1987. *Rhetoric and Reality.* Carbondale, IL: Southern Illinois University Press.

———. ed. 1984. *Reclaiming the Imagination: Philosophical Perspective for Writers.* Portsmouth, NH: Boynton/Cook Publishers.

Berthoff, Ann E. 1988. *Forming/Thinking/Writing.* 2d ed. Portsmouth, NH: Boynton/Cook Publishers.

Bissex, Glenda. 1980. *GNYS at Work: A Child Learns to Read and Write.* Cambridge, MA: Harvard University Press.

Bissex, Glenda, and Richard Bullock, eds. 1987. *Seeing for Ourselves: Case Study Research by Teachers of Writing.* Portsmouth, NH: Heinemann.

Boomer, Garth. 1985. *Fair Dinkum Teaching and Learning.* Portsmouth, NH: Boynton/Cook Publishers.

————. 1985. *Negotiating the Curriculum*. Sydney: Ashton Scholastic.

————. 1988. *Metaphors and Meanings*. Hawthorn, Victoria, Australia: Australian Association for the Teaching of English.

Brannon, Lil, Melinda Knight, and Vara Neverow-Turk. 1982. *Writers Writing*. Portsmouth, NH: Boynton/Cook Publishers.

Britton, James, et al. 1975. *The Development of Writing Abilities, 11-18*. London: Macmillan Education.

Britton, James, Robert Shafer, and Ken Watson, eds. 1990. *Teaching and Learning English Worldwide*. Multilingual Matters, Ltd., available through the National Council of Teachers of English, Urbana, IL.

Brooks, Cleanth, and Robert Penn Warren. 1938. *Understanding Poetry*. New York: Holt, Rinehart and Winston.

Busching, Beverly A., and Judith I. Schwartz, eds. 1983. *Integrating the Language Arts in the Elementary School*. Urbana, IL: National Council of Teachers of English.

Byron, Ken. 1986. *Drama in the English Classroom*. New York: Methuen.

Calkins, Lucy. 1986. *The Art of Teaching Writing*. Portsmouth, NH: Heinemann.

Cambourne, Brian. 1988. *The Whole Story: Natural Learning and the Acquisition of Literacy in the Classroom*. Auckland: Scholastic.

Chater, Pauline. 1984. *Marking and Assessment in English*. New York: Methuen.

Chomsky, Noam. 1972. *Language and Mind*. Orlando, FL: Harcourt Brace Jovanovich.

Chukovskii, Kornei. 1963. *From Two to Five*. Berkeley, CA: University of California Press.

Clark, Roy Peter. 1987. *Free to Write: A Journalist Teaches Young Writers*. Portsmouth, NH: Heinemann.

Clegg, A. B., ed. 1972. *The Excitement of Writing*. New York: Schocken Books.

Cooper, Charles. 1981. *The Nature and Measurement of Competency in English*. Urbana, IL: National Council of Teachers of English.

Cooper, Charles, and Lee Odell, 1977. *Evaluating Writing: Describing, Measuring, Judging*. Urbana, IL: National Council of Teachers of English.

Copperud, Roy. 1980. *American Usage and Style: The Consensus*. New York: Van Nostrand Reinhold.

Corcoran, Bill, Mike Hayhoe, and Gordon M. Pradl. 1994. *Knowledge in the Making: Challenging the Text in the Classroom*. Portsmouth, NH: Boynton/Cook Publishers.

Corcoran, William, and Emrys Evans, eds. 1987. *Readers, Texts, Teachers*. Portsmouth, NH: Boynton/Cook Publishers.

Creber, J. W. Patrick. 1965. *Sense and Sensitivity in Teaching English*. London: University of London. Reprinted by the Exeter Curriculum Study Centre, St. Luke's, College of Education, Exeter, U.K.

Daniels, Harvey A., ed. 1990. *Not Only English: Affirming America's Multilingual Heritage*. Urbana, IL: National Council of Teachers of English.

Daniels, Harvey A., and Steven Zemelman. 1985. *A Writing Project: Training Teachers of Writing from Kindergarten to College*. Portsmouth, NH: Heinemann.

D'Arcy, Pat. 1989. *Making Sense, Shaping Meaning: Writing in the Context of a Capacity-Based Approach to Learning*. Portsmouth, NH: Boynton/Cook Publishers.

Davis, James, and James D. Marshall, eds. 1988. *Ways of Knowing*. Iowa City, IA: Iowa Council of Teachers of English.

Dewey, John. 1956. *The School and Society*. Chicago: University of Chicago Press.

Dillard, J. L. 1972. *Black English: Its History and Usage in the United States*. New York: Random House.

Dixon, John. 1976. *Growth Through English,* 2d ed. Urbana, IL: NCTE/NATE, 1968. London: Oxford University Press.

Donaldson, Margaret. *Children's Minds*. 1978. New York: Norton.

Donovan, Timothy R., and Ben W. McClelland, eds. 1980. *Eight Approaches to Teaching Composition*. Urbana, IL: National Council of Teachers of English.

Douglas, Wallace. 1963. *An Introduction to Some Basic Processes in Composition*. Evanston, IL: Northwestern University Curriculum Center in English.

Duke, Charles. 1974. *Creative Dramatics and the Teaching of English*. Urbana, IL: National Council of Teachers of English.

Dyson, Anne Haas. 1989. *Collaboration Through Reading and Writing: Exploring Possibilities*. Urbana, IL: National Council of Teachers of English.

Eagleton, Terry. 1983. *Literary Theory: An Introduction*. Minneapolis: University of Minnesota Press.

Elbow, Peter. 1981. *Writing with Power: Techniques for Mastering the Writing Process*. New York: Oxford.

Elbow, Peter, and Pat Belanoff. 1989. *A Community of Writers*. New York: Random House.

Emig, Janet. 1971. *The Composing Process of Twelfth Graders*. Urbana, IL: National Council of Teachers of English.

Fader, Daniel, and Elton McNeil. 1965. *Hooked on Books: Program and Proof*. New York: Putnam.

Farmer, Marjorie, ed. 1986. *Consensus and Dissent: Teaching English Past, Present and Future*. Urbana, IL: National Council of Teachers of English.

Farr, Marcia, and Harvey Daniels, eds. 1986. *Language Diversity and Writing Instruction*. Urbana, IL: National Council of Teachers of English and ERIC.

Farrell, Edmond J., and James R. Squire, eds. 1990. *Transactions with Literature: A Fifty-Year Perspective*. Urbana, IL: National Council of Teachers of English.

Farrell, Pamela B., ed. 1989. *The High School Writing Center: Establishing and Maintaining One*. Urbana, IL: National Council of Teachers of English.

Freedman, Sarah Warshauer, ed. 1987. *Response to Student Writing*. Urbana, IL: National Council of Teachers of English.

Fox, Mem. 1986. *Teaching Drama to Young Children*. Portsmouth, NH: Heinemann.

———. 1985. *The Politics of Education*. South Hadley, MA: Bergen.

Freire, Paulo. 1988. *The Pedagogy of the Oppressed*. New York: Continuum.

Gardner, Howard. 1983. *Frames of Mind: The Theory of Multiple Intelligences*. New York: Basic Books.

Genisti, Celia, and Anne Haas Dyson. 1984. *Language Assessment in the Early Years*. Norwood, NJ: Ablex.

Gere, Anne. 1987. *Writing Groups*. Carbondale, IL: Southern Illinois University Press.

Goodman, Kenneth, Smith E. Brooks, Robert Meredith, and Yetta Goodman. 1987. *Language and Thinking in School: A Whole-Language Curriculum*. New York: Richard Owen.

Goodman, Kenneth, Yetta Goodman, and Wendy J. Hood, eds. 1988. *The Whole Language Evaluation Book,* Portsmouth, NH: Heinemann.

Goswami, Dixie, and Peter Stillman, eds. 1987. *Reclaiming the Classroom: Teacher Research as an Agency for Change*. Portsmouth, NH: Boynton/Cook Publishers.

Graves, Donald. 1983. *Writing: Teachers and Children at Work*. Portsmouth, NH: Boynton/Cook Publishers.

Hacker, Diane. 1997. *Pocket Manual of Style*. Boston: Bedford Books.

Halpern, Jeanne, and Sarah Liggett, eds. 1984. *Computers and Composing*. Carbondale, IL: Southern Illinois University Press.

Hansen, Jane. 1987. *When Writers Read*. Portsmouth, NH: Heinemann.

Harris, Muriel. 1986. *Teaching One-to-One: The Writing Conference*. Urbana, IL: National Council of Teachers of English.

Harste, Jerome C., Kathy G. Short, and Carolyn Burke. 1988. *Creating Classrooms for Authors: The Reading-Writing Connection*. Portsmouth, NH: Heinemann.

Heath, Shirley Brice. 1983. *Ways with Words: Language, Life, and Work in Communities and Classrooms.* Cambridge: Cambridge University Press.

Hillocks, George, Jr. 1986. *Research on Written Composition: New Directions for Teaching.* Urbana, IL: National Council of Teachers of English.

Hirsch, E. D. 1987. *Cultural Literacy: What Every American Needs to Know.* Boston: Houghton Mifflin.

Holbrook, David. 1967. *Children's Writing.* Cambridge: Cambridge University Press.

Holdaway, Don. 1979. *The Foundations of Literacy.* Portsmouth, NH: Heinemann.

Hynds, Susan, and Donald L. Rubin, eds. 1990. *Perspectives on Talk and Learning.* Urbana, IL: National Council of Teachers of English.

Illich, Ivan. 1971. *Deschooling Society.* New York: Harper & Row.

Jackson, David. 1982. *Continuity in Secondary English.* New York: Methuen.

Jensen, Julie, ed. 1984. *Composing and Comprehending.* Urbana, IL: National Council of Teachers of English and ERIC.

———. 1988. *Stories to Grow On: Demonstrations of Language Learning in K–8 Classrooms.* Portsmouth, NH: Heinemann.

Johnson, Brian. 1983. *Assessing English.* Sydney: St. Clair Press.

Kirby, Dan, and Tom Liner. 1988. *Inside Out.* 2d ed. Portsmouth, NH: Boynton/Cook Publishers.

Kirschenbaum, Howard, Sidney B. Simon, and Rodney W. Napier. 1971. *Wad-Ja-Get: The Grading Game in American Education.* New York: Hart.

Klonsky, Milton. 1975. *Speaking Pictures: A Gallery of Pictoral Poetry from the Sixteenth Century to the Present.* New York: Harmony Books.

Knowles, Malcolm S. 1986. *Using Learning Contracts.* San Francisco: Jossey-Bass.

Kohl, Herbert. 1981. *A Book of Puzzlements: Play and Invention with Language.* New York: Schocken Books.

Kozol, Jonathon. 1985. *Illiterate America.* Garden City, NJ: Anchor/Doubleday.

Kuhn, Thomas S. 1962. *The Structure of Scientific Revolutions.* Chicago: University of Chicago Press.

Langer, Judith A., and Arthur N. Applebee. 1987. *How Writing Shapes Thinking: A Study of Teaching and Learning.* Urbana, IL: National Council of Teachers of English.

Langer, Susanne. 1957. *Philosophy in a New Key: A Study in the Symbolism of Reason, Rite, and Art.* Cambridge: Harvard University Press.

Lee, Dorris, and Roach Van Allen. 1963. *Learning to Read Through Experience.* New York: Appleton-Century-Crofts.

Lloyd-Jones, Richard, and Andrea A. Lunsford, eds. 1989. *The English Coalition Conference: Democracy Through Language.* Urbana, IL: National Council of Teachers of English.

Lutz, William, ed. 1989. *Beyond 1984: Doublespeak in a Post-Orwellian Age.* Urbana, IL: National Council of Teachers of English.

Macrorie, Ken. 1988. *The I-Search Paper.* Portsmouth, NH: Boynton/Cook Publishers.

Mandel, Barret, ed. 1980. *Three Language Arts Curriculum Models: Pre-Kindergarten Through College.* Urbana, IL: National Council of Teachers of English.

Marshall, Sybil. 1965. *An Experiment in Education.* Cambridge: Cambridge University Press.

Masterman, Len. 1988. *Teaching About Television.* London: Macmillan Education.

Mayher, John S., Nancy B. Lester, and Gordon Pradl. 1983. *Learning to Write/Writing to Learn.* Portsmouth, NH: Boynton/Cook Publishers.

McClelland, Ben, and T. R. Donovan. 1985. *Research and Scholarship in Composition.* New York: Modern Language Association.

Medway, Peter. 1980. *Finding a Language.* London: Chameleon.

Moffett, James. 1983. *Teaching the Universe of Discourse.* Portsmouth, NH: Boynton/Cook Publishers.

Moffett, James, and Betty Jane Wagner. 1991. *A Student-Centered Language Arts Curriculum, K-12.* 4th ed. Portsmouth, NH: Boynton/Cook Publishers.

Murray, Donald. 1968. *A Writer Teaches Writing: A Practical Method of Teaching Composition.* Boston: Houghton Mifflin.

Myers, Miles. 1985. *The Teacher Researcher: How to Study Writing in the Classroom.* Urbana, IL: National Council of Teachers of English and ERIC.

Nelms, Ben F., ed. 1988. *Literature in the Classroom: Readers, Texts, and Contexts.* Urbana, IL: National Council of Teachers of English.

Newman, Judith M. 1985. *Whole Language: Theory in Use.* Portsmouth, NH: Heinemann.

North, Stephen M. 1987. *The Making of Knowledge in Composition: Portrait of an Emerging Field.* Portsmouth, NH: Boynton/Cook Publishers.

Nurnberg, Maxwell. 1972. *Fun with Words.* New York: Pocket Books.

Ong, Walter. 1982. *Orality and Literacy: The Technologizing of the Word.* New York: Methuen.

Orwell, George. 1946. "Politics and the English Language." In *Shooting an Elephant and Other Essays.* New York: Harcourt Brace.

Pattison, Robert. 1982. *On Literacy: The Politics of the Word from Homer to the Age of Rock.* New York: Oxford University Press.

Peetoom, Adrian. 1986. *Shared Reading.* Toronto: Scholastic.

Piaget, Jean. 1985. *The Language and Thought of the Child.* New York: New American Library.

Plimpton, George, ed. 1962. *Writers at Work: The Paris Review Interviews.* 2d series. New York: Viking.

Polanyi, Michael. 1953. *Personal Knowledge: Towards a Post-Critical Philosophy.* Chicago: University of Chicago Press.

Pooley, Robert. 1945. *Understanding English Usage.* New York: Appleton.

Pradl, Gordon M., ed. 1982. *Prospect and Retrospect: Selected Essays of James Britton.* Portsmouth, NH: Boynton/Cook Publishers.

Probst, Robert. 1988. *Response and Analysis: Teaching Literature in Junior and Senior High School.* Portsmouth, NH: Boynton/Cook Publishers.

Purves, Alan C., Theresa Rogers, and Anna O. Soter. 1990. *How Porcupines Make Love II: Teaching a Response-Centered Curriculum.* New York: Longman.

Rigg, Pat, and Virginia C. Allen, eds. 1989. *When They Don't All Speak English.* Urbana, IL: National Council of Teachers of English.

Romano, Tom. 1987. *Clearing the Way: Working with Teenage Writers.* Portsmouth, NH: Heinemann.

Rose, Mike. 1984. *Writer's Block: The Cognitive Dimension.* Carbondale, IL: Southern Illinois University Press.

Rosenblatt, Louise. [1938] 1995. *Literature as Exploration.* New York: Modern Language Association.

———. 1978. *The Reader, the Text, and the Poem: The Transactional Theory of the Literary Work.* Carbondale, IL: Southern Illinois University Press.

Rouse, John. 1978. *The Completed Gesture.* New Jersey: Skyline Books.

Rousseau, J. J. 1961. *Émile, ou, de l'Éducation.* Paris: Garnier.

Shannon, Patrick. 1990. *The Struggle to Continue: Progressive Reading Instruction in the United States.* Portsmouth, NH: Heinemann.

Shaughnessy, Mina. 1977. *Errors and Expectations: A Guide for the Teacher of Basic Writing.* New York: Oxford University Press.

Shor, Ira, ed. 1987. *Freire for the Classroom: A Sourcebook for Laboratory Teaching.* Portsmouth, NH: Boynton/Cook Publishers.

Shuman, R. Baird, and Denny Wolfe. 1990. *Teaching English Through the Arts.* Urbana, IL: National Council of Teachers of English.

Shuy, Roger D. 1974. *Discovering American Dialects*. Urbana, IL: National Council of Teachers of English.

Smith, Frank. 1971. *Understanding Reading: A Psycholinguistic Analysis of Reading and Learning to Read*. New York: Holt, Rinehart, and Winston.

———. 1985. *Reading Without Nonsense*. New York: College Press.

———. 1998. *Joining the Literacy Club: Further Essays into Education*. Portsmouth, NH: Heinemann.

Smitherman, Geneva. 1977. *Talkin and Testifyin: The Language of Black America*. Boston: Houghton Mifflin.

Snow, C. P. 1964. *The Two Cultures*. Cambridge: The Cambridge University Press.

Suhor, Charles, and Christopher Thaiss, eds. 1984. *Speaking and Writing K-12*. Urbana, IL: National Council of Teachers of English.

Summerfield, Geoffrey. 1965. *Topics in English*. London: Batsford.

Taylor, Denny. 1983. *Family Literacy: Young Children Learning to Read and Write*. Portsmouth: NH: Heinemann.

Tchudi, Stephen. 1984. *The Burg-O-Rama Man*. New York: Delacorte.

———. 1985. *Language, Schooling, and Society*. Portsmouth, NH: Boynton/Cook Publishers.

———. 1986. *English Teachers at Work: Ideas and Strategies from Five Countries*. Portsmouth, NH: Boynton/Cook Publishers.

———. 1990. *Planning and Assessing the Curriculum in the English Language Arts*. Alexandria, VA: National Association for Supervision and Curriculum Development.

———. 1991. *Travels Through the Curriculum*. Toronto: Scholastic.

Tchudi, Stephen, with Lillian Hassler, Betty Swiggett, Jan Loveless, and Carol Kuykendall. 1991. *The English Language Arts Curriculum: A Guide to Planning and Assessment*. Alexandria, VA: Association for Supervision and Curriculum Development.

Tchudi, Stephen, Margie Huerta, Joanne Yates, and Susan Tchudi. [1984] 1986. *Teaching Writing in the Content Areas*. 4 vols. Washington, DC: National Education Association.

Tchudi, Stephen, and Susan Tchudi. 1984. *The Young Writer's Handbook*. New York: Scribner's.

Tchudi, Susan. 1994. *Integrated Language Arts in the Elementary School*. Glendale, CA: Wadsworth.

Tchudi, Susan, and Stephen Tchudi. 1980. *Gifts of Writing*. New York: Scribner's.

Van Allen, Roach. 1976. *Language Experiences in Communication*. Boston: Houghton Mifflin.

Vygotsky, Lev. 1962. *Thought and Language*. Cambridge: MIT Press.

Walshe, R. D., ed. 1986. *Writing and Learning in Australia*. Melbourne: Oxford/Delasta.

Ward, Geoff. 1988. *I've Got a Project On . . .* Rozelle, New South Wales: Primary English Teaching Association of New South Wales and Portsmouth, NH: Heinemann.

Weaver, Constance. 1990. *Understanding Whole Language*. Portsmouth, NH: Heinemann.

Wells, Gordon. 1986. *The Meaning Makers: Children Learning Language and Using Language to Learn*. Portsmouth, NH: Heinemann.

Whitehead, Alfred North. 1929. *The Aims of Education*. New York: Macmillan.

# Index